D. Haggarty
May 2004

Tuscany

Paintings and sketches by Douglas Smith

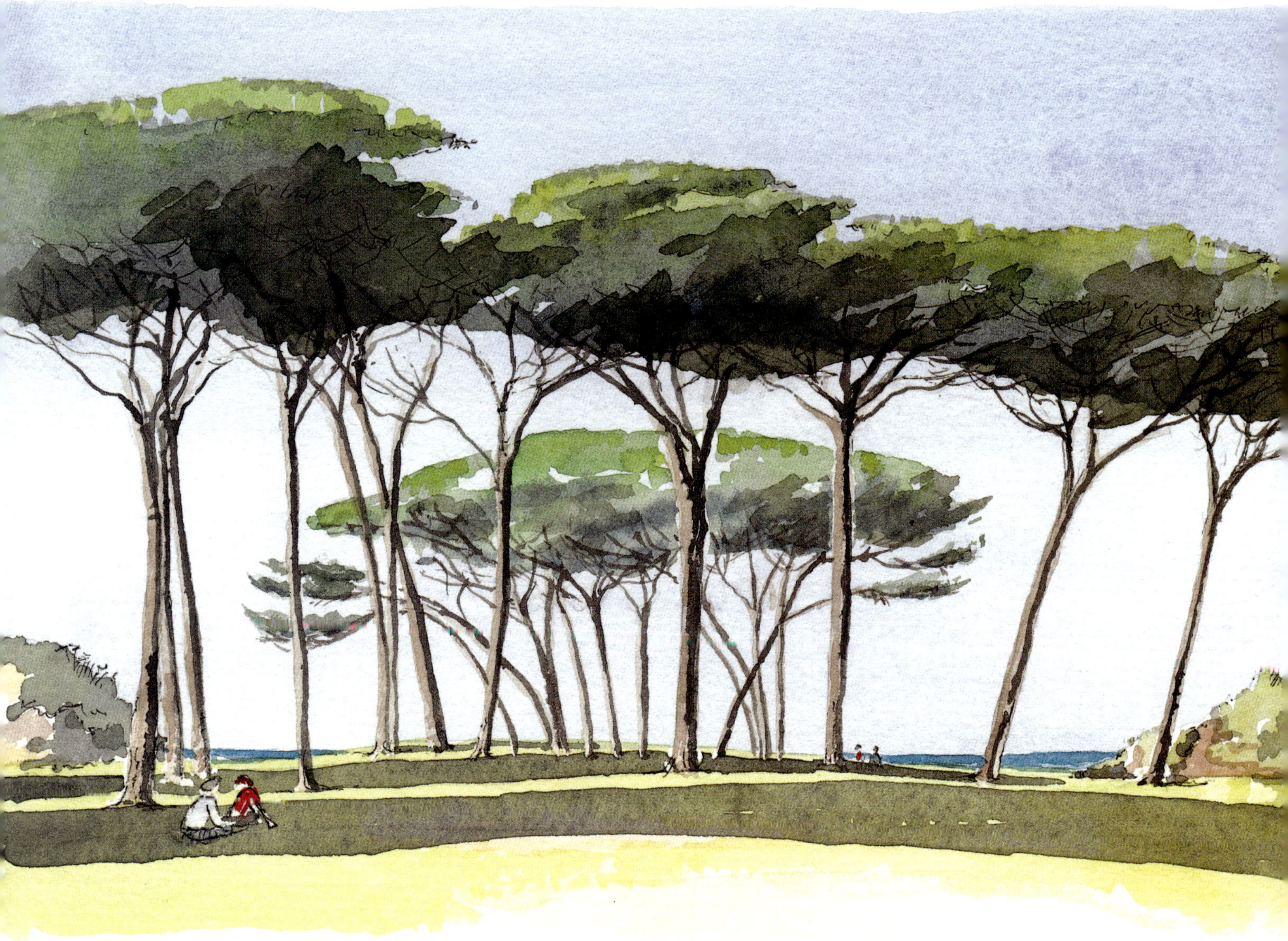

Tuscany

Paintings and sketches by Douglas Smith

Douglas Smith, an artist architect travelling with sketchbook, explores the dazzling countryside, fascinating architecture and art of Tuscany.

Other books by the same author

FRANCE Paintings and sketches	ISBN 0-9538124-1-3
LEICESTER Paintings and sketches	ISBN 0-9538124-2-1
ARCHITECTURE INTERIOR LANDSCAPE	ISBN 0-9538124-0-5
HOTEL RESTAURANT DESIGN	ISBN 0-435-86501-3

Acknowledgments

This book is dedicated to the challenges of the art, architecture and diverse landscape of Tuscany and to Ron Haylock who planted the seed for this publication, for his encouragement and positive support.

I would like to thank Bryan Organ for writing the Foreword, Edward Moody for the graphic design, and Traphouse Design & Reproduction Limited for scanning the paintings and drawings with great skill.

I am indebted to Hilary Smith, Shirley Smith and Veronica Rawson for their editing and typing skills, who have put me right when I have got it wrong.

I am pleased to acknowledge the following sources for the quotations.

Dante
Eliot, T S
Gautier, Théophile
James, Henry
Lawrence, D H
Michelangelo
Tennyson, Alfred, Lord
Varsari, Giorgio

Tuscany

Paintings and sketches by Douglas Smith

Published in the United Kingdom 2003
Douglas Smith Stimson Partnership Limited
53 Spencefield Lane
Leicester LE2 6HH

Graphic Design
Edward Moody Design
169 Knighton Road,
Leicester LE2 3TS

Printed and bound in the United Kingdom by B B H Colourprint Group Ltd

ISBN 0-9538124-3-X

Contents

Preface

'We shall not cease from exploration
And the end of all our exploring
Will be to arrive where we started
And know the place for the first time.'

T S Eliot

My aim through paintings and sketches is to illustrate the rich and diverse appeal of Tuscany that has compelled me to return so many times. It still has the same power, as to those in the past, to participants on the 'Grand Tour', to writers, poets, painters and travellers since the start of the Renaissance.

However familiar you are with Tuscany, nothing fascinates more than by looking at buildings, art and the diverse landscape of this unique corner of the world through other eyes. My aim is therefore to stimulate a re-examination at the start of the new millennium.

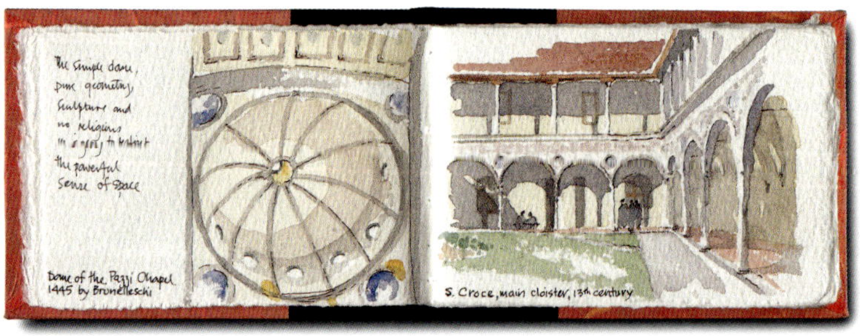

Pages from a sketch book of Tuscany
by Douglas Smith

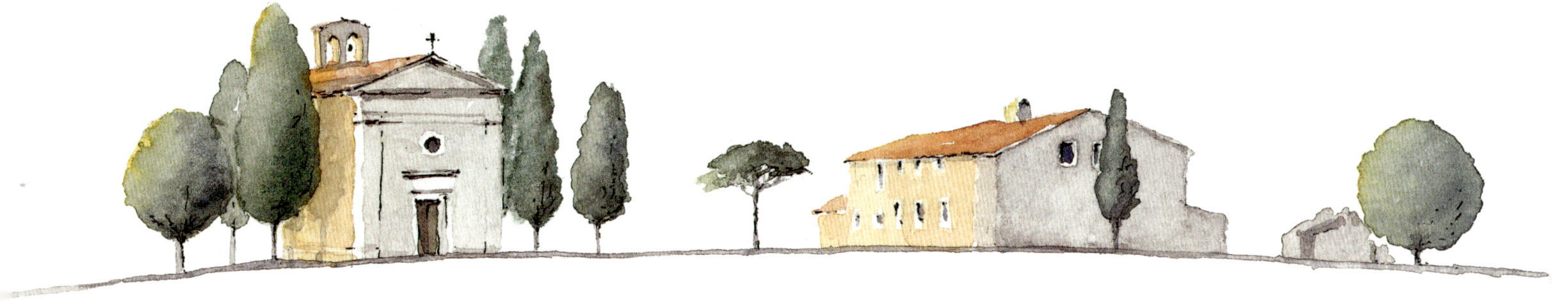

Hamlet on the ridge between Pienza and San Quirico d'Orcia

Foreword

It is a great pleasure for me as an old friend and fellow artist to see that Douglas has given us another sketchbook of his travels.

This time he takes us to Tuscany recording with tremendous enthusiasm and energy the architecture, landscape, light and colour in a series of detailed studies in this very special part of Italy.

Bryan Organ

Tuscan order

Columns and proportions have a direct relationship to Classical Roman and Greek architecture.

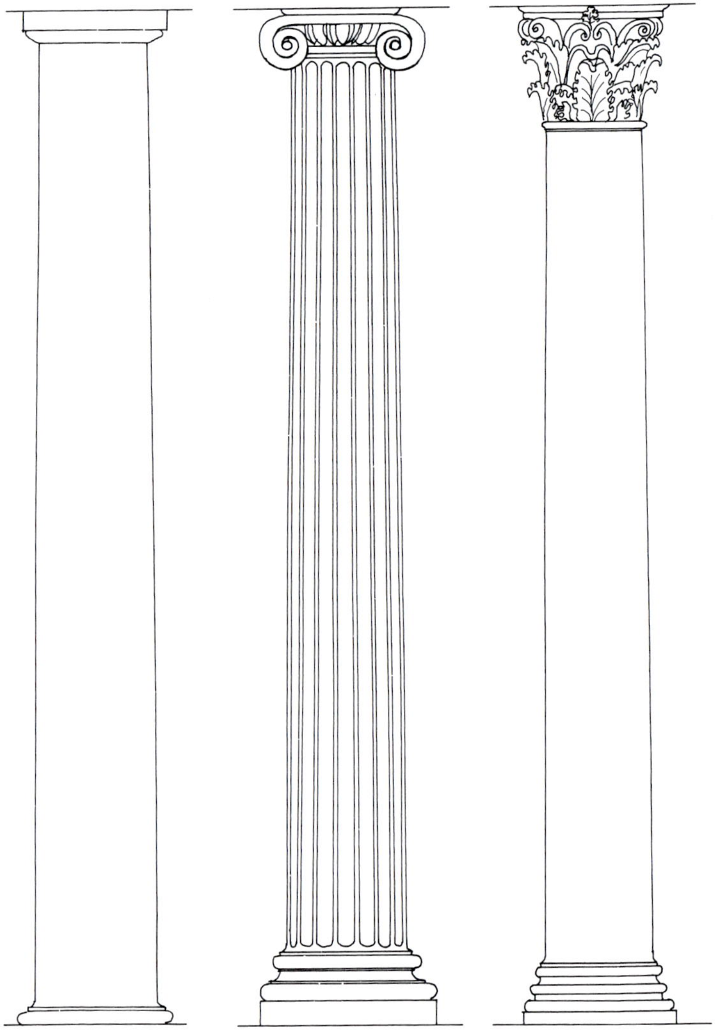

Doric Ionic Corinthian

The vocabulary and language of classical architecture were based on the three original 'orders' Doric, Ionic and Corinthian established by the Greeks and developed by the Romans. The theory of Platonic geometry of mathematical proportions was absolute.

It was applied and optically corrected in the Parthenon in Athens.

The proportion of these 'orders' were studied and prescribed by the Roman architect Vitruvius in the first century AD. By this time the Etruscans and the Romans had added the development of the arch and the vault.

In the thirteenth century Italy emerged from the 'Dark Ages' and Florence turned to Classical Rome for inspiration and the birth of the Renaissance occurred.

Introduction

'...to enter Tuscany, where one
discovers an azure panorama
of plains, mountains, and villages;
a horizon dotted with cities and villas,
shimmering in light and shade.'

Théophile Gautier

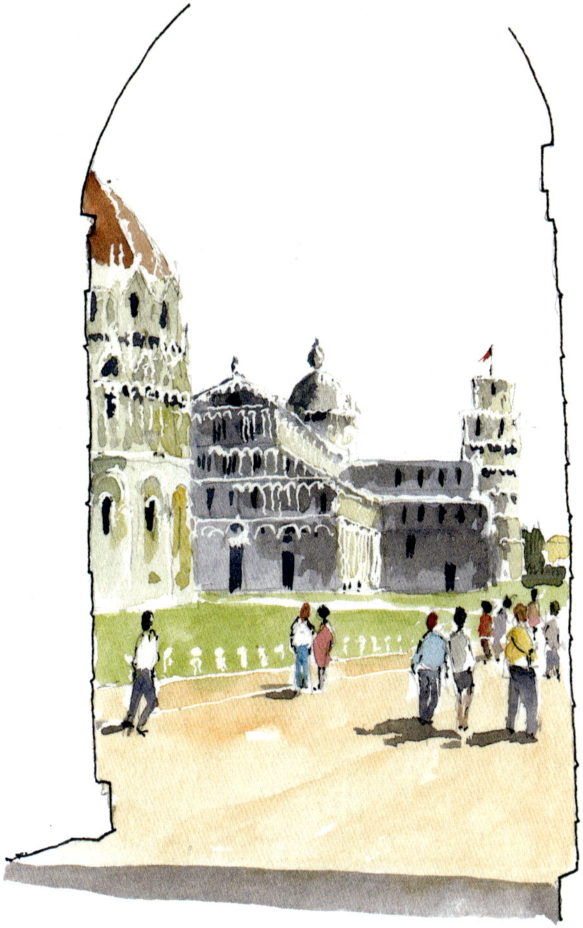

Campo dei Miracoli, Pisa

Italy has been a fascination and a magnet for me. In the course of my studies for my first degree in Architecture at the Cheltenham College of Art, it was necessary to study a special period of 'The history of architecture'. I chose the Greek and Roman period as a good foundation. Later I found it was a constant source of inspiration and invaluable when travelling in Europe. Greece must be regarded as the root of literary and artistic inspiration that has influenced European art. The Romans adopted the columnar and trabeated (column, beam and entablature constructions) style of the Greeks but never, in my opinion, surpassed the subtlety of the architecture started by them. However, they developed the arch, vault and dome of the Etruscans and it was the Romans who spread the classical movement over Europe. It was the Romans, not the Greeks, who inspired the Renaissance. In classical design, first came the Doric followed by the Ionic, then the Corinthian and finally the Composite orders.

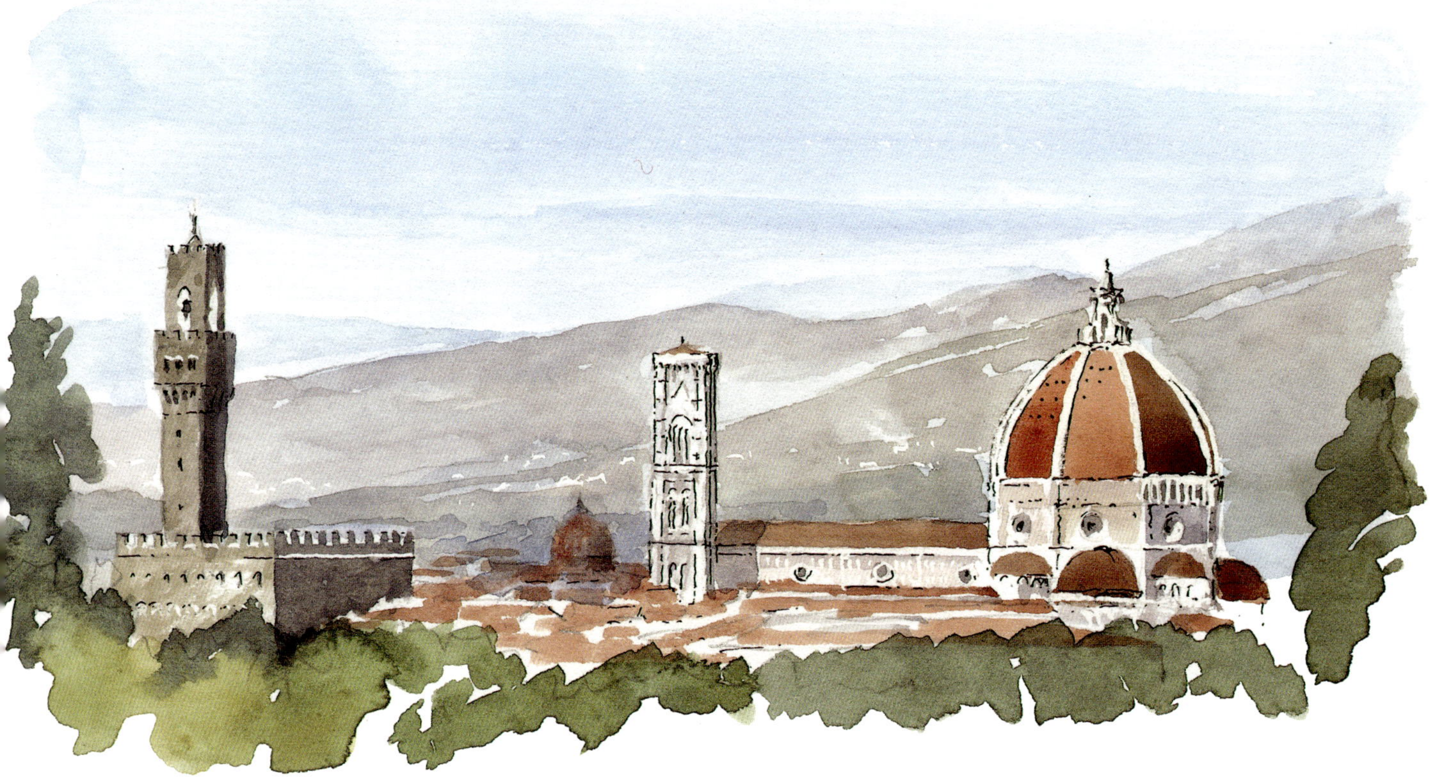

Florence from Piazzale Michelangelo

While studying for my second degree at Leicester School of Architecture, four students from different disciplines and one fellow student of architecture joined with me to purchase an old London taxi for a relatively small sum, which was redeemed when we sold it on our return. It enabled us to make a Grand Tour of France, Switzerland, Italy, Austria and Germany. However, it was a few years later that I went to Tuscany, an area that had an immediate attraction that has continued ever since, spanning more than the next forty plus years.

Florence was the first city of Tuscany I visited. This was on my honeymoon in 1957 and the impact was instant. I discovered piazza after piazza linked by narrow roads each with their individual character, a stimulating challenge to the eye. (Free use of Italian and English place names have been used, please see brief glossary). The excitement of the first impression of paintings in the Uffizi Gallery; the superb

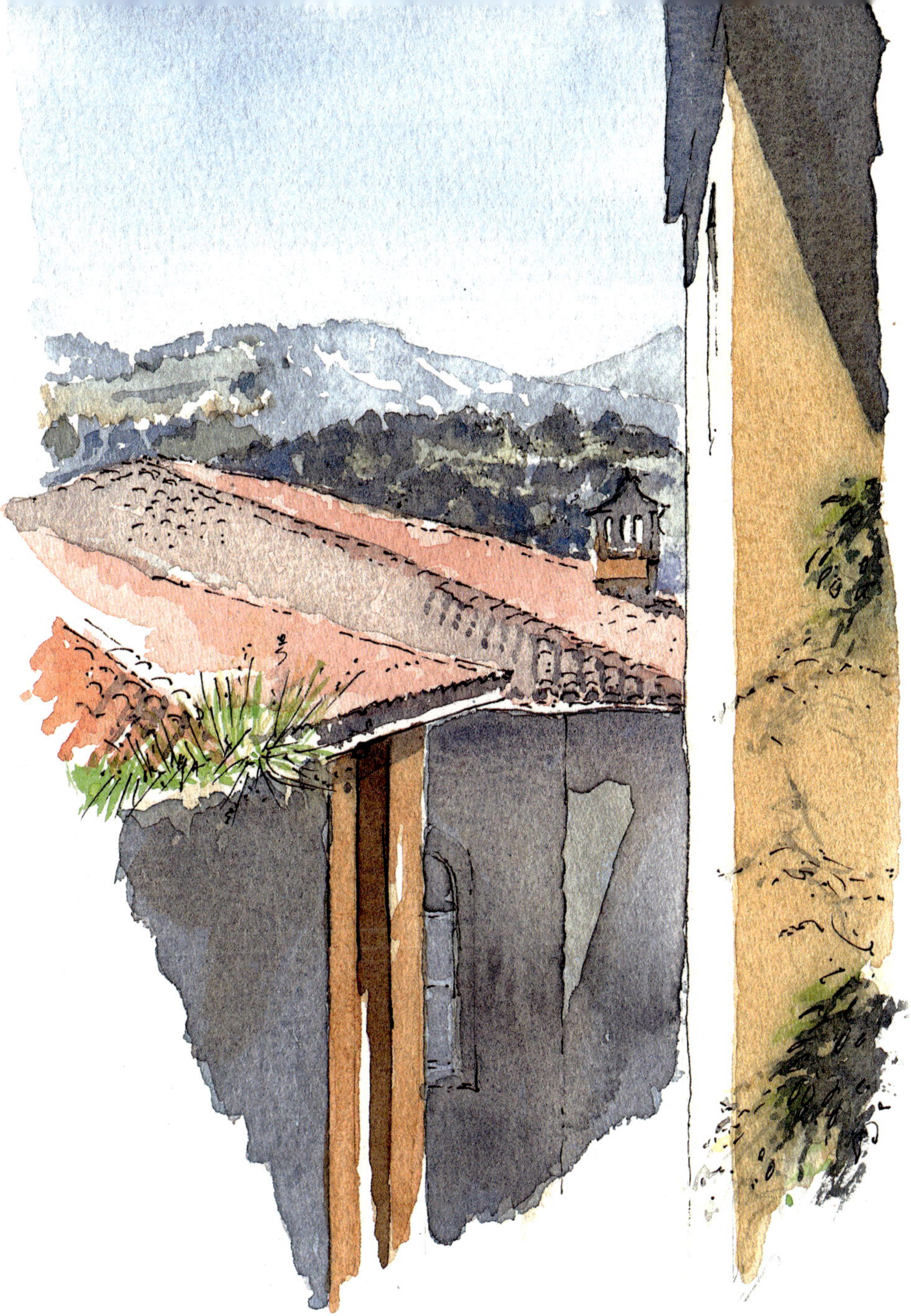

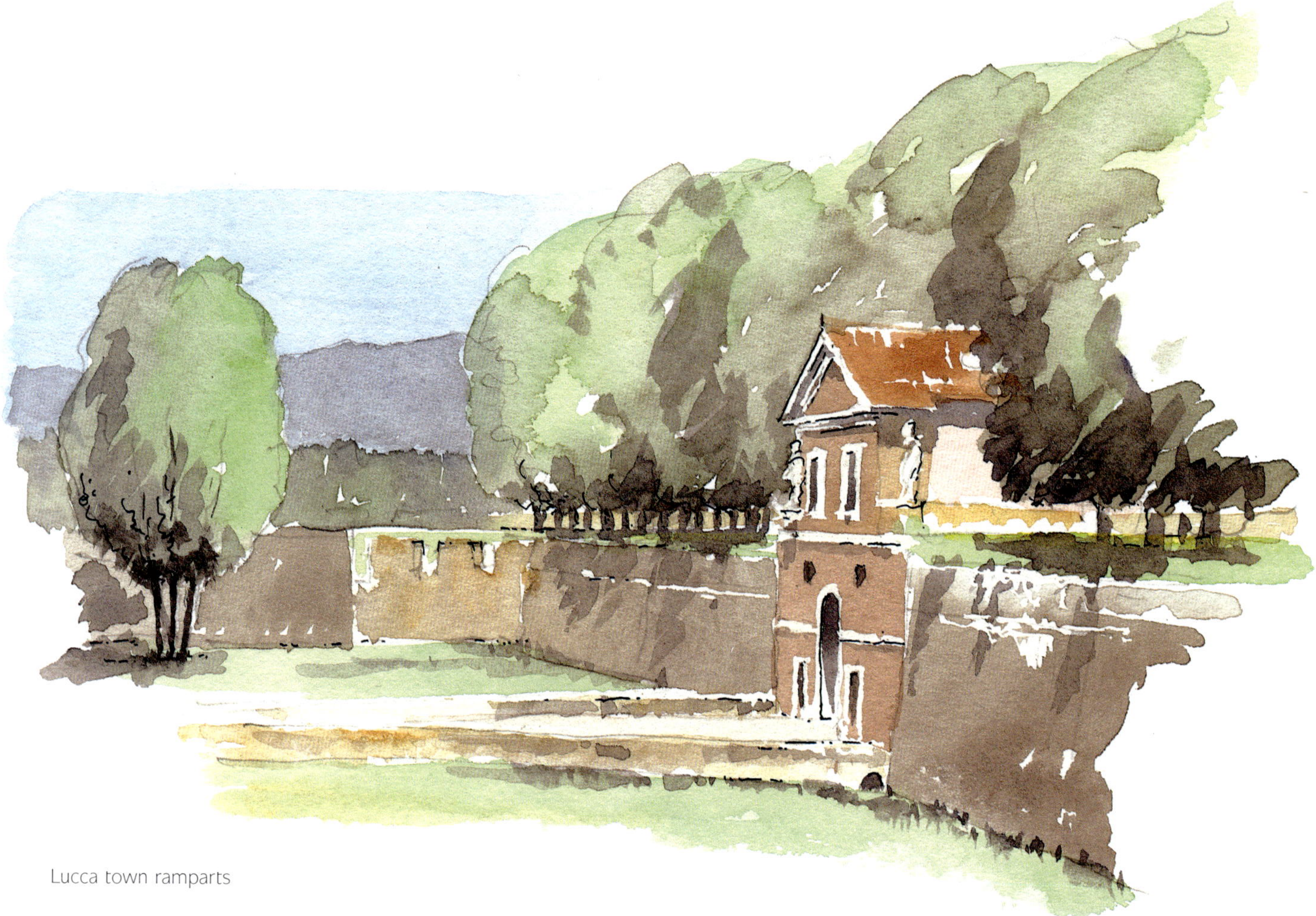

Lucca town ramparts

sculptures by Michelangelo of David in the Accademia and the Medici tombs in the New Sacristy of the church of San Lorenzo, made one want to search out more and more gems. It is easy to try to see too much but less is more, leaving many to explore next time, attracting one back again and again. There is an art in avoiding the intrusion of tourists and the trappings of tourism by concentrating on views, to fully experience the wonderful spaces created by the Great Renaissance Architects such as the Piazza della Signoria with its buildings and sculpture or the juxtaposition of the Baptistery and the Duomo. Climb up to the exquisite San Miniato and return to the breathtaking view over the city from Piazzale Michelangelo. A city made for people where it is possible to wonder, eat and drink, in a built environment with sculpture inside and outside where one can soak up the sun and atmosphere in exquisite space, leaving one with vivid memories of a unique city. However, this is only a tiny part of Tuscany.

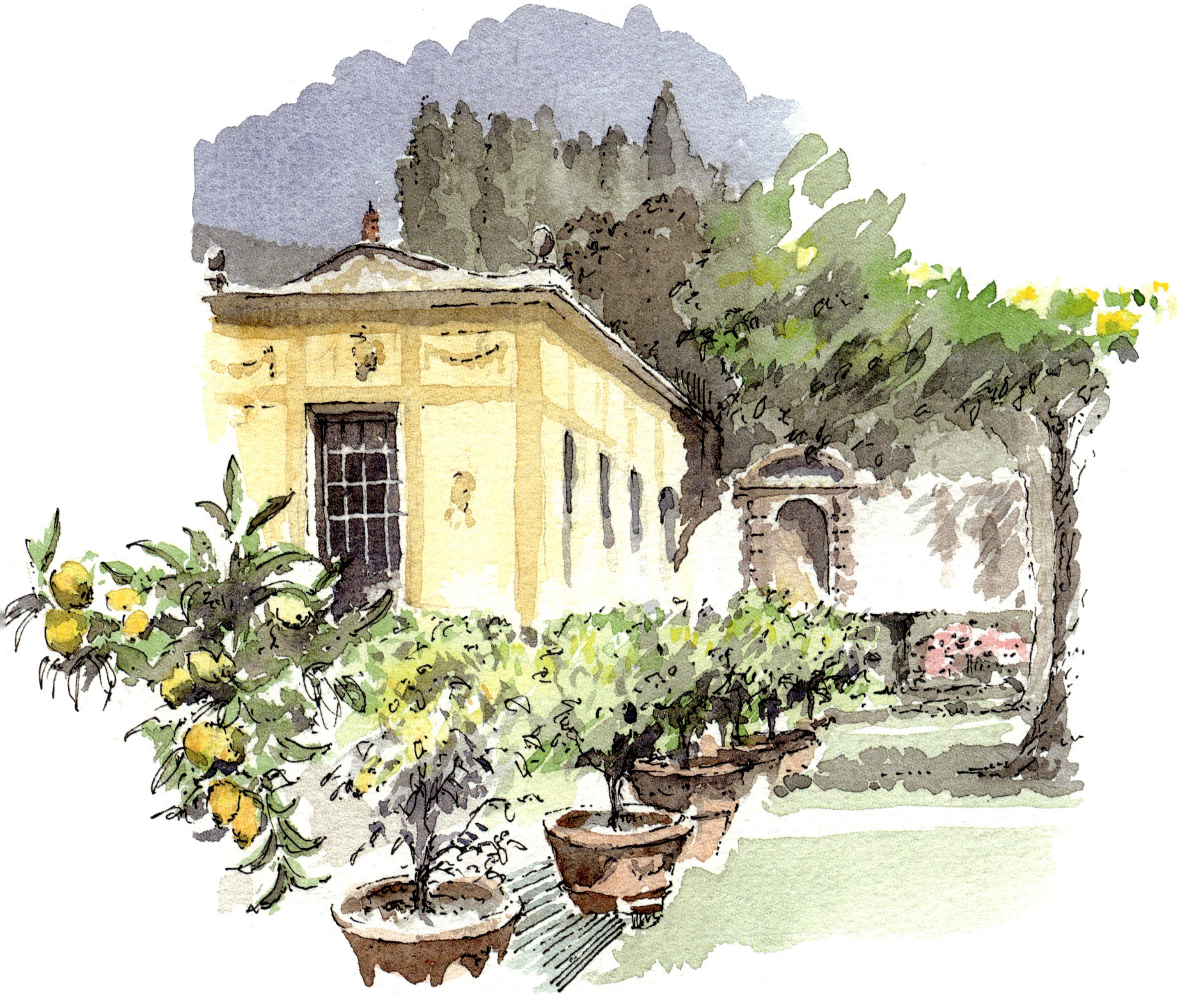

The garden lemon house of the
Villa Medici at Fiesole

Siena is a nearby city of a very different character. On entering the town one is struck by brown/pink hue of a great medieval town centred on the beautiful shell shaped Piazza del Campo. In contrast the white and black striped marble Duomo dominates the skyline.

In contrast to Siena is San Gimignano, built with tall medieval windowless towers dominating this unique hillside.

For a long time, visitors flying to Tuscany have arrived at Pisa. It was also an important port in Roman times and therefore has a tradition of welcoming visitors. Campo dei Miracoli is difficult to miss with the two familiar 'icons', the Baptistery and the Leaning Tower together with the Duomo, Camposanto and the two museums.

Nearby is Lucca with the 16th century town wall placing a complete collar round the old town, and hence preserving its character, charm and attraction.

History from time to time produces significant events where so many things happen together. Tuscany was one such place in the Renaissance. The Medici family became the magnet for a prosperous medieval trade centre. However, they were not only great traders but also outstanding patrons of the arts. Palaces, villas and gardens emerged from this family that are admired by, and are an inspiration for the western world. At the same time, being the home of great artists, architects and writers like Giotto and Ghiberti, Brunelleschi, Masaccio, Piero della Francesca and Michelangelo, Dante and Donatello. In the same period Leonardo, the creative and inventive genius of the Renaissance, was born in Vinci.

The beauty of wild mountain scenery, Carrara marble quarries, fascinating coastline and islands contrasting with the rolling hills, beautiful valleys, olives, sunflowers, vines and cypress trees attract one back, again and again, to explore the hidden secrets of a unique area of the world.

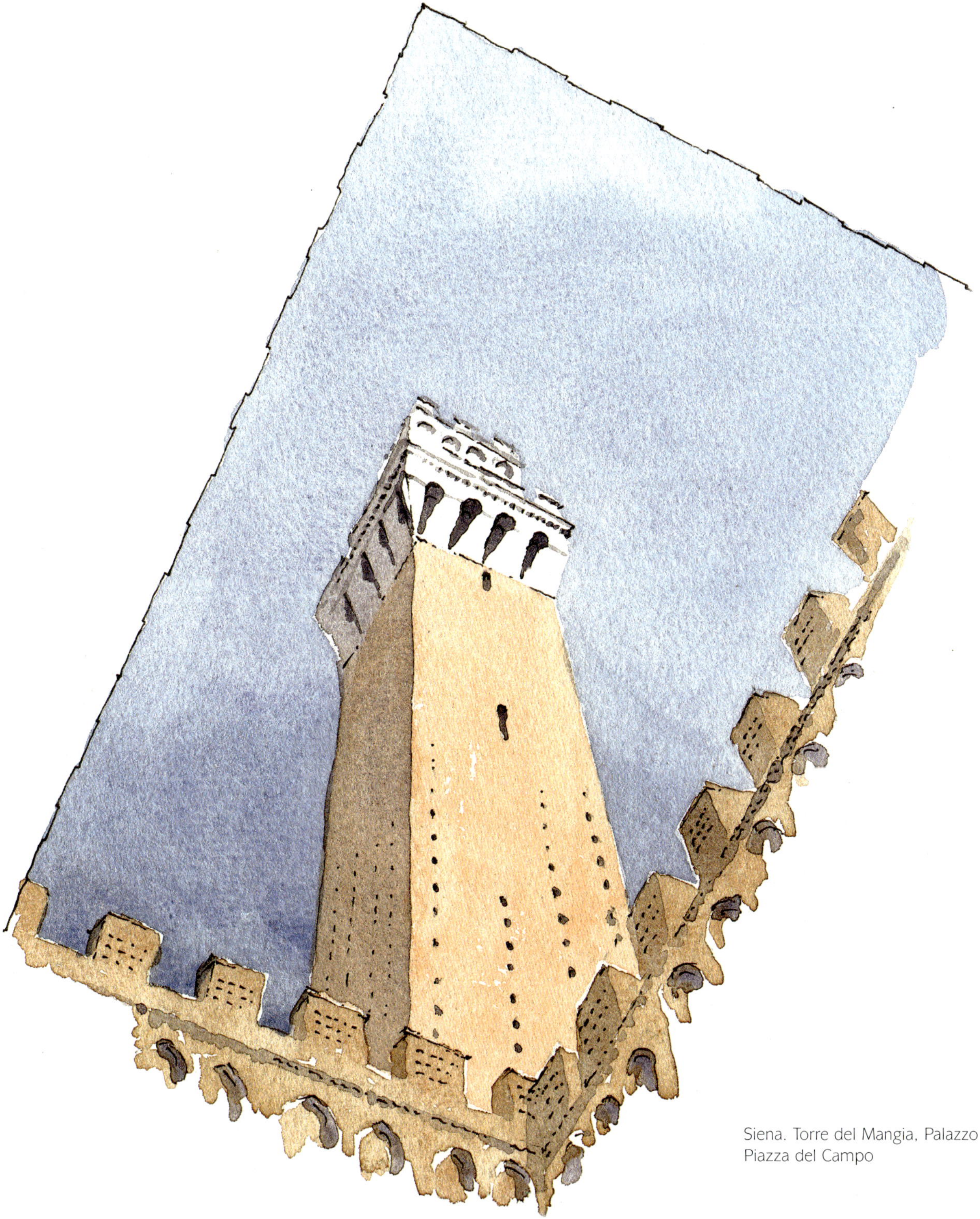

Siena. Torre del Mangia, Palazzo Pubblico on Piazza del Campo

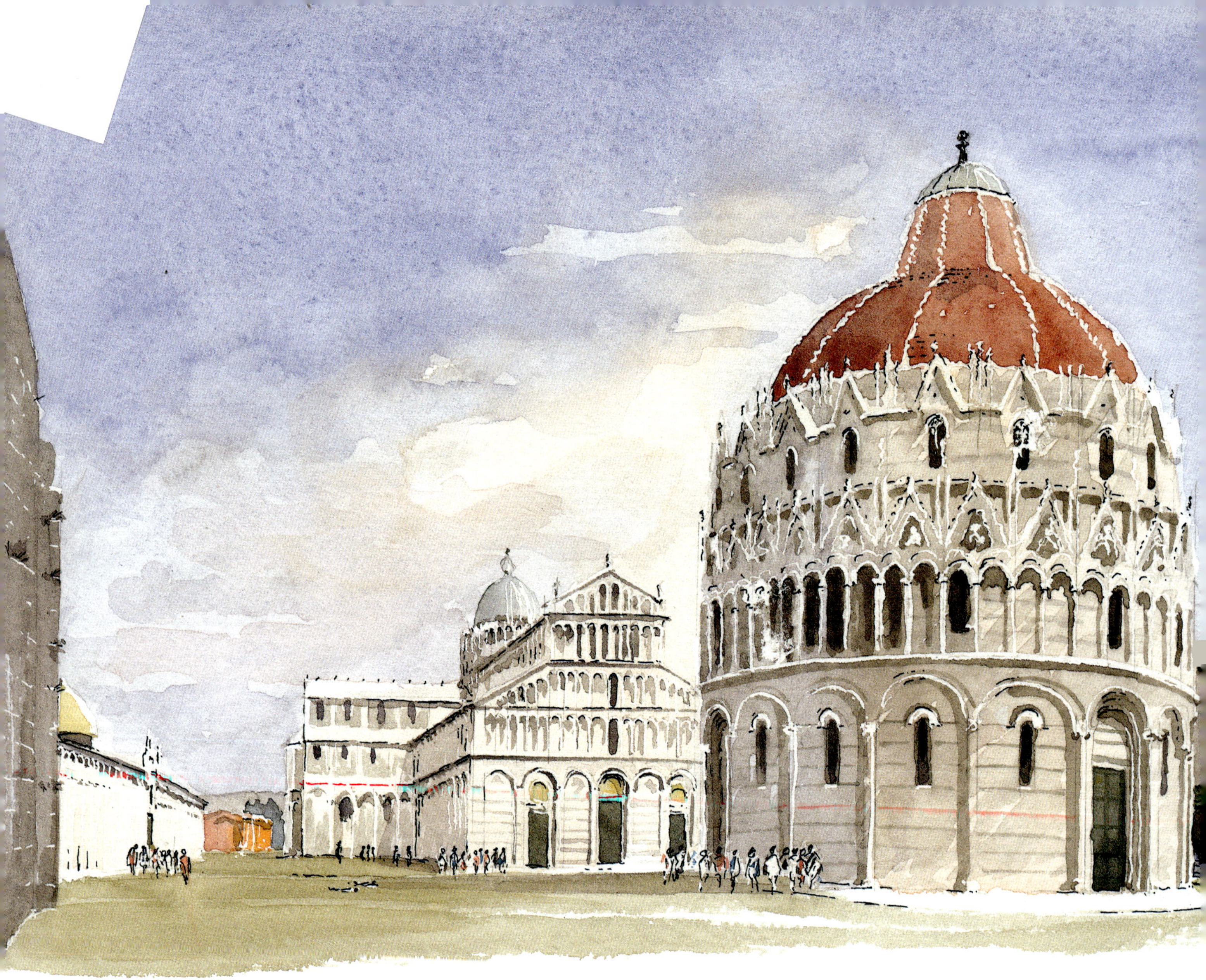

Baptistery, Duomo and Camposanto in
Campo dei Miracoli

Gateway to Tuscany - Pisa and surrounding countryside

Location is the key to success; the Etruscans followed by the Romans had a natural instinct when they chose the site for the important port of Pisa at the mouth of the Arno on the coast. Founded in the 7th century BC it was ideal for a maritime power. In the Middle Ages its location established a powerful maritime republic and a significant impact was made on the Mediterranean. These merchant warriors traded with countries as far away as North Africa and Spain, resulting in Fibonacci a Pisan mathematician, who introduced Arabic numerals to the West. It helped to change the architects' concept of geometry, enabling them to experiment with new forms and decoration of buildings.

Trade to and from Tuscany was conveyed along the Arno bringing wealth and a scientific cultural revolution to Pisa. Trading reached its peak in the 12th century and first half of the 13th century. Wealth brought a building spree with the construction of the Duomo, Baptistery, Camposanto Cemetery and the Camponile. All were built in the same period and were set on a beautiful grass Campo dei Miracoli adjacent to the northern section of the town wall. The town expanded and it is possible to explore the narrow streets in the direction of the river, passing the oldest botanical garden in Europe, Orto Botanico. The major buildings are in white marble complementing houses painted in yellow, pink and ochre. Absorb the atmosphere and stumble across two gothic gems the church of Santa Maria della Spina and San Paolo a Ripa d'Arno.

In 1284 Pisa was defeated by the Genoese and it became dependent on Florence. Although it eventually recovered economically, the Renaissance passed by with little impact on a city trapped in a time warp.

Campo dei Miracoli, 'Field of Miracles' is still a succinct description in translation for this formidable

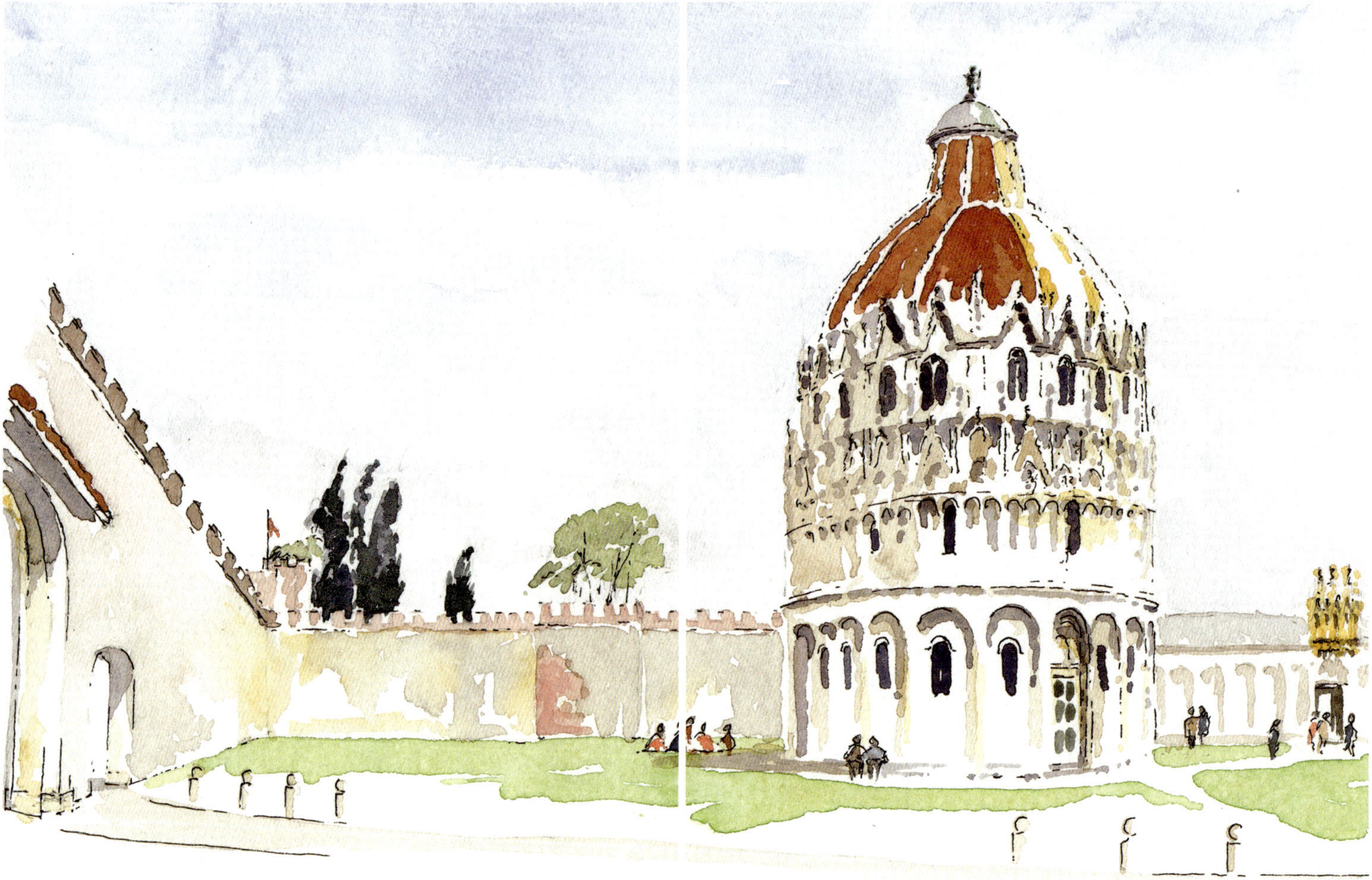

Exploring Campo dei Miracoli

White vertical lines through the paintings on pages 18, 19 and 20 show where there are paper folds on the original sketch.

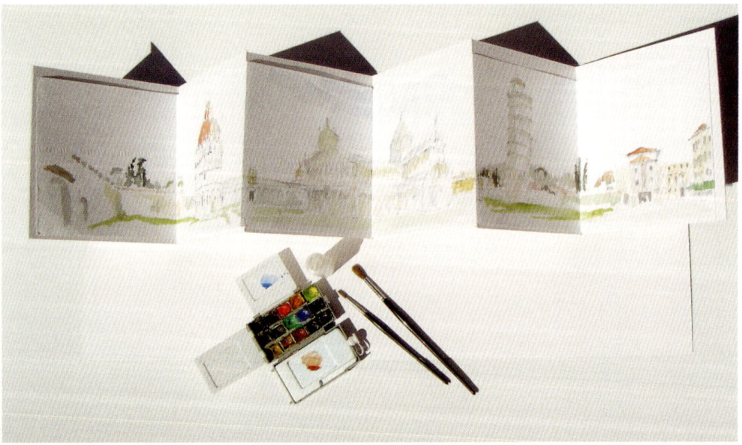

Photograph of the original sketch

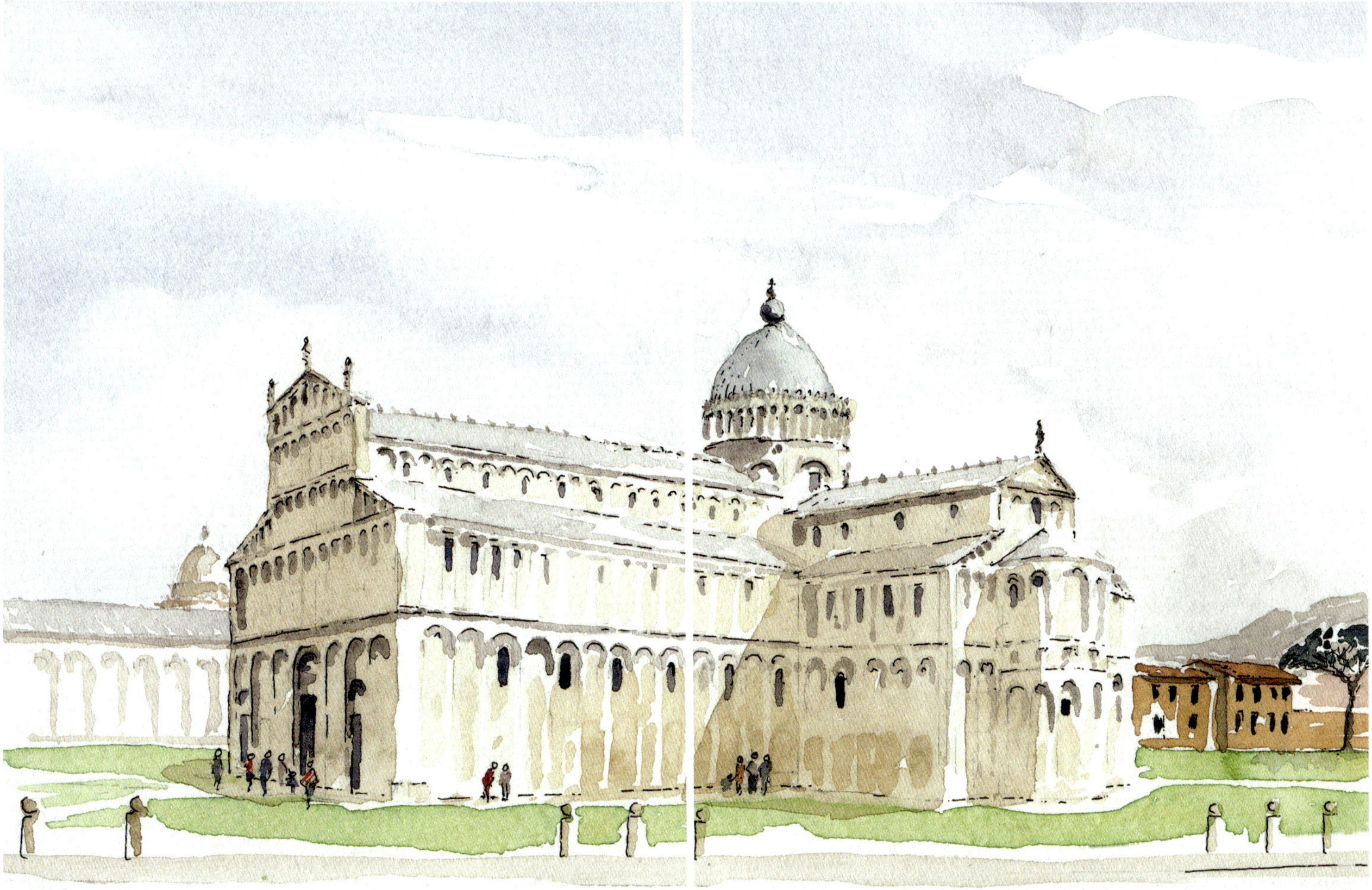

group of elegant religious buildings set on an immaculate green lawn. The Duomo was built in 1063 by two architects, first Buscheto and finished by Rainaldo, who produced a fine Romanesque building. Look at the detail of the west façade and the exquisite pulpit by Giovanni Pisano.

The Baptistery 1152–1284 originally designed by Diotisalvi, was altered and completed by Nicola and Giovanni Pisano. See the fine pulpit set on columns resting on lions, supporting beautifully carved panels by Nicola Pisano.

Camposanto the Cemetery, 1278, is a beautiful Gothic cloistered designed by Giovanni di Somone.

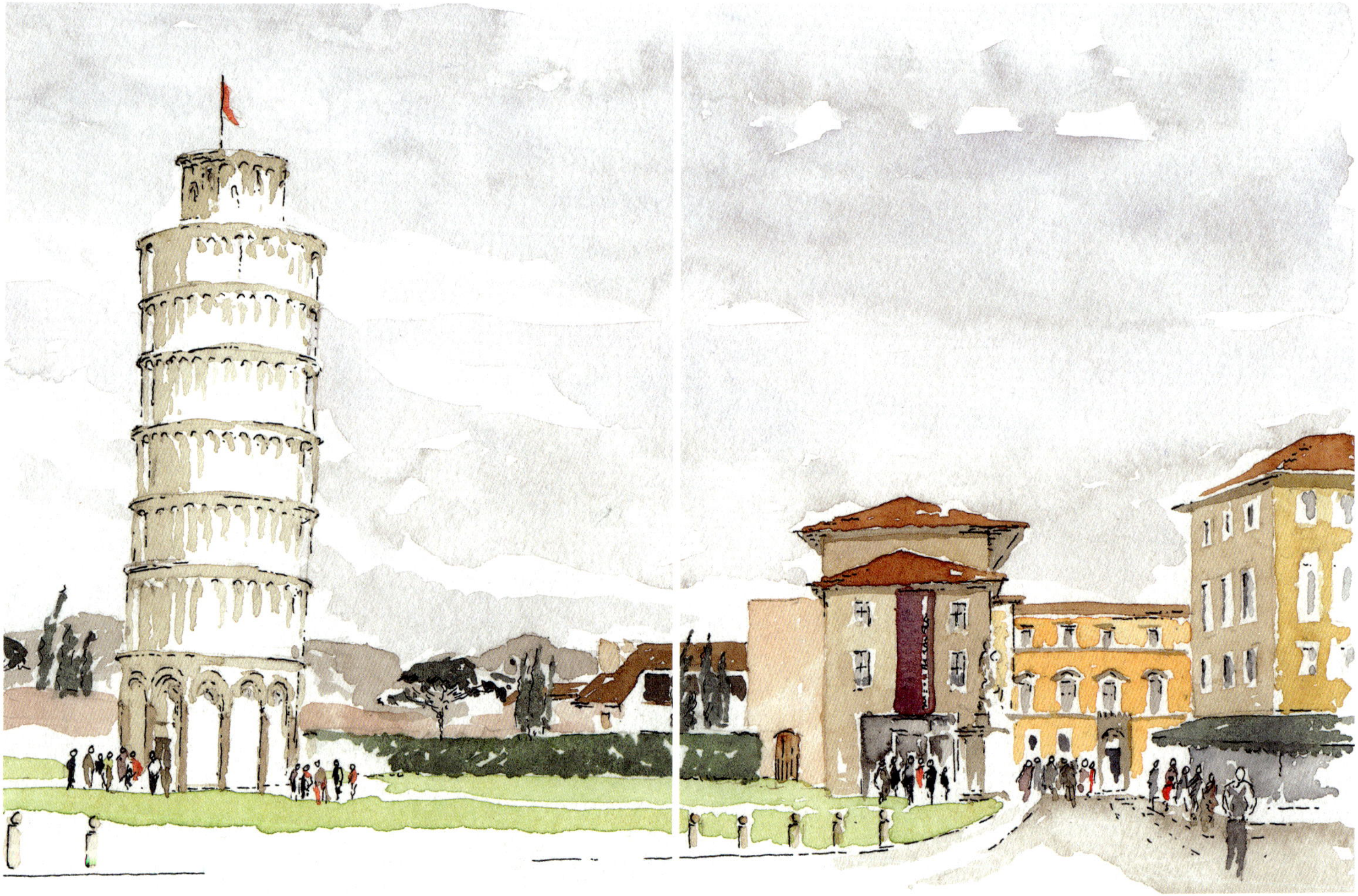

The Crusaders claim to have brought earth from the Holy Land for the cemetery.

The bell tower of the Duomo is Pisa's famous landmark affectionately named the Leaning Tower that was started in 1173, but fortunately not built in one operation as when it started to lean it would have collapsed. Before the fourth storey was added in 1350 the tilt had occurred and the bell tower was added still later bringing it to a height of 54.5 metres. However, by 1993 it was 5.4 m from the vertical and recent work has now stabilised the structure. Although still leaning, it is again open to the public.

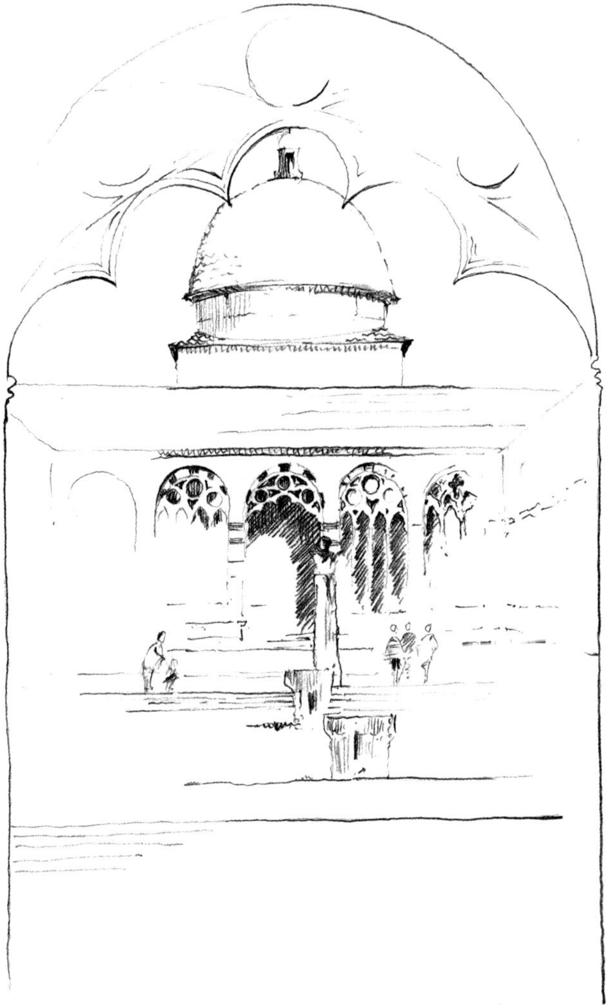

Detail of Camposanto cemetery

This group of buildings was influenced by ideas brought back from the Middle East. Moorish elements of inlaid marble in geometric patterns named Arabesque emerged through the trade that was active between East and West at that time.

The Museo della Sinopie, formally a hospice in the 13th century, displays the 'under drawing' of the Camposanto frescoes that were damaged by bombing in 1914. They are now restored, some experts think over restored; however they make an impressive display. Frescoes are painted on fresh plaster and once dried cannot be changed. However to enable the work to be completed quickly the artist would draw ideas

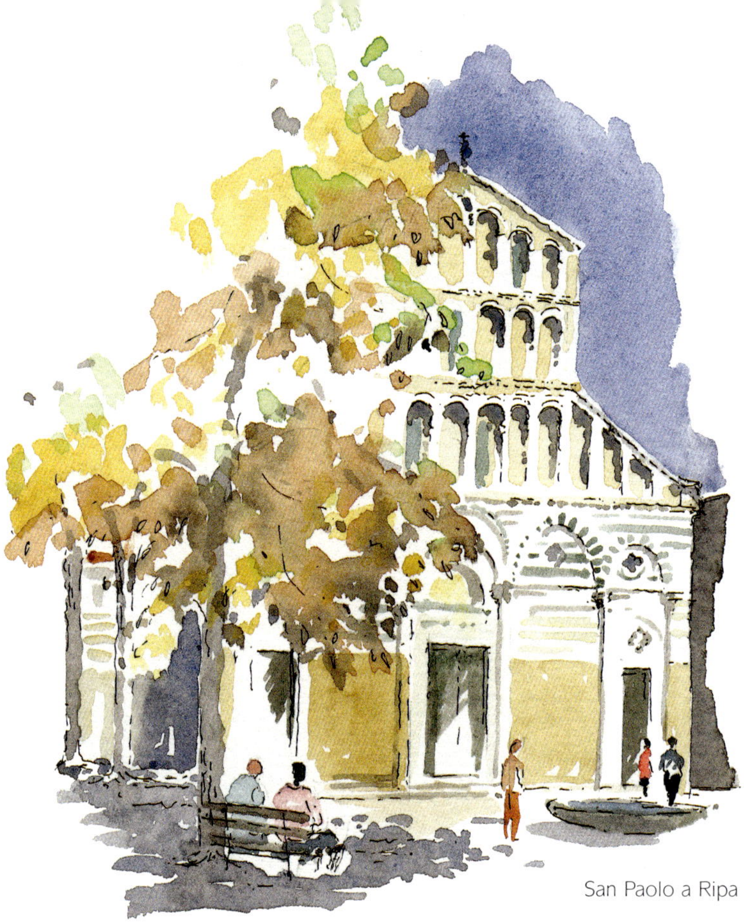

San Paolo a Ripa d'Arno

first and these are called 'under drawing' (sinopie). They remain hidden unless a fresco is removed.

A beautiful church, San Piro a Grado, can be found nearer the coast. It is claimed to be the place where St Peter is believed to have first set foot on Italian soil in AD 42. Foundations of a Roman port found under the church and the present structure dates from 1004. The Nave capitals are interesting coming from an ancient Roman building and fine wall paintings adorn the walls.

The Arno was the main artery linking Florence and Tuscany. Industry developed metalwork, furniture and textiles. Main roads and the autostrada have emerged following the line of the river.

The industrial development along the valley is not attractive, however there are still gems to be found between Pisa and Florence. The unspoilt hilltop town of San Miniato traces its roots back to the Holy Roman Empire. It has a fine Romanesque cathedral with a massive Matilda belltower of the 12th century. Close by, the frescoes and sgraffito of the 17th century Seminary dominate the remarkable Piazza del Seminario. Allegories of Virtue's are painted on the facades with quotations from key

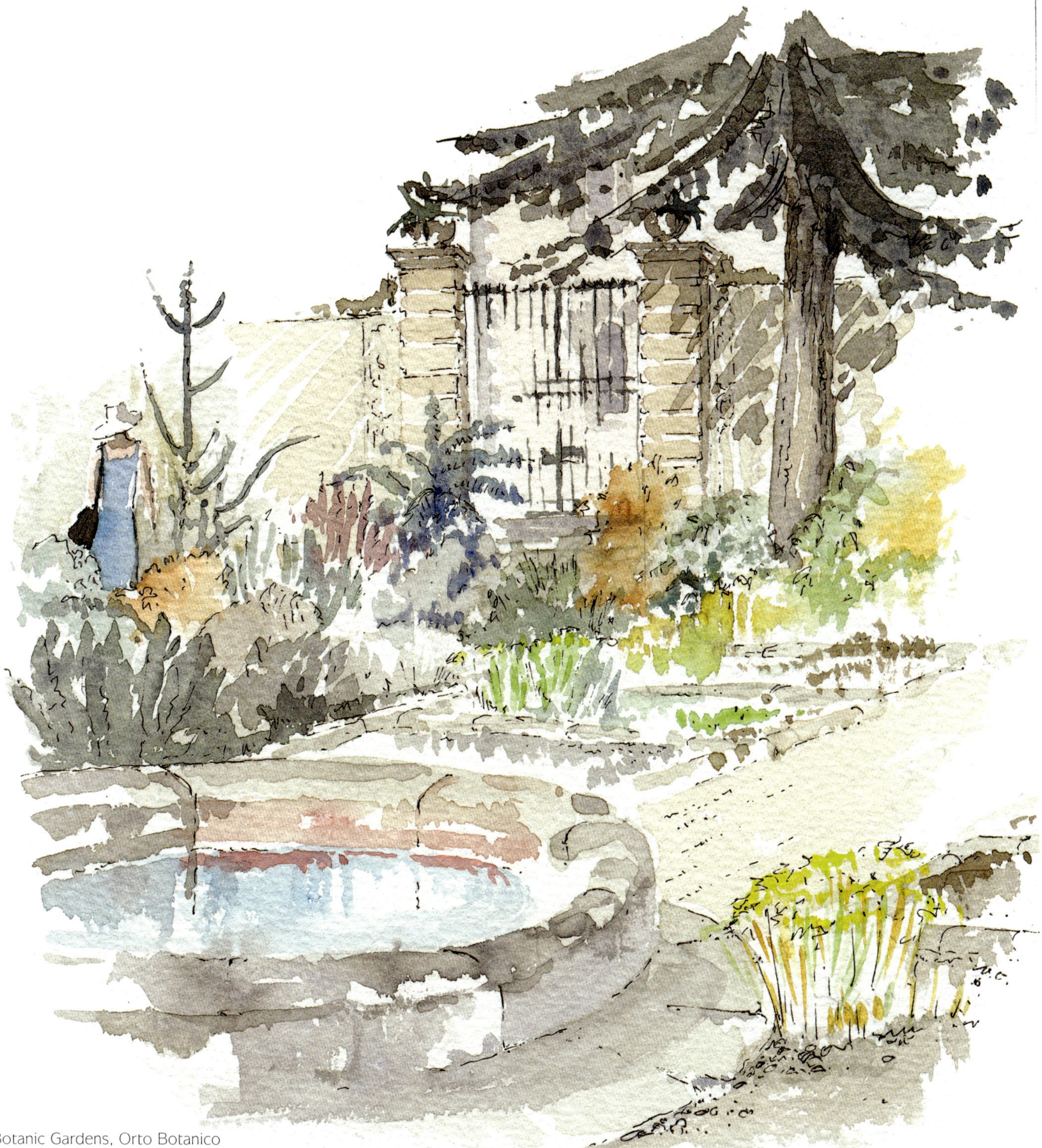

Pisa Botanic Gardens, Orto Botanico

religious texts including writings of Pope Gregory of 540–604.

Vinci is a hilltop village where Leonardo da Vinci was born in 1452. His actual birthplace was amongst the olive groves and vineyards surrounding the village. The 11th century castle has been converted into a museum with a fascinating collection of 100 models of machines built to his designs. Five hundred years later in 2003 Television Channel 4 organised the reproduction of the glider to his specification and it flew like a bird. Medical science is applying his theory of vortex formation to solve problems with the heart valve. Leonardo's great genius of the past continues to influence many developments and inventions of the present today.

The Romans first exploited the hot springs from volcanoes in various parts of Tuscany. Spa towns in these locations, Montecatini Terme was one, expanded in the period of the art Nouveau style of 1915 with elegant spas and beautiful Parks that continue to attract people today. There is a matching railway station of the same period. The original spa is on the top of the hill – Montecatini Alto.

A surprise is to be found in the industrial town of Pistoia where interesting medieval streets surround the central Piazza del Duomo. The cathedral di San Zeno has an enormous tower that was originally the watchtower in the 12th century city walls. In this sector of the town is the Ospedale del Ceppo built in the 13th century with an interesting 16th century portico decorated with a glazed terracotta frieze by Giovanni della Robbia, illustrating the Seven deeds of Charity with decorative medallions above each column. Pistoia is the birthplace of Marino Marini, one of Italy's famous artists of the 20th century. The impressive collection of his work is to be found in a converted ancient church in Florence.

Little remains of the Etruscan and Roman town of Prato that is now a large industrial city. However the old mediaeval centre survives and still has its charm centred on the cathedral Piazza Duomo. San

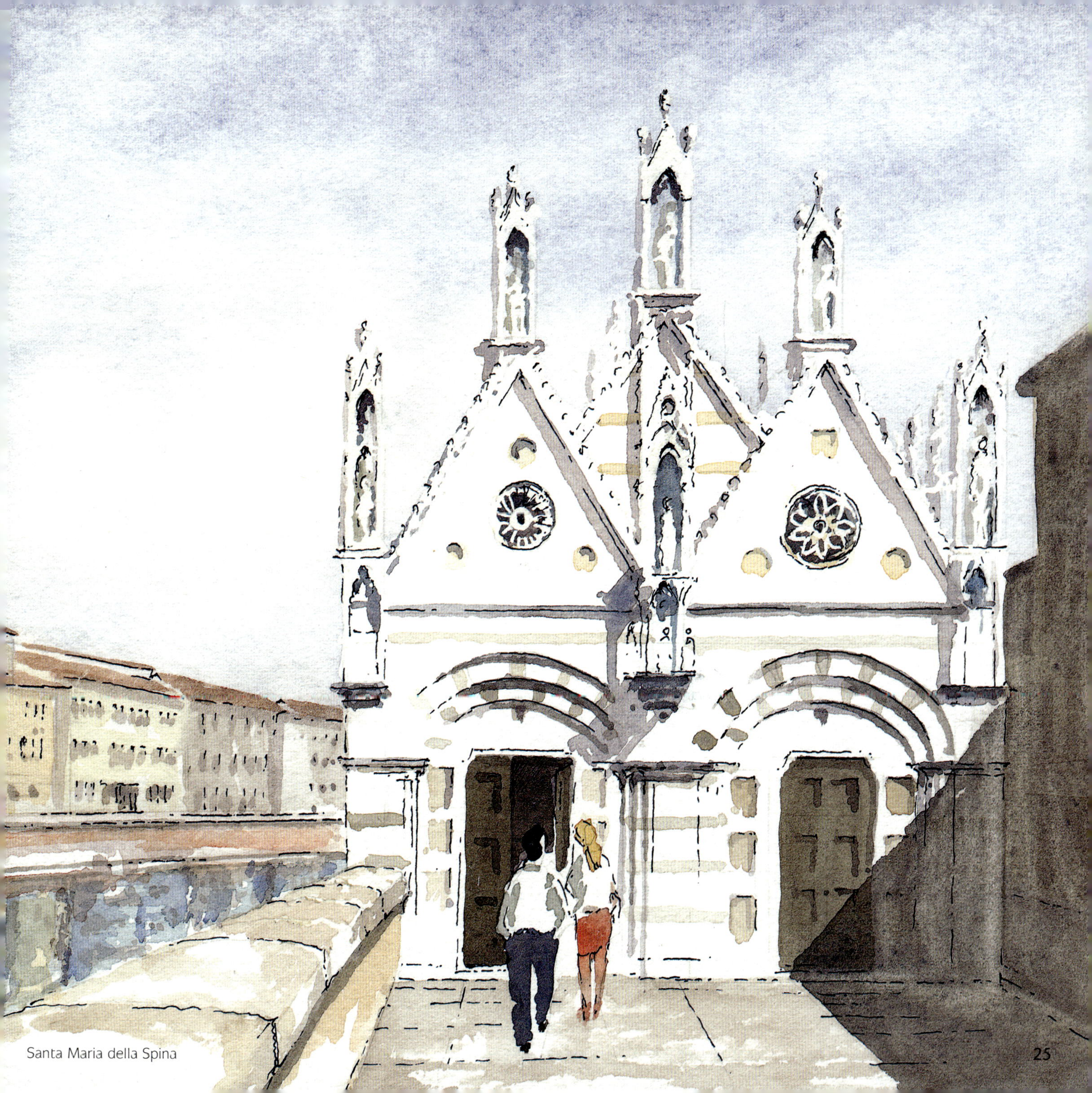

Santa Maria della Spina

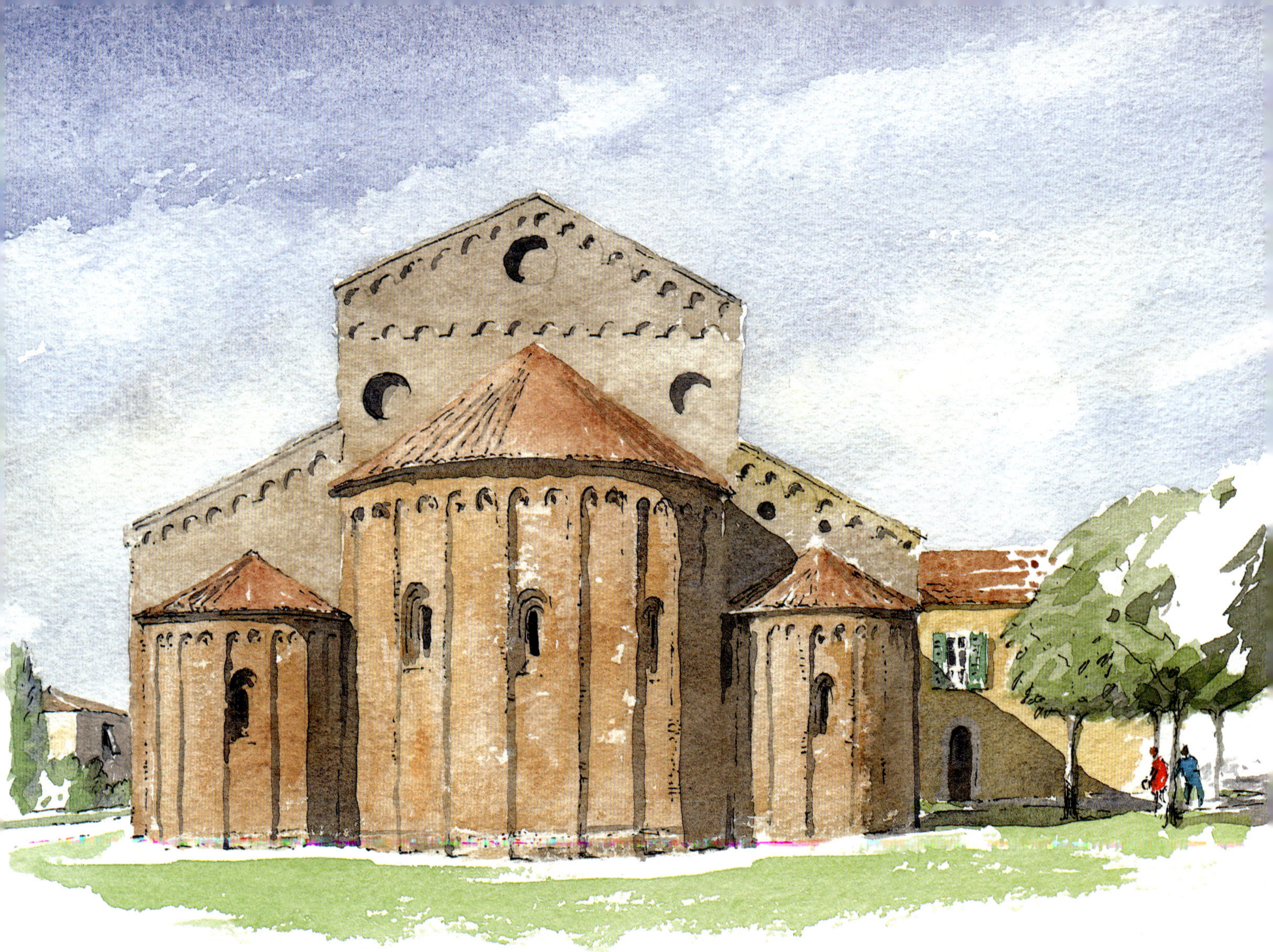

On the coast near Pisa San Piro a Grado
11th century Romanesque basilica

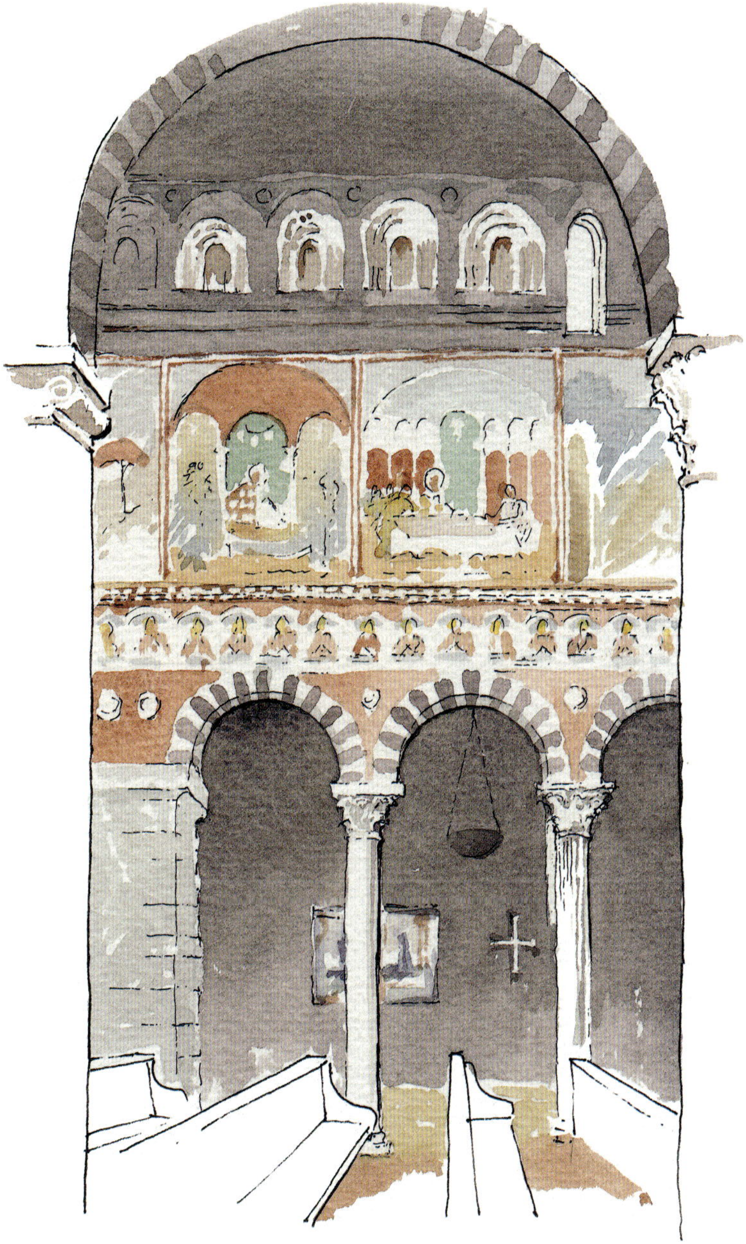

Interior of the Basilica with some
foundation and columns from
the Roman Period

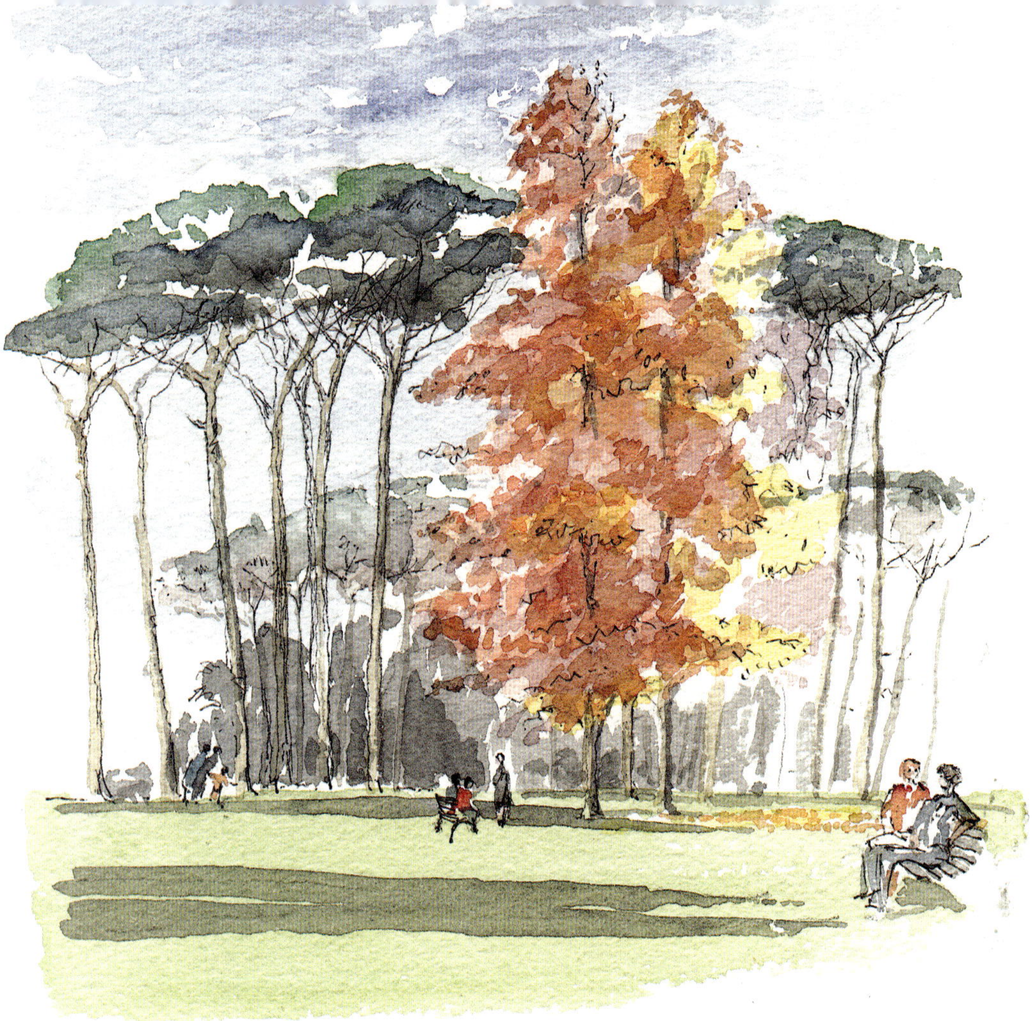

A Park, Montecatini Terme

Stefano has an impressive external pulpit of the Holy Girdle by Danotello 1438 on the corner of the main façade. It acts as a visual counterbalance to the tower. Inside is to be found 'The life of John the Baptist' 1452 by Filippo Lippi and his Madonna and Child altarpiece 1453 is now to be found in the City museum. The nearby Palazzo Pretorio 13th to 14th century is huge, and illustrates their love of power expressed without shame in their buildings. Castello dell Imperatore is an imposing castle built by the German Holy Roman Emperor, Frederick II, in 1237 during his campaign to conquer Italy. It was fascinating to find that the City had honoured the friendship between Marini and Henry Moore with a

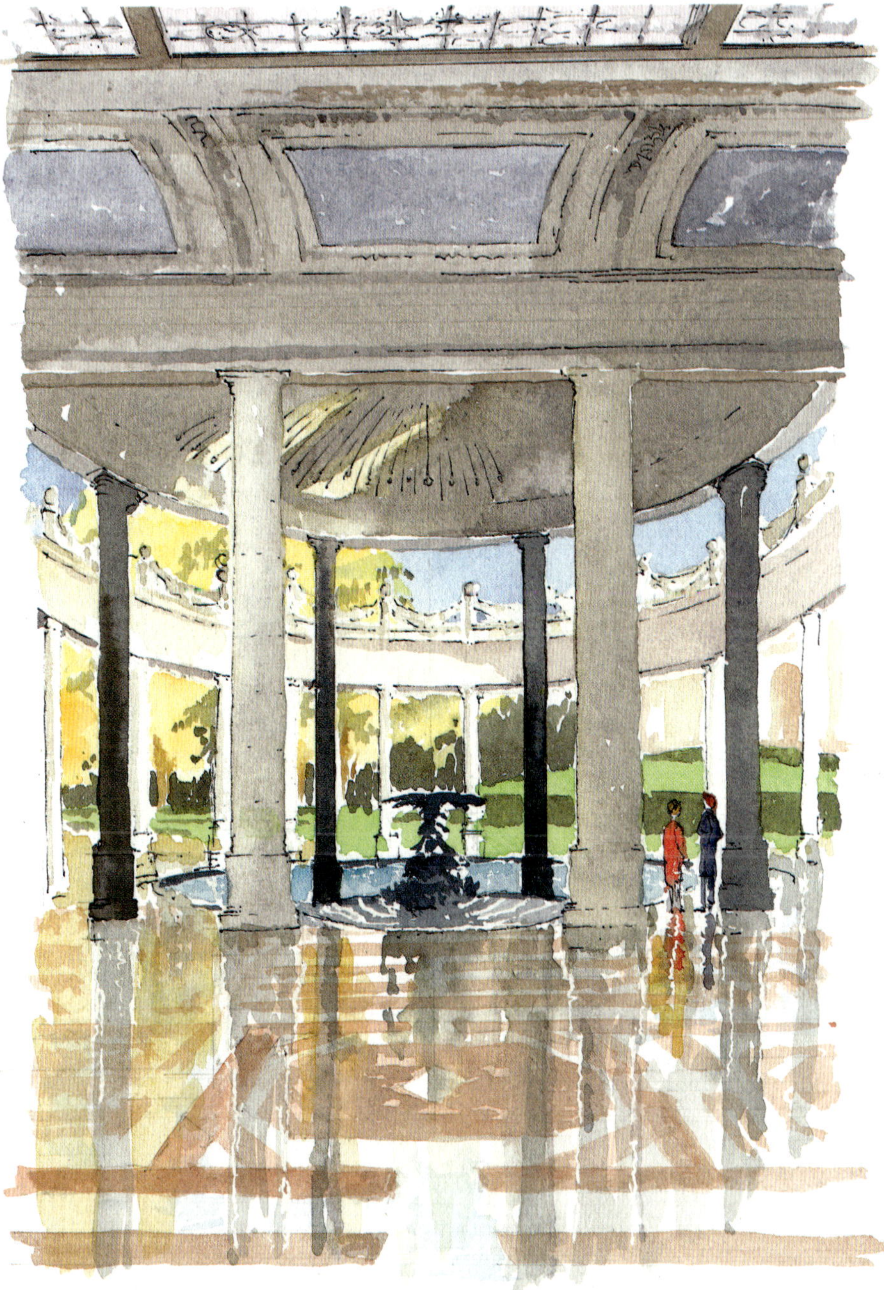

Tettuccio Spa, Montecatini

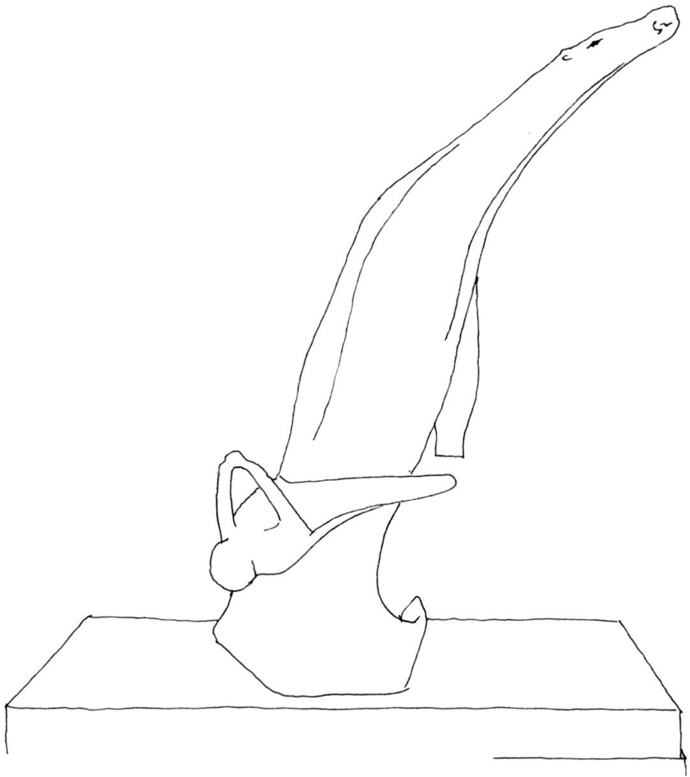

Bronze sculpture of horseman falling off his horse by Marino Marini 1953 in the courtyard of Palazzo del Comune

Pistoia

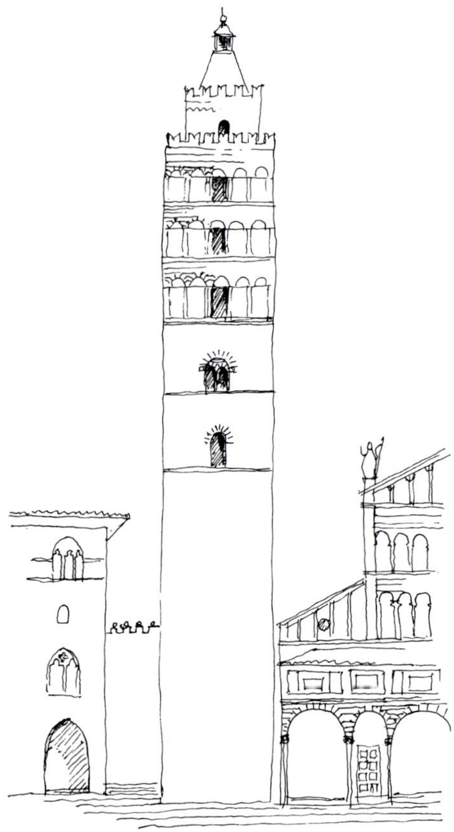

13th century Tower flanked by the Duomo and Palazzo del Comune

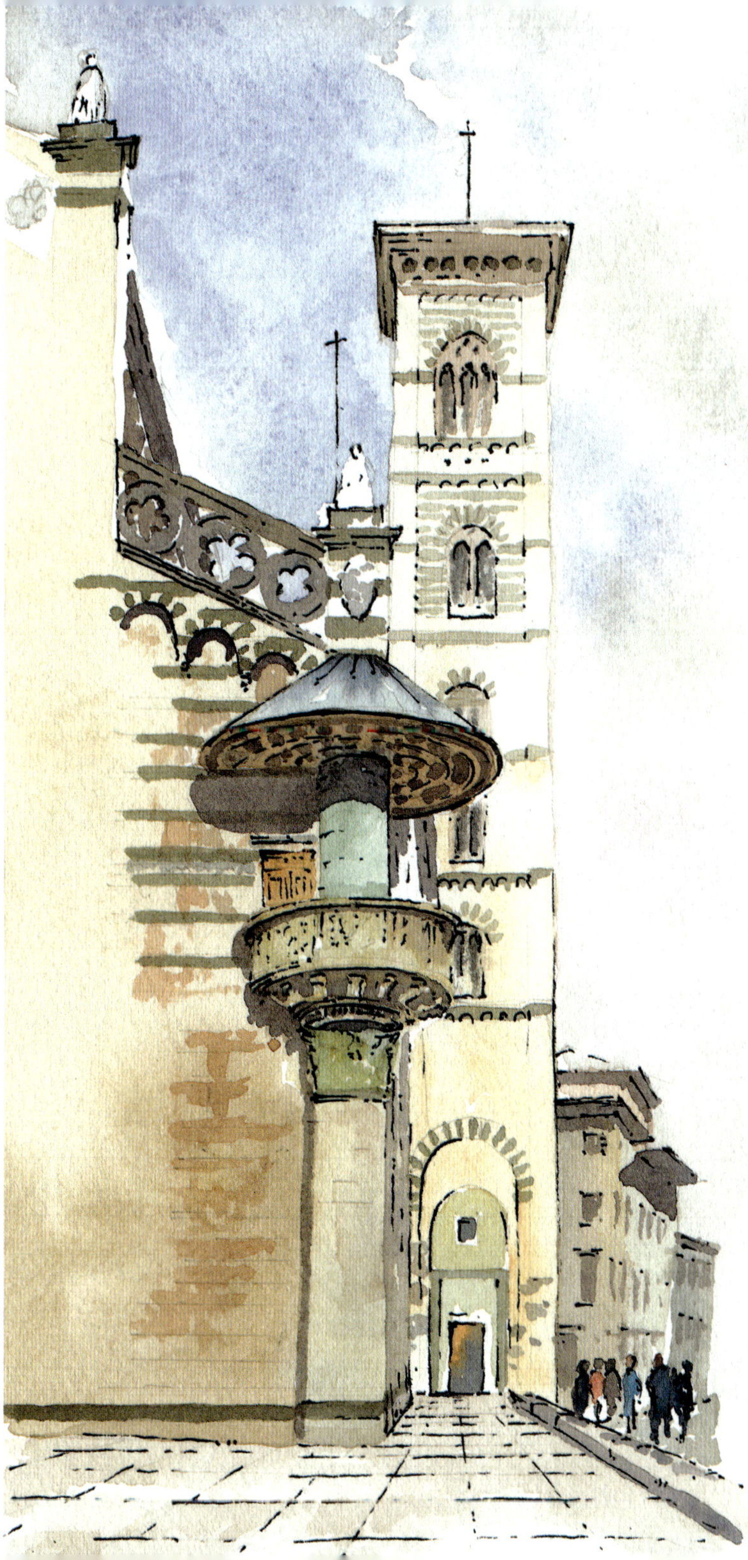

Duomo San Stefano, Prato

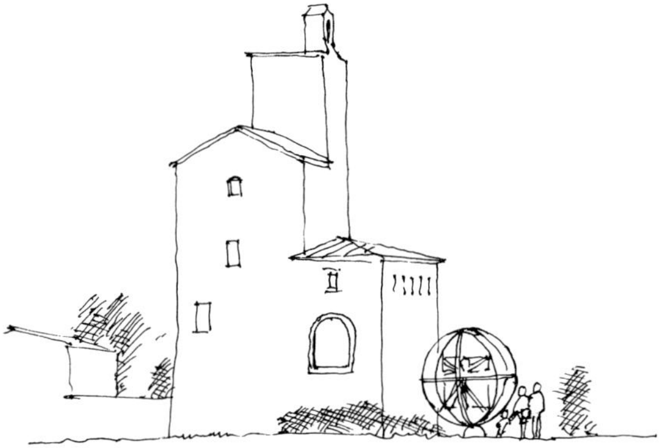

Leonardo da Vinci Museum, Vinci

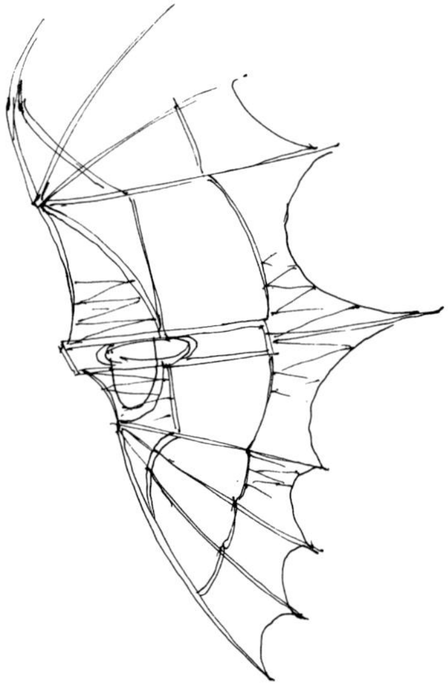

Model of a flying machine

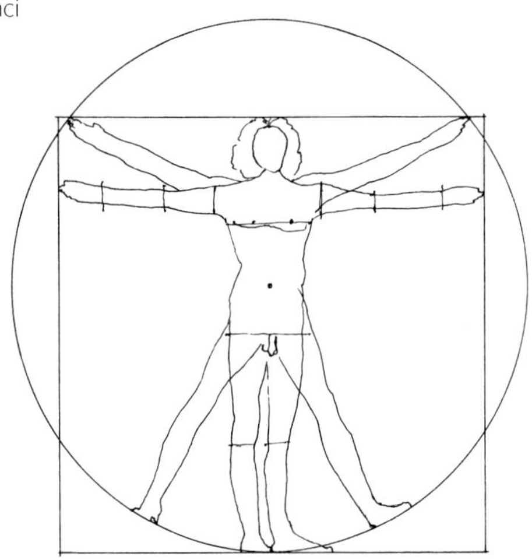

Drawing and three-dimensional concept of the relationship of the human figure to the circle, first studied by Vitruvius AD 1, in the Renaissance by Alberti and Leonardo da Vinci

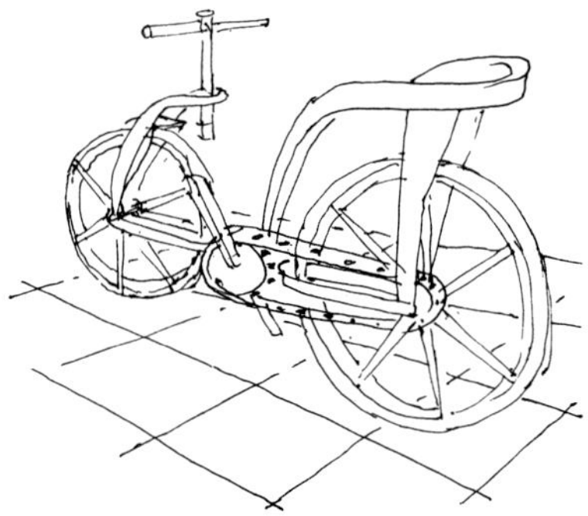

Model of bicycle

large-scale sculpture 'square shape with cut' in Piazza San Marco. It was refreshing to find an impressive museum of contemporary art. – Luigi Pecci Museum where they stage large travelling exhibitions. At the time of my visit in 2002 the works of Paladino, an important Italian artist were exhibited, showing the painting and sculpture obtained from collections around the world. A new work 'New York' conceived after September 11, 2002, was centre stage. In the grounds of the museum is a powerful sculpture

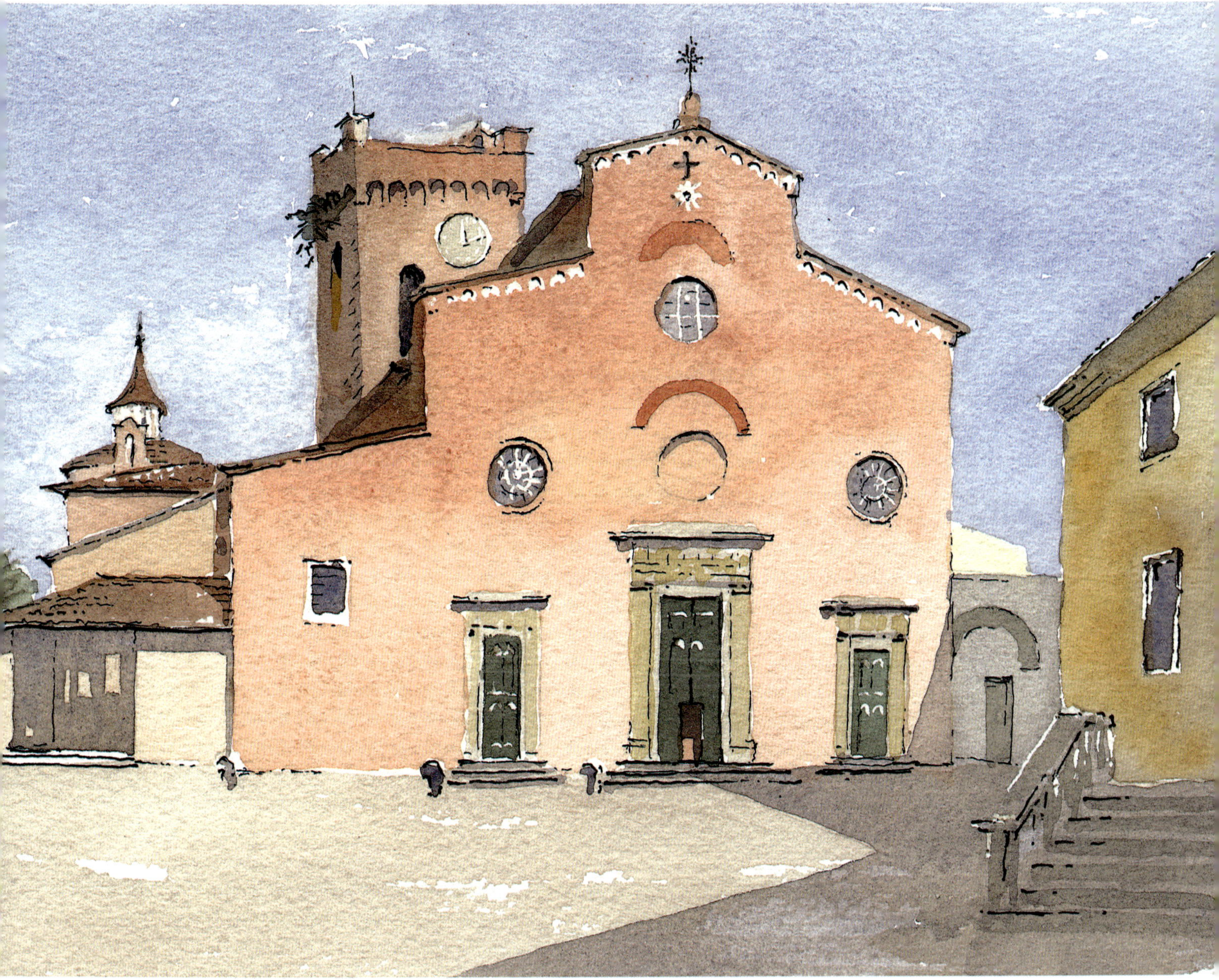

San Miniato

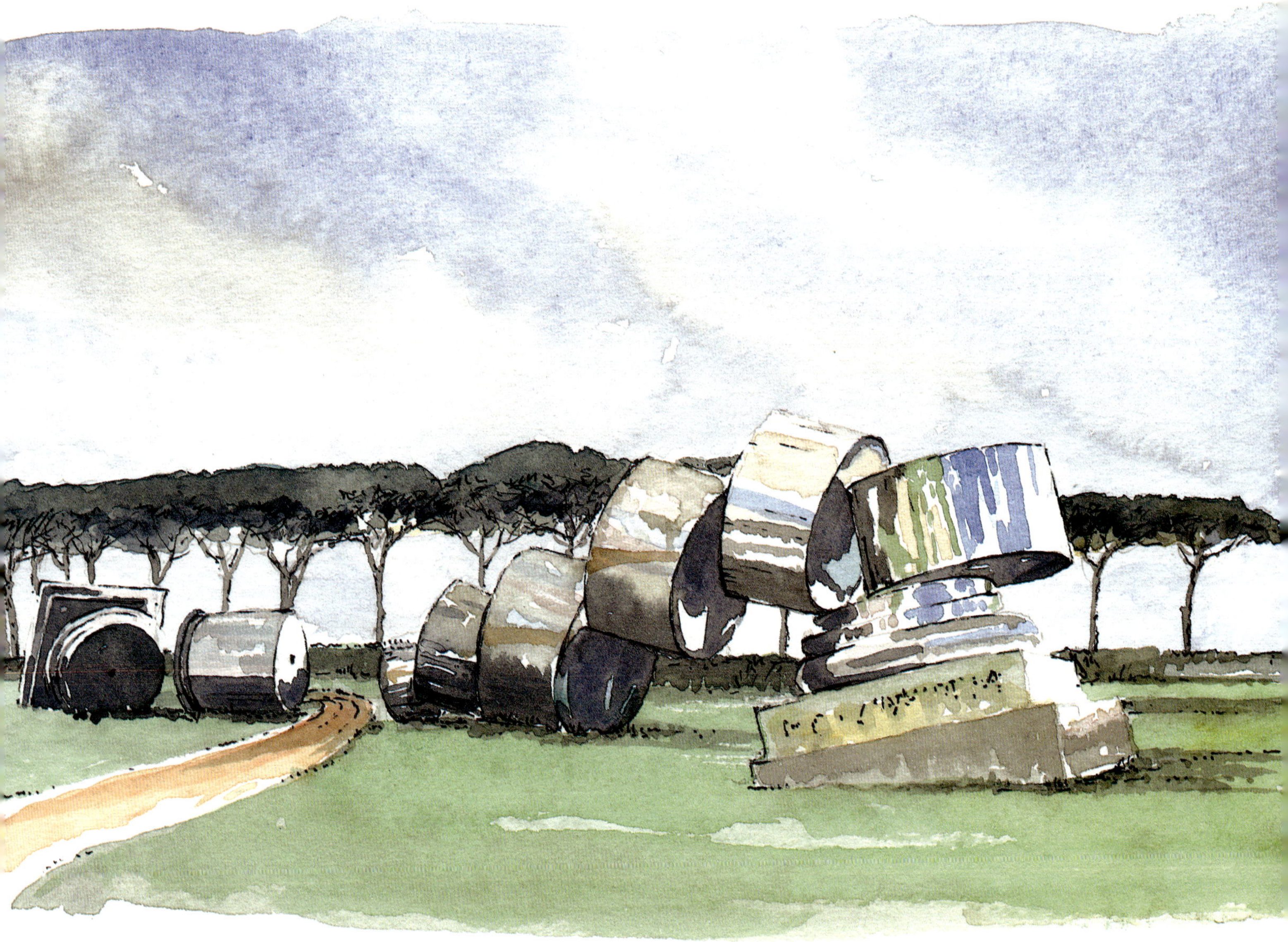

 Sculpture in the garden of Luigi Pecci Museum, Prato

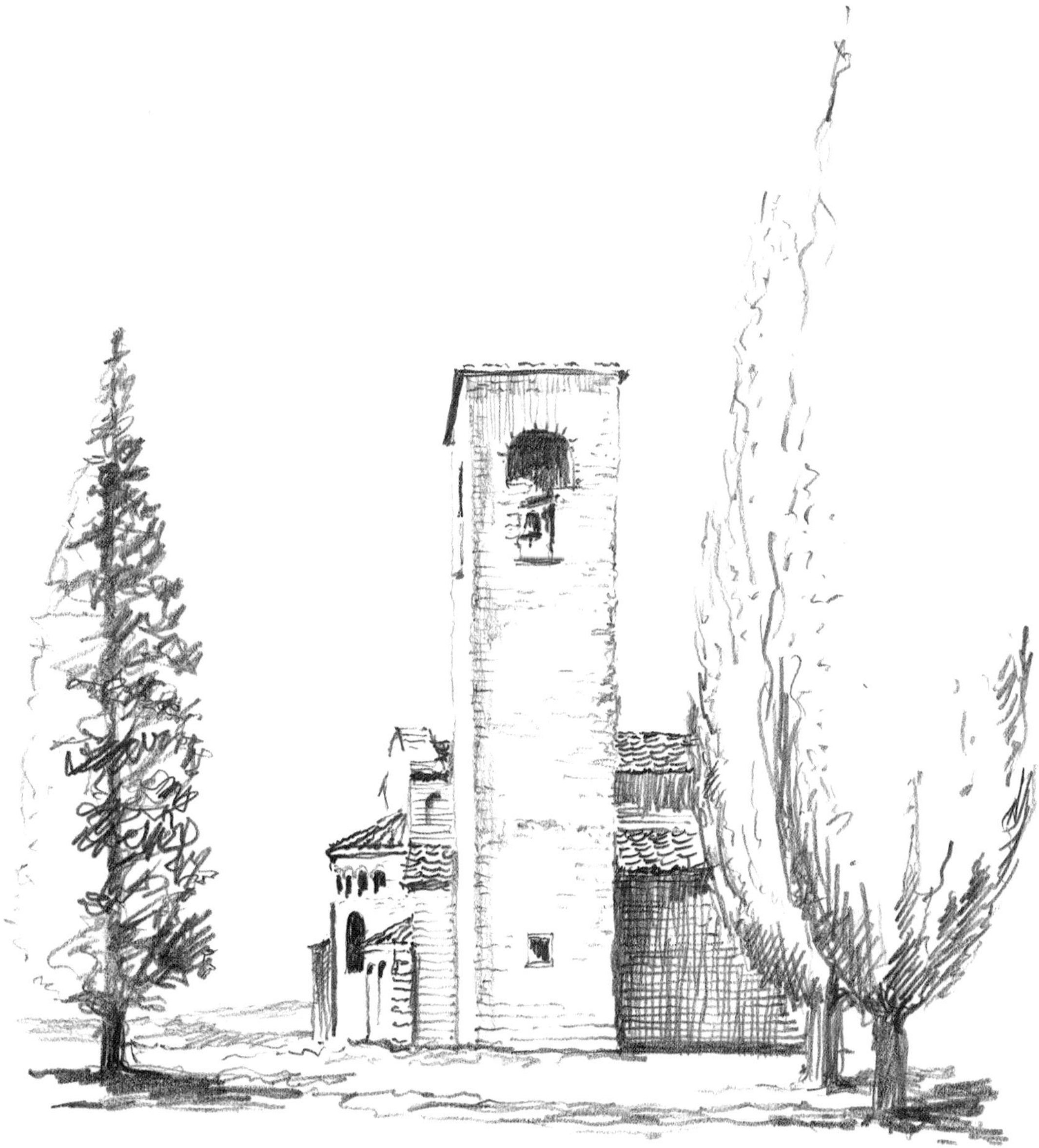

The church of San Leonardo, Artimino

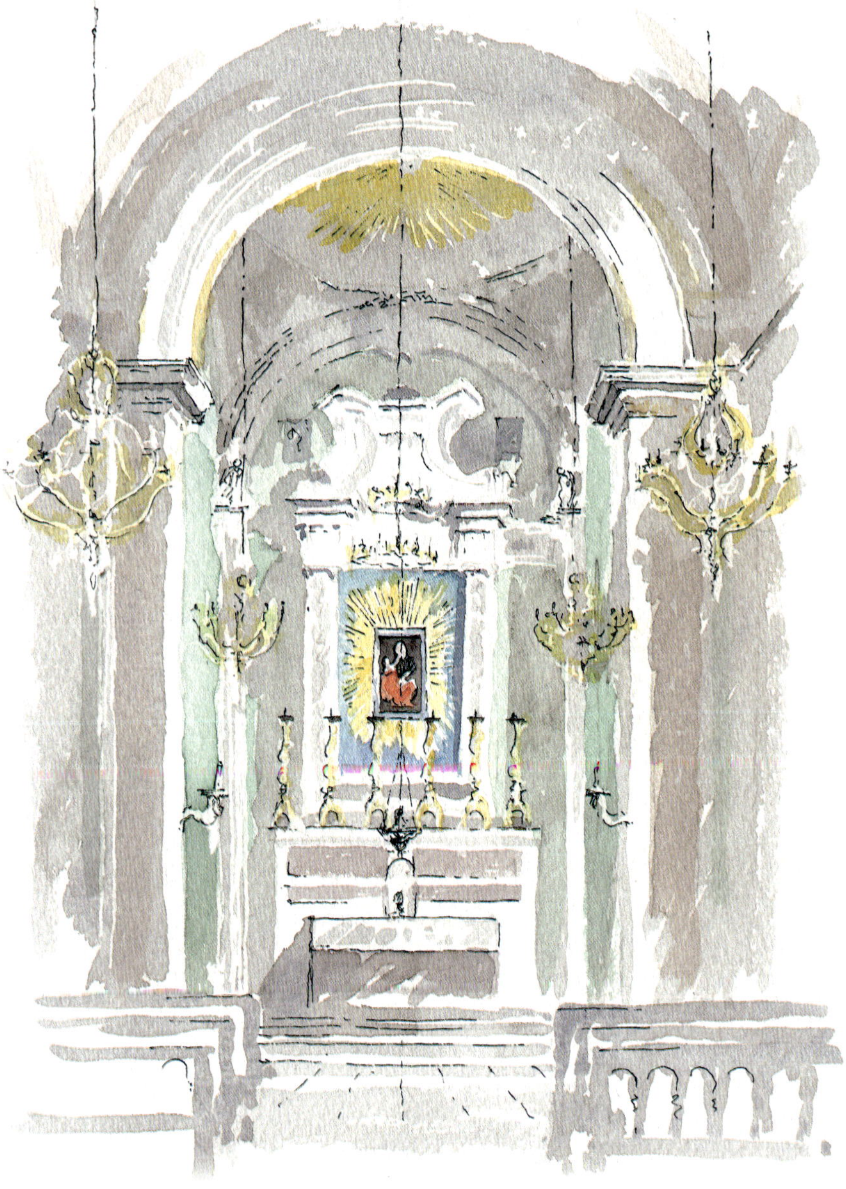

Baroque Chapel of Madonna della Rocca in the old borgo of Villa Saletta with a copy of the stolen picture of the Madonna della Rocca above the altar

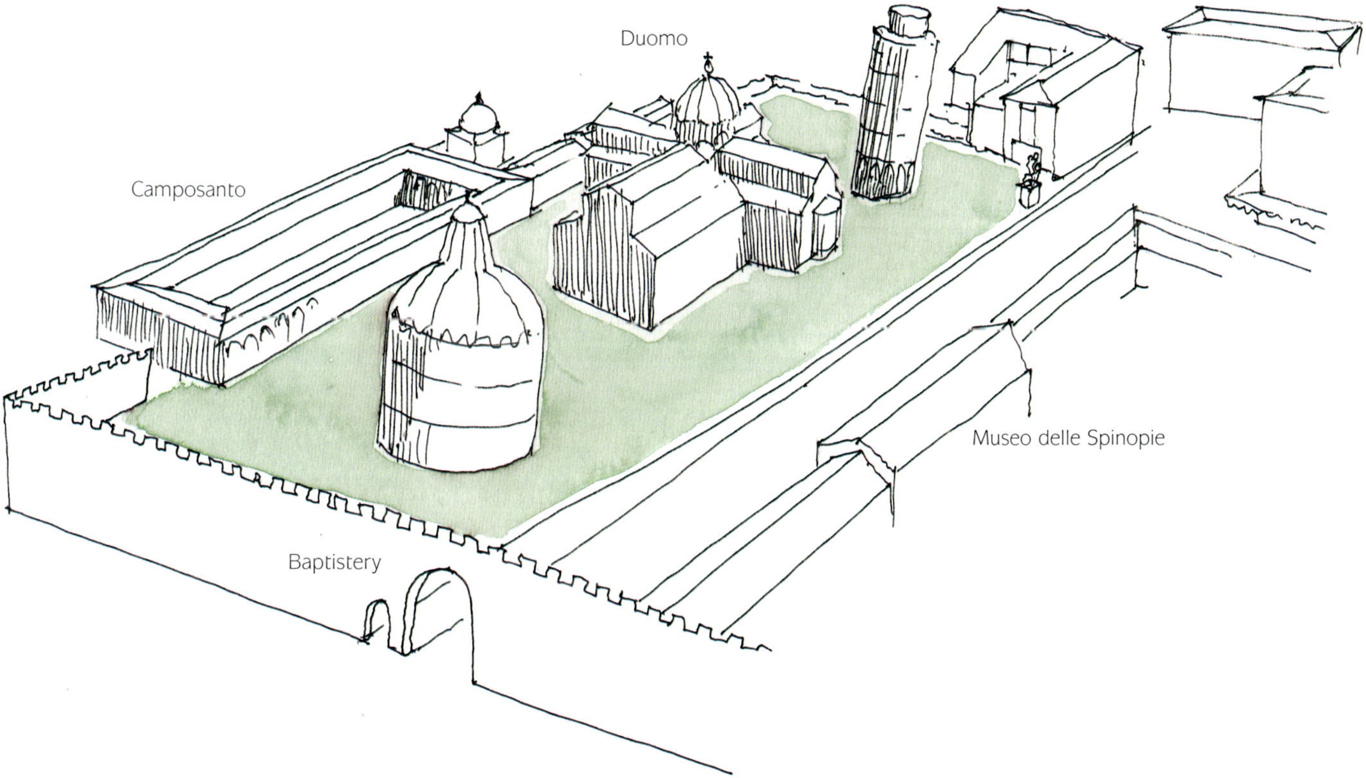
Leaning Tower
Duomo Museum
Duomo
Camposanto
Museo delle Spinopie
Baptistery

Pisa

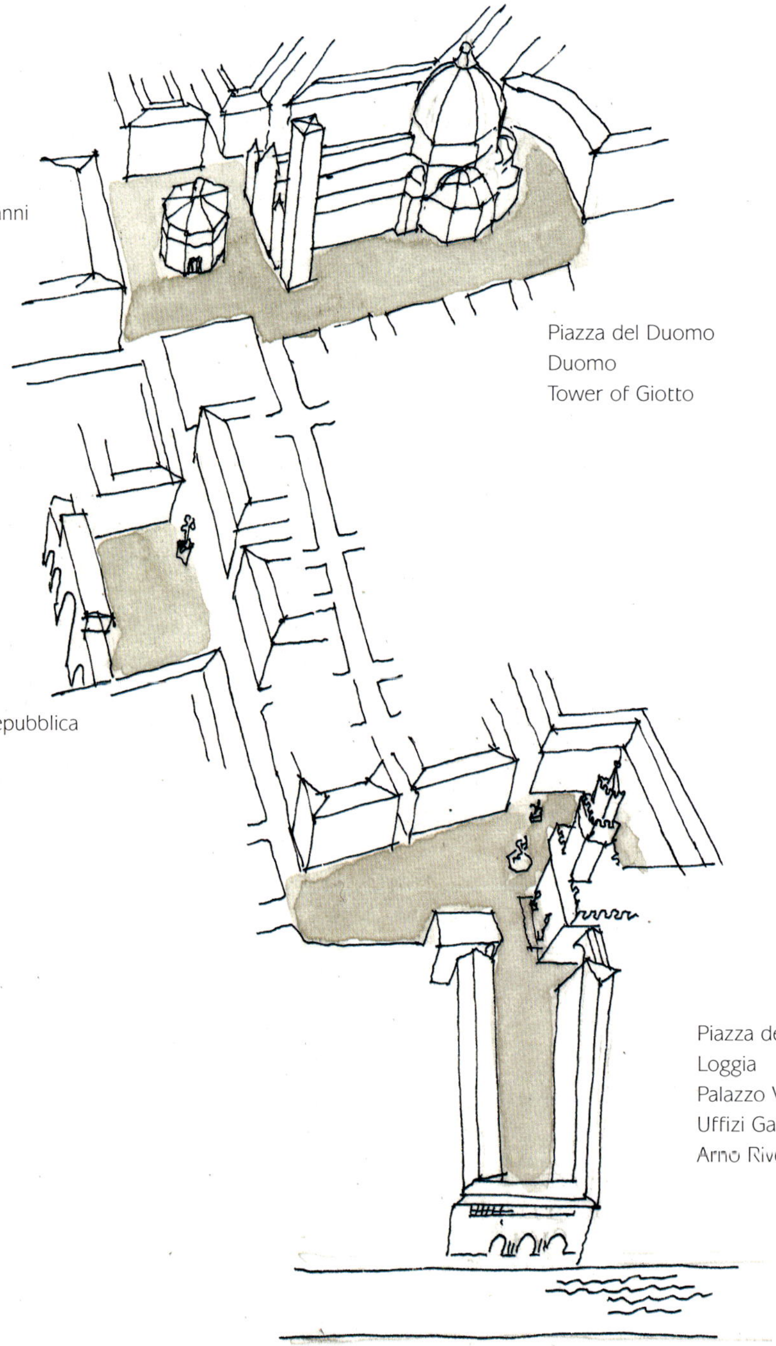
Piazza di S Giovanni
Baptistery
Piazza del Duomo
Duomo
Tower of Giotto
Piazza della Repubblica
Piazza della Signoria
Loggia
Palazzo Vecchio
Uffizi Gallery
Arno River

Florence

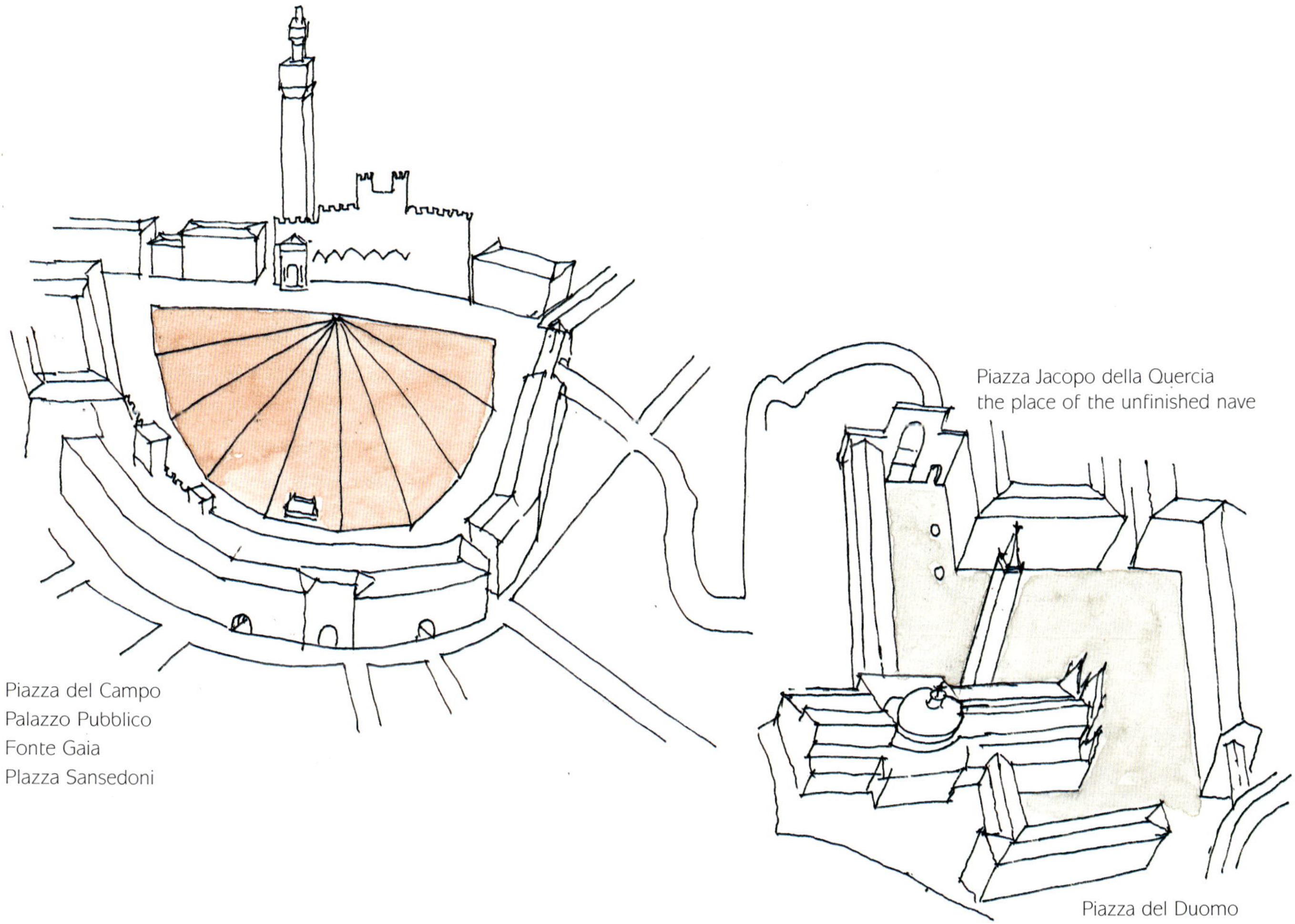
Piazza Jacopo della Quercia
the place of the unfinished nave
Piazza del Campo
Palazzo Pubblico
Fonte Gaia
Plazza Sansedoni
Piazza del Duomo
Duomo

Siena

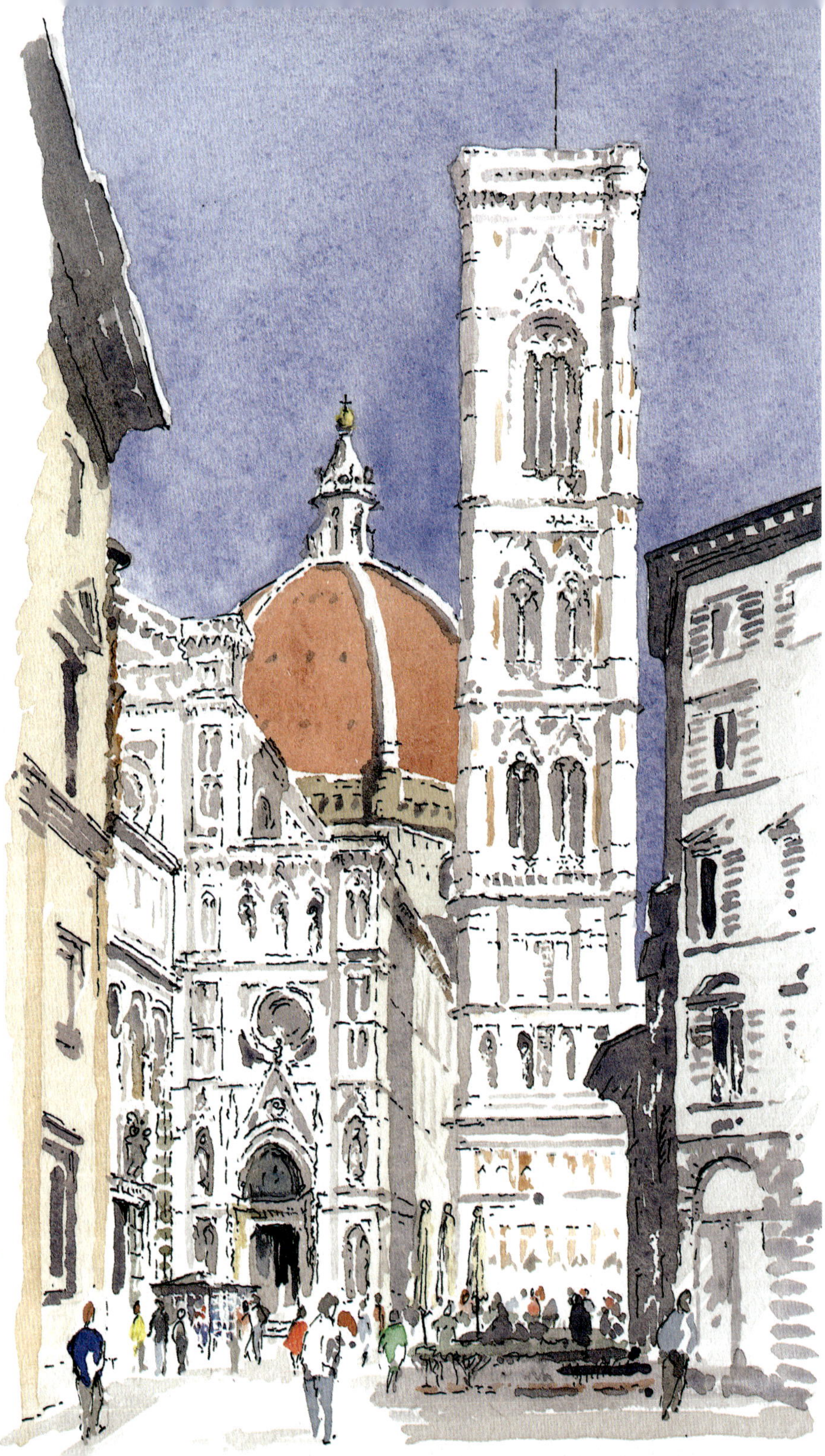

Duomo, Baptistery and
Giotto's Campanile

Florence

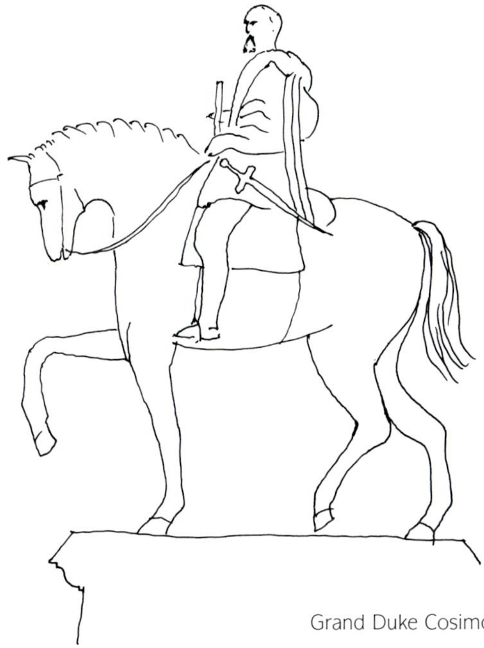

Grand Duke Cosimo I

Tennyson wrote

'In bright vignettes, and each complete,
Of towers or duomo summer sweet,
Or palace, how the city glittered,
Through cypress avenues at our feet.'

The Renaissance was to change the face of Florence. The coming together in the 13th century of enlightened clients and sponsors, highly creative, intellectual, dynamic artists and architects culminating in a dramatic change and the greatest achievements the art world has witnessed. This 'age of genius' was sponsored by the humanist Medici dynasty that looked to classical Rome to gain inspiration by reading Horace and Pliny, and not seeking authority from the church.

Florence immediately became the epicentre of the Renaissance and this new movement spread rapidly throughout Europe in the 15th century. Explore and discover not only the buildings and works of art, but absorb the atmosphere created by the fascinating piazzas of great variety sometimes punctuated by a range of large outdoor sculptures and linked by narrow streets and surprising vistas.

Examine Santa Maria Novella, close to the railway station, a gothic church built 1297–1350. Inside a masterpiece 'The Trinity' by Masaccio, challenges art and architecture by the use of perspective for the first time, making suggestions in three dimensions, thereby forming an invitation for the architect to solve the construction of the barrel vault that lead to the birth of the Renaissance.

As the magic of the city unfolds, narrow streets link beautiful buildings set in superb spaces. One such area is the Piazza di San Giovanni and the Piazza del Duomo where the Baptistery, Duomo and

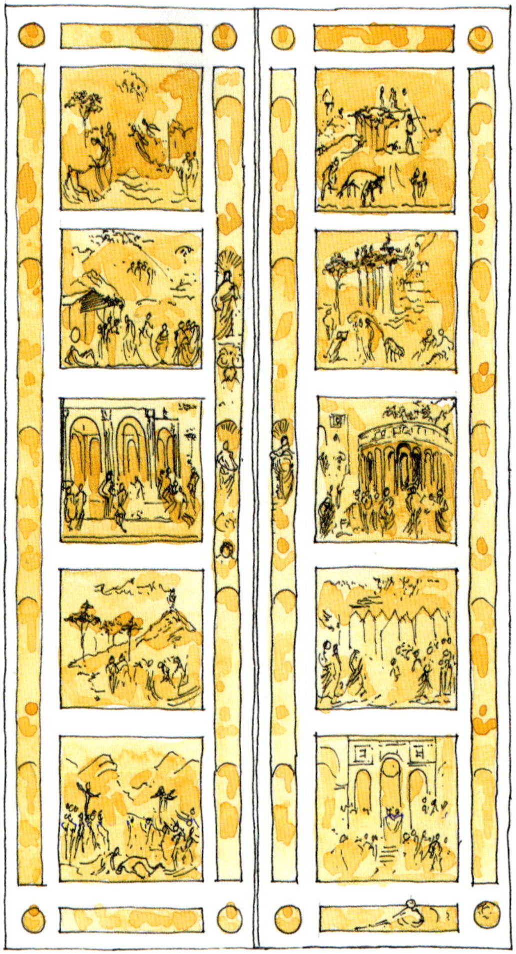

Baptistery the 'Gates of Paradise' by Lorenzo Ghiberti, the originals are in the Museo dell'Opera del Duomo. An early example of perspective to achieve an illusion of depth on a flat surface

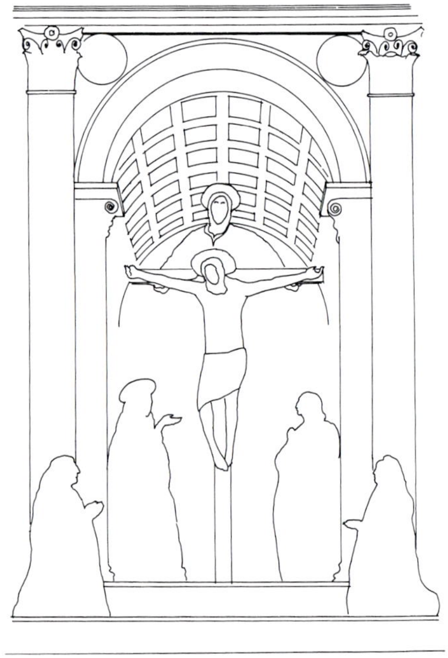

'The Trinity' 1425-27 by Masaccio in Santo Maria Novella

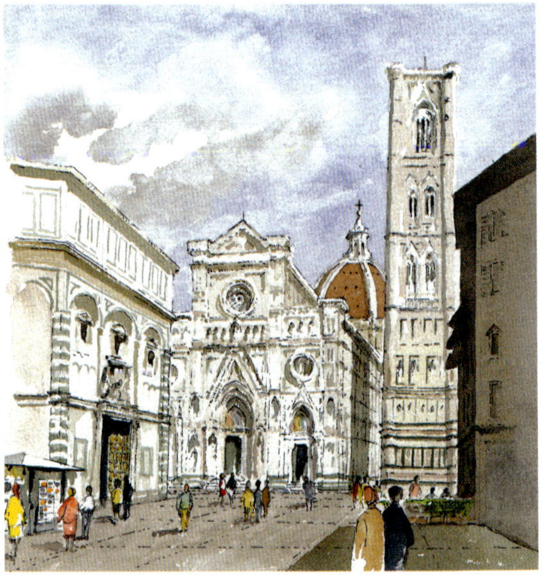

A collage to explore the Baptistery, Duomo and Campanile

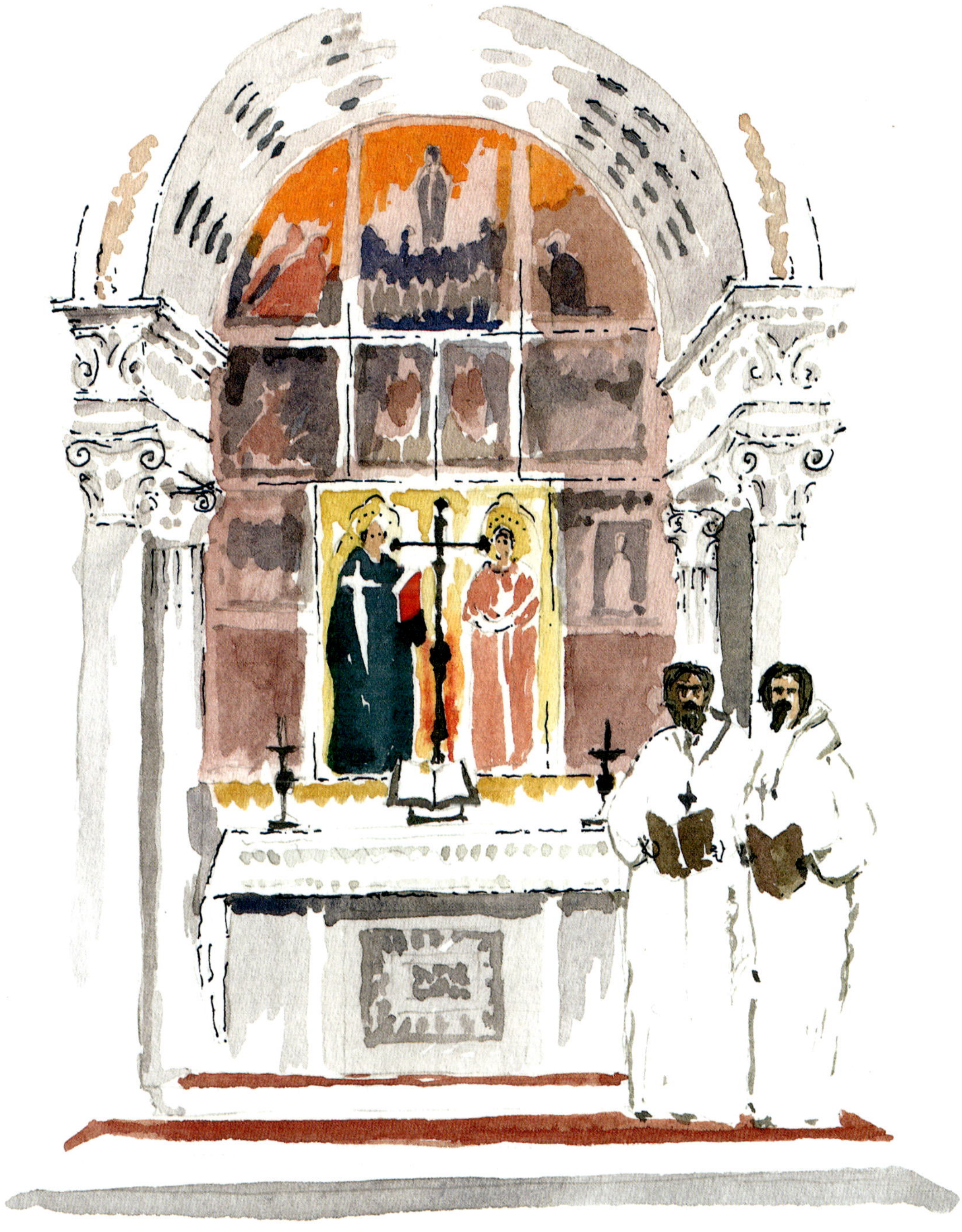

Interior of San Miniato al Monte

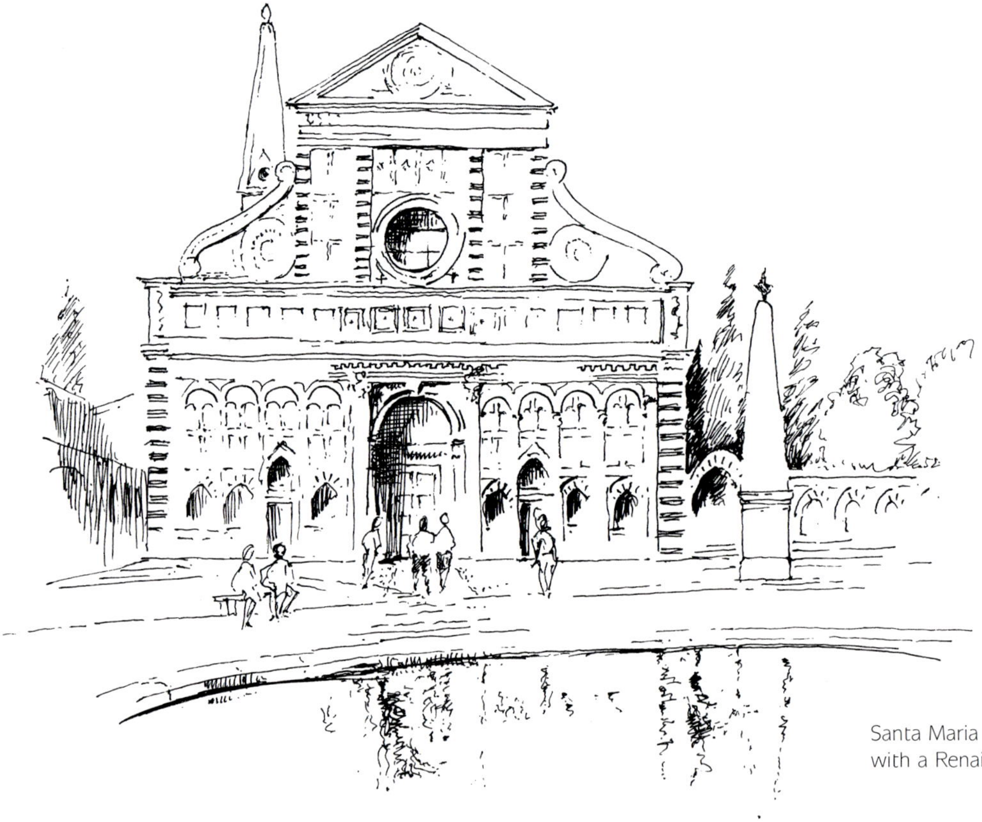

Santa Maria Novella Romanesque
with a Renaissance façade by Alberti

the Camponile are situated. A static view does not reveal the beauty or the spaces experienced by moving through the two Piazzas. The one view point or set piece misses the experience of the place.

The Baptistery is a Romanesque building from the 11th century with the famous bronze door panels by Ghiberti conveying stories of the old Testament in sculpture. Remember the originals are in the Museo dell' Opera del Duomo. A beautiful interior with work attributed to Cimabue.

Santa Maria del Fiore, the Duomo, was started in the 13th century. A vast plan without a design solution to roof the huge space of the sanctuary. Brunelleschi submitted an untried design in 1420 of flattened domes linked by a series of arches and buttresses to produce a masterpiece for the roof that demonstrates the spirit of the Renaissance. Vasari described it as 'an architectural genius sent down from heaven to bring new form to an architecture that had gone astray'. The campanile by Giotto completes and articulates the spaces.

To the north is San Lorenzo, a complex to explore and for me the main attractions are the tombs symbolising Night, Day, Dawn and Dusk by Michelangelo. His design of the staircase of the main entrance

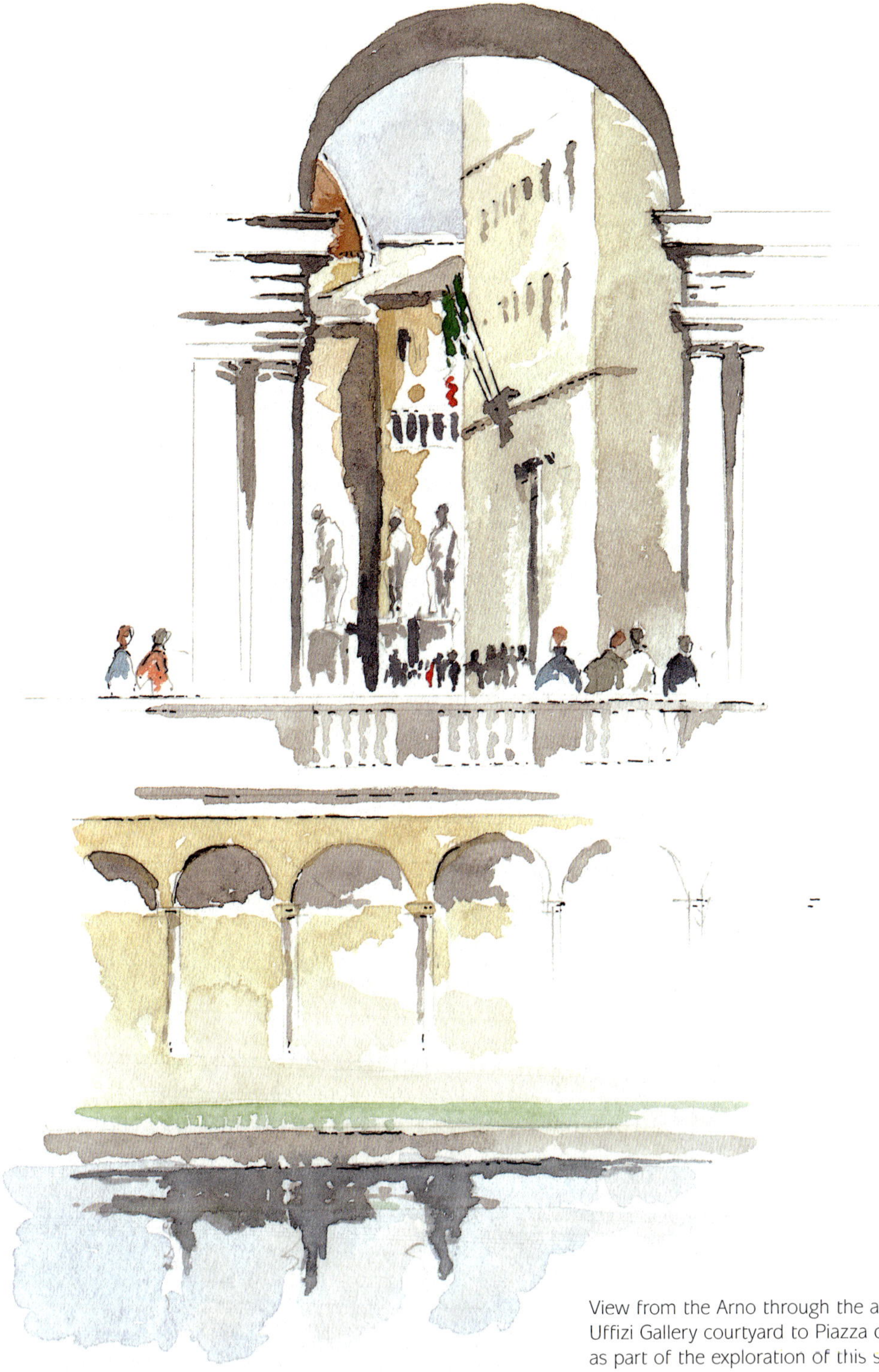

View from the Arno through the arches of the Uffizi Gallery courtyard to Piazza della Signoria as part of the exploration of this space

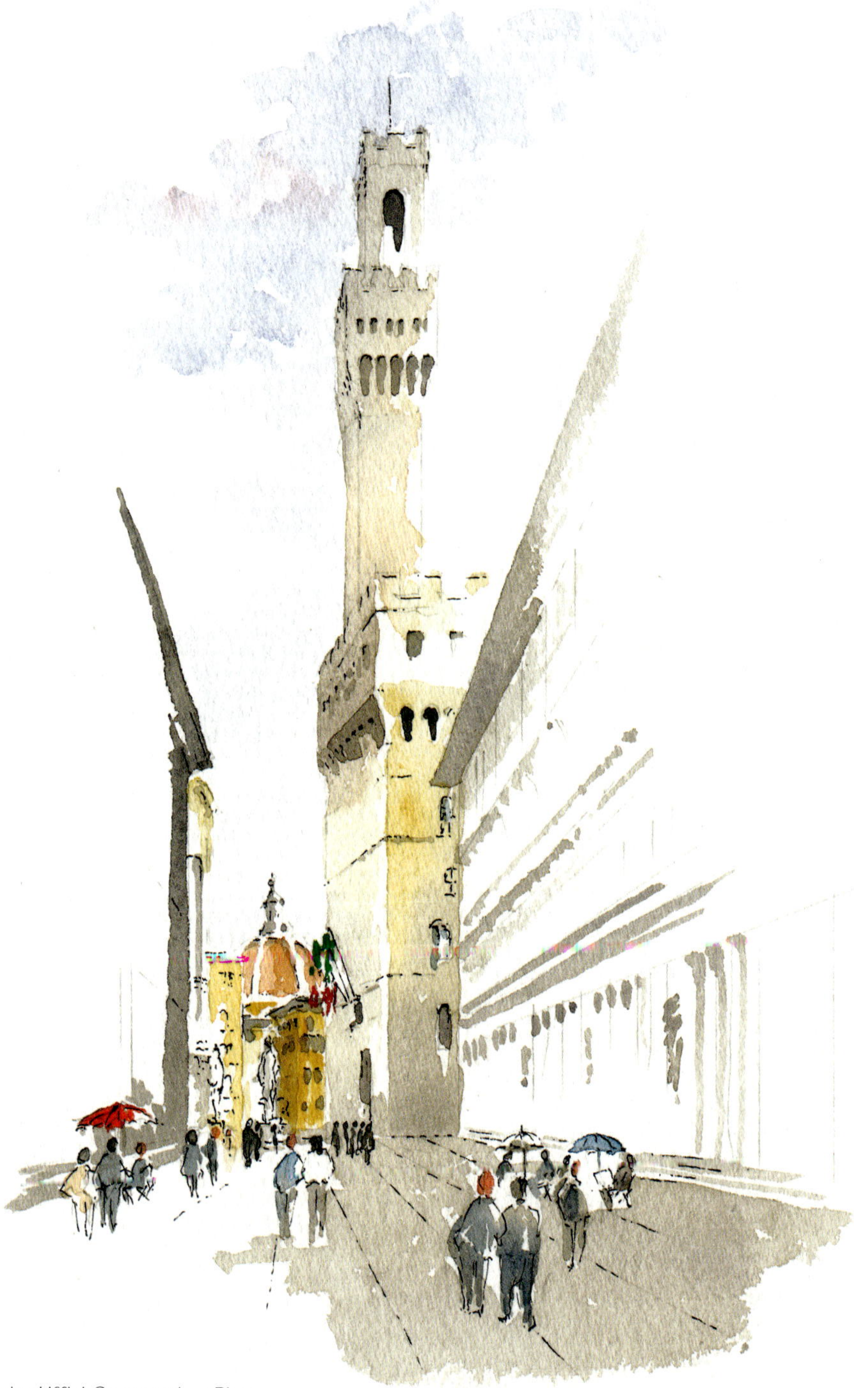

From the courtyard of the Uffizi Courtyard to Piazza della Signoria with Palazzo Vecchio and the dome of the Duomo in the distance

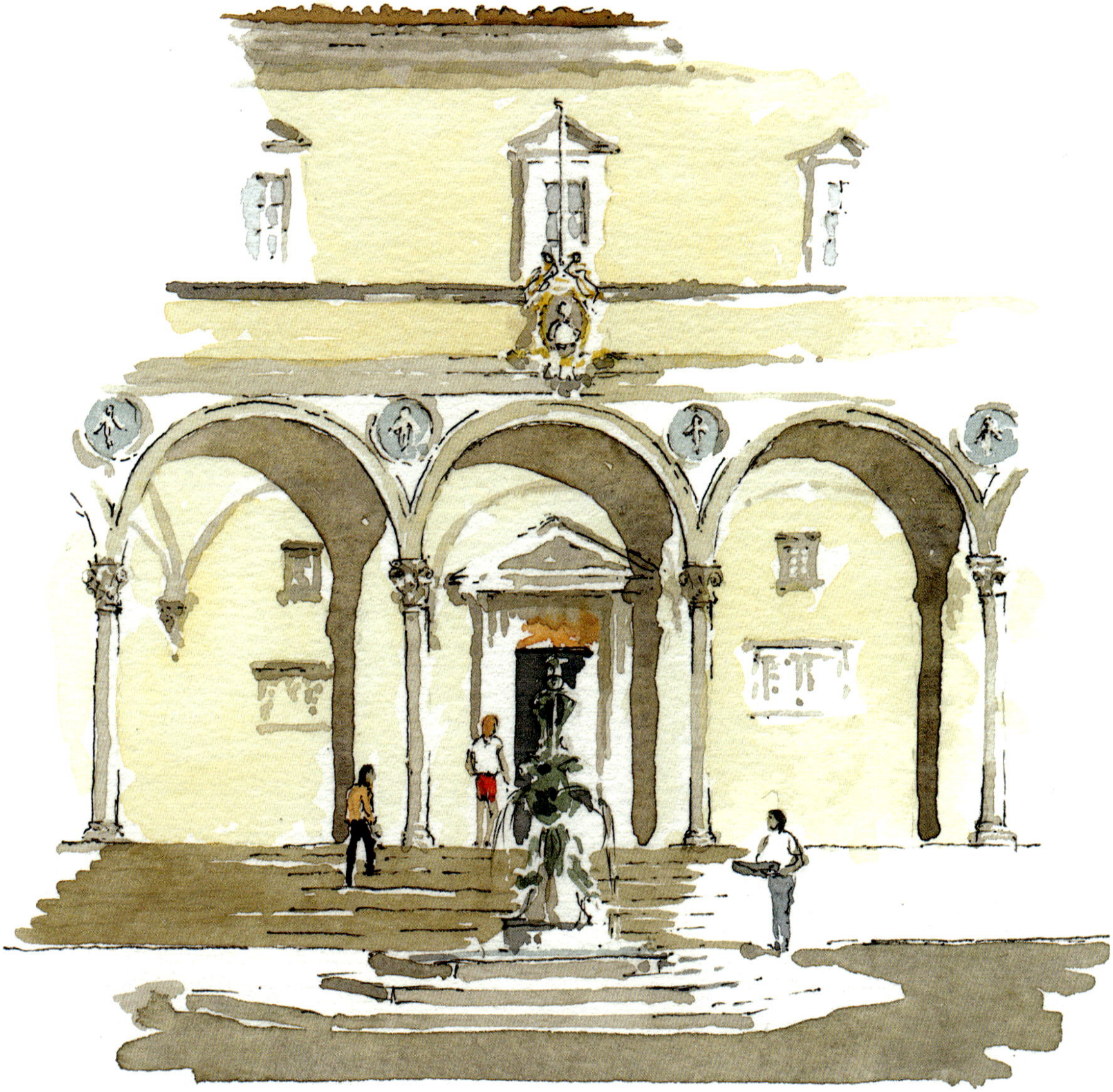

Ospedale degli Innocenti. Brunelleschi designed a pioneering idea of early town planning with uniformity to the square as a whole. In 1463 Andrea della Robbia added the ceramic medallions

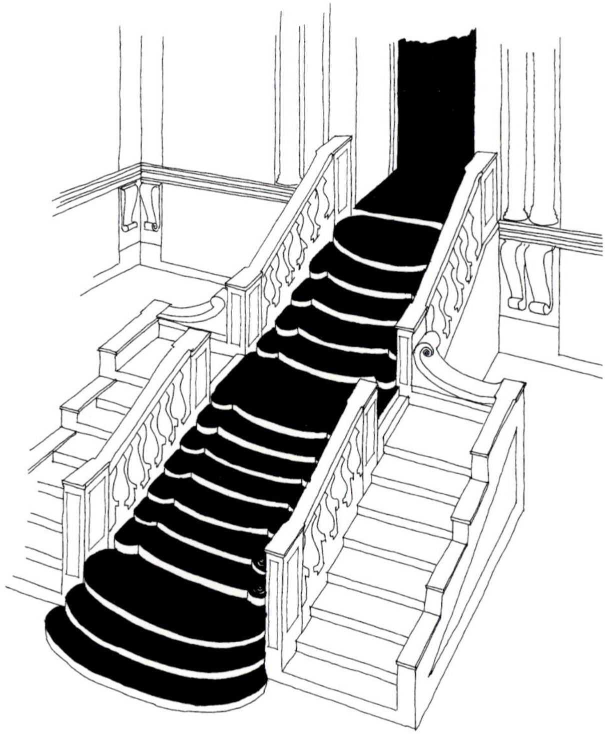

Entrance to the Laurenziana library by Michelangelo 1559 with access from the Cloister of San Lorenzo. The beautiful staircase is a good example of timeless design in clarity of form and shape

to the Laurenziana library is timeless and approached from the serene cloister. Nearby is the Galleria dell'Accademia displaying the famous sculpture of 'David' again by Michelangelo who made it sound so easy to produce by saying 'The figure is in the stone; you have only to let it out.' In this part of the city is one of the early Renaissance masterpieces by Brunelleschi who in 1419 designed the portico of Spedale degli Innocenti that has inspired many portico façades in Tuscany and beyond.

Medieval streets link the Piazza della Duomo to the Piazza della Signoria. Ignore the tourists and their trimmings and explore the space. From the narrow streets the Piazza opens out and is dominated by the vast buildings of Palazzo Vecchio and a group of powerful sculpture. First the equestrian statue of the Grand Duke Cosimo I, then the Neptune Fountain, David and Hercules and the Carey leads the eye to the Uffizi and the Loggia dei Lanzi. In the Loggia are the bronze statue of Perseus and the Rape of the Sabine Woman by Giambologna. In reverse, from the South bank of the Arno a penetrating view through the central arch of the Uffizi Façade is a view that directs the eye back to Piazza della Signoria.

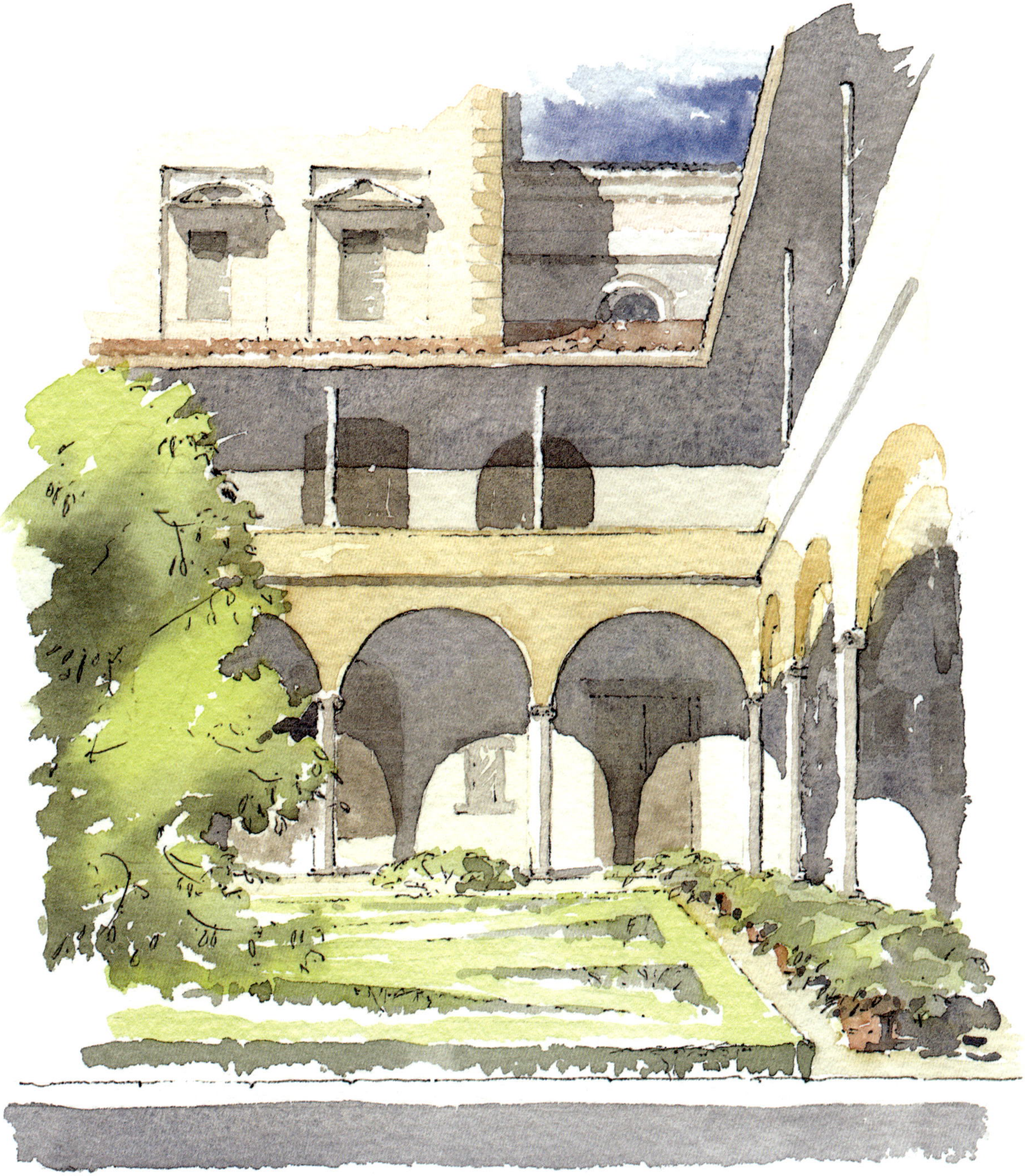

Cloister of San Lorenzo by Manetti with the Biblioteca Mediceo-Laurenziana in the background

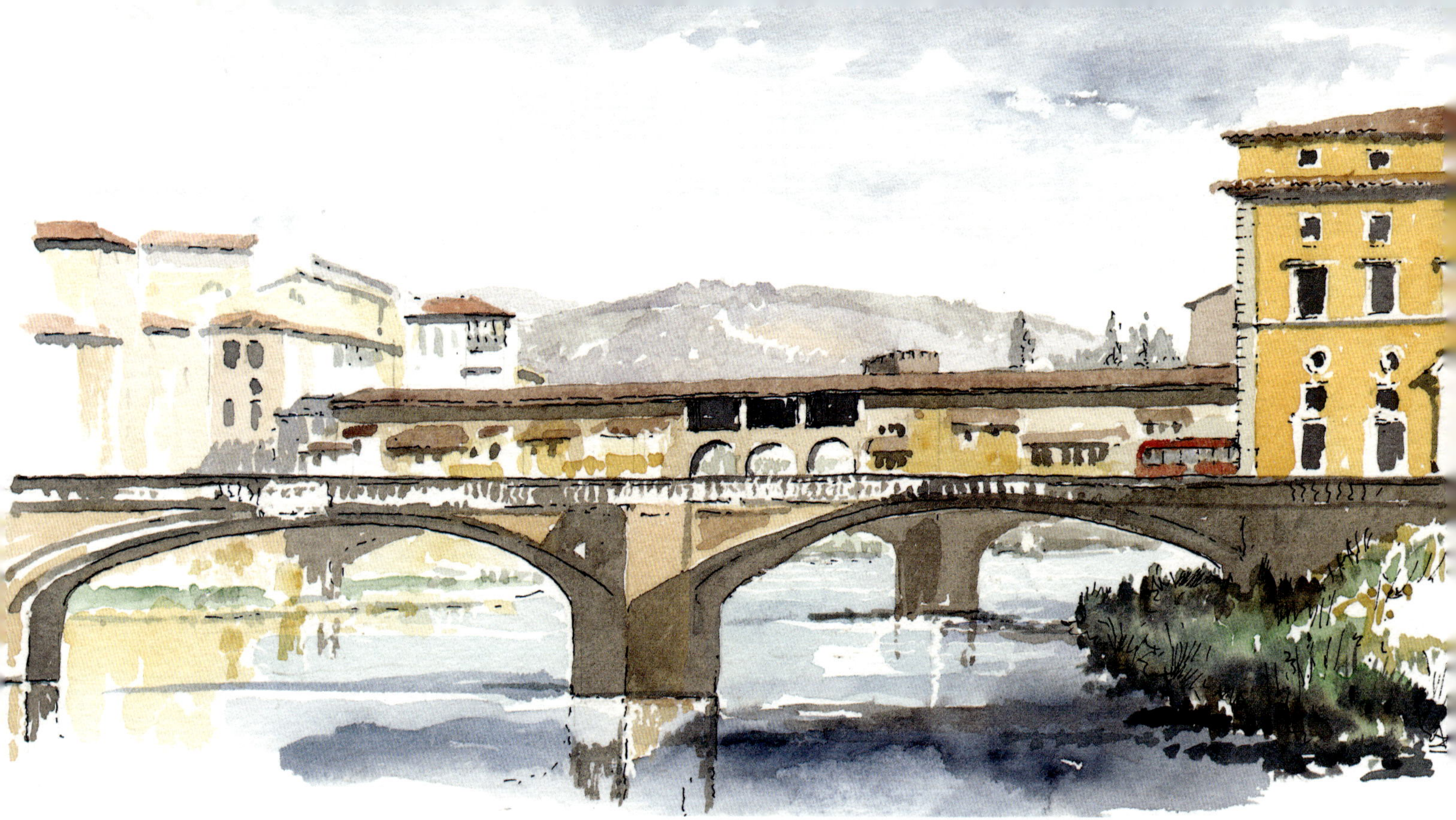

Ponte San Trinità in the foreground of Ponte Vecchio, view from Ponte alla Cattaia

Cosimo Medici I commissioned architect Vasari in the 1560s to design the Uffizi Gallery that houses one of the worlds greatest collection. It is, in my opinion better to choose in advance the picture you wish to see, remember less is more. There are important works by Giotto, Botticelli, Filippo Lippi,, Michelangelo, Leonardo da Vinci, Raphael and in particular Titian, the artist that changed the art world not only for the subject matter as 'The Venus of Urbino' but also for his use of colour and light.

Divert to the Franciscan Gothic Church of Santa Croce to look for the Death of St. Francis by Giotto in the Bardi Chapel. Also in the museum is a painted crucifix by Cimabue. However, it is the Pazzi Chapel by Brunelleschi 1443 that we come to study a remarkable early Renascence building.

View the Ponte Vecchio and then on to the Pitti Palace designed by Brunelleschi for the other wealthy banking family Luca Pitti. The original building was smaller and unfinished when through financial problems they were forced to sell to their rival Eleonore Medici the wife of Cosimo I. They enlarged the palace and the garden. More details in the Villas and garden section.

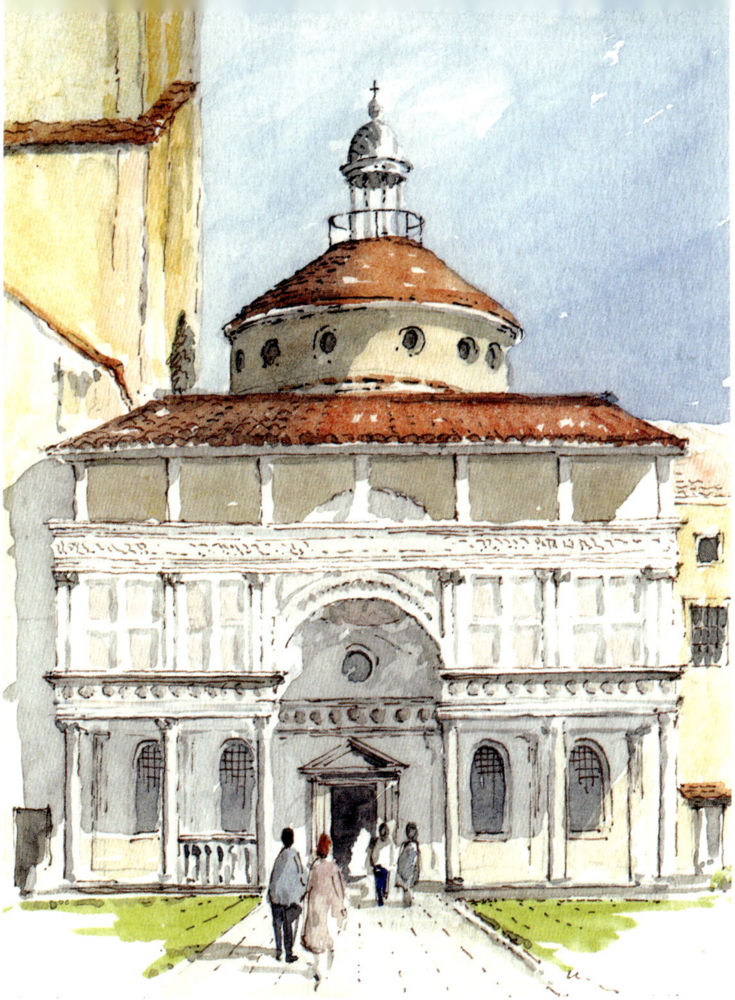

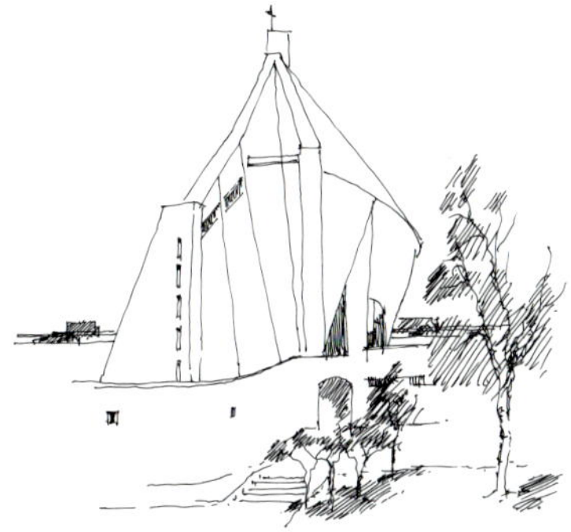

San Giovanni Battista 1964 by Giovanni Michelucci, Autostrada del Sole and dedicated to those who died building the Autostrada

Pazzi Chapel by Brunelleschi 1430

A must is the Santa Maria del Carmine to see the beautifully restored frescoes in the Brancacci Chapel by Masolino and his pupil Masaccio from 1424. These works were soon to influence such great artists as Leonardo da Vinci and Michelangelo.

Returning towards the station we find one of the oldest churches in Florence, San Pancrazio, which had become redundant, but which has been converted skillfully by architects Lorenzo Papi and Bruno Sacchi. It is reminiscent of the superb conversion of the old castle of Verona into a museum by Carlo Scarpa. San Pancrazio is a stunning setting for the work of the great 20th century sculptor Marino Marini after whom the museum is now named. The Italians are never afraid to exploit the new and to complement the old with the new.

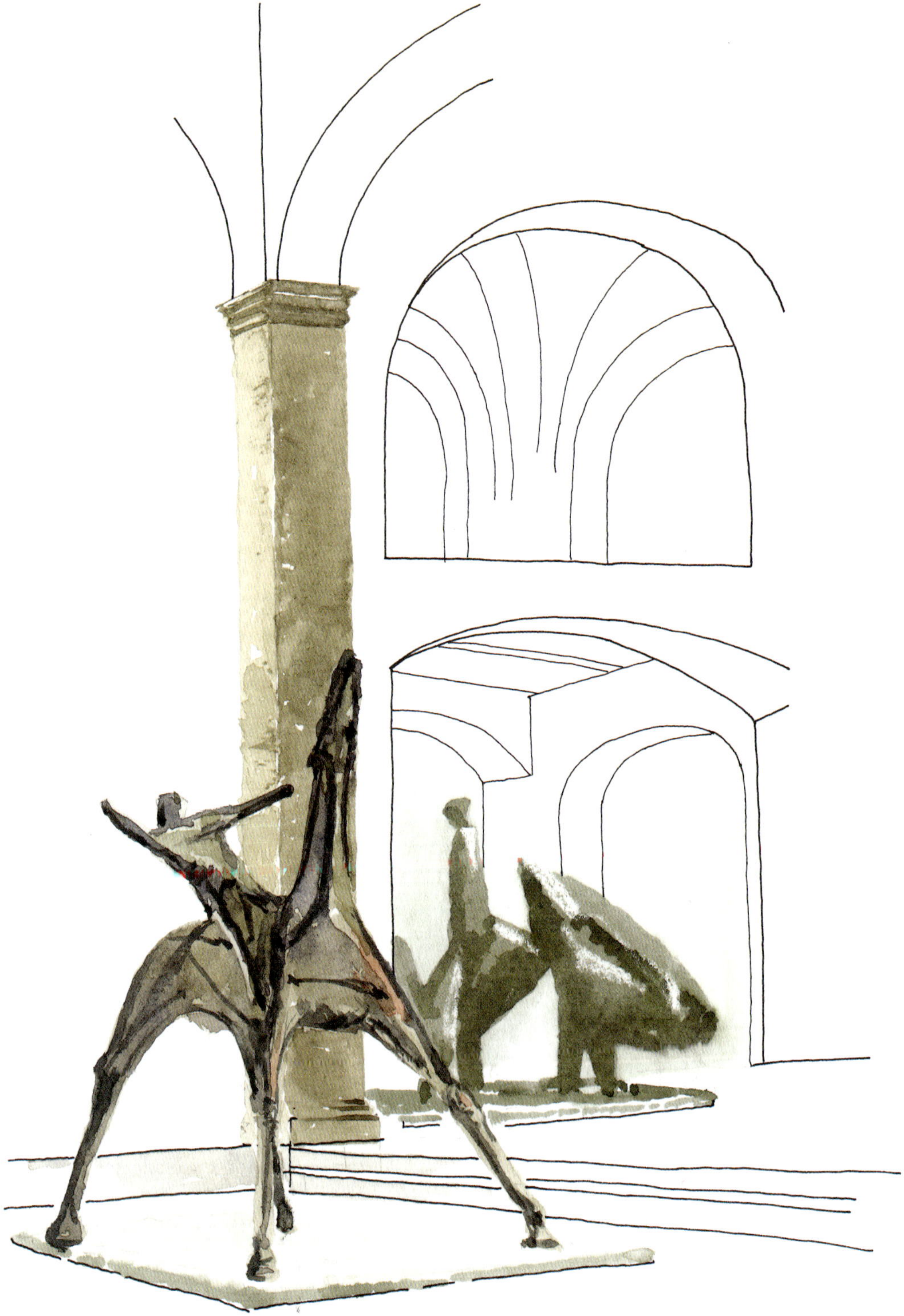

Interior of Museo Marino Marini
in San Pancrazio

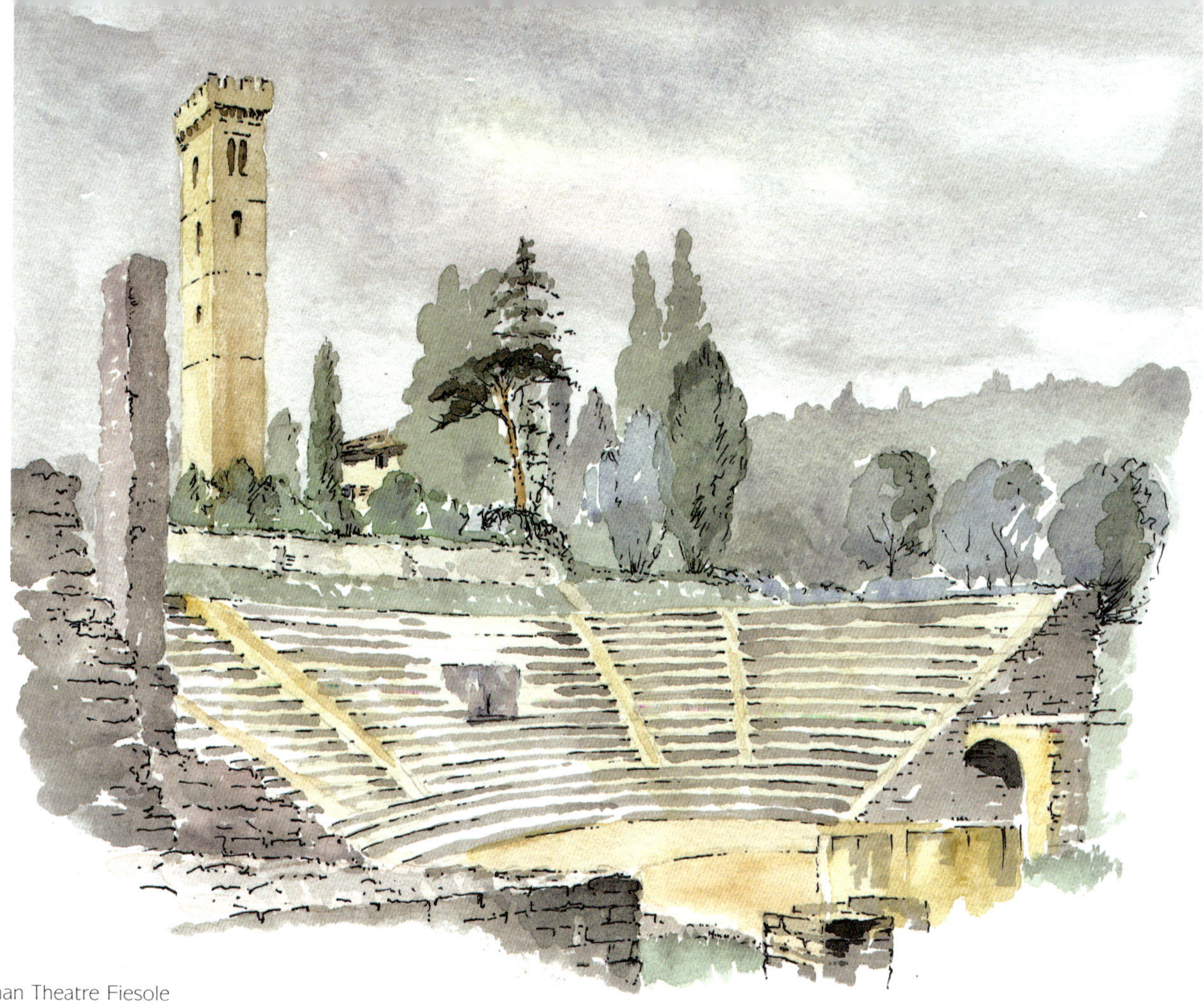

Roman Theatre Fiesole

There are memorable views from Piazzale Michelangelo and fascinating challenges to identify the great landmarks of the city. A little further up the hill is San Miniato al Monte, a Romanesque church of the 11–12th century.

Fiesole, founded by the Etruscans in the 7th century BC, became one of the larger settlements in northern Etruria. The Romans also established an important base here and the remains of their theatre are impressive. However it also became an important part in the establishment of the Renaissance. Chosen by the Medici family for an avant-garde Villa and garden overlooking the City of Florence, details of this can be seen in villas and gardens section of the book.

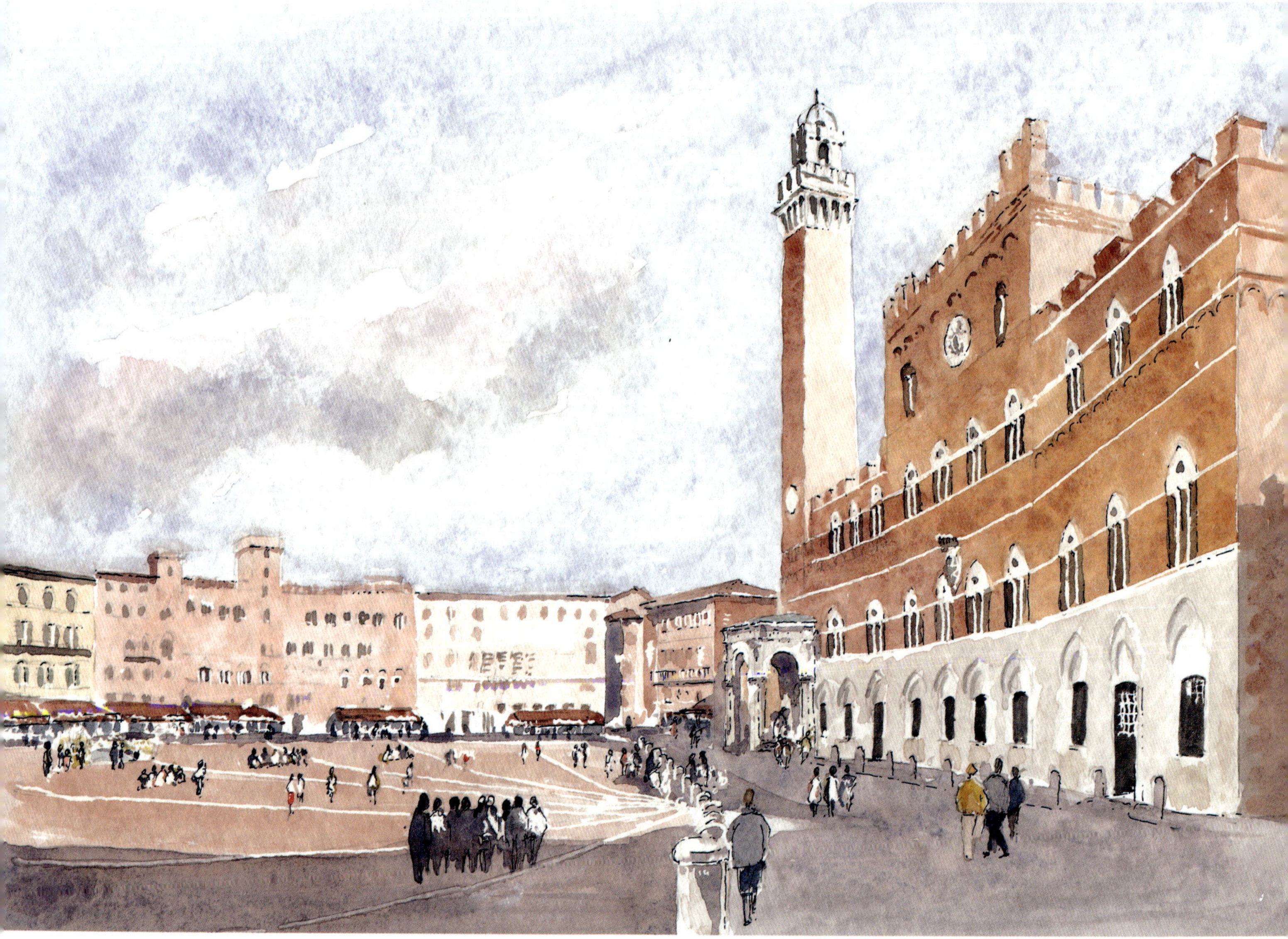

Piazza del Campo. It has been the setting for battles, riots, bullfights and the Palio

Siena

A great medieval city with fine Gothic buildings that retains its original atmosphere and character. Unfolding narrow streets reflect the shape of the central fan shape space of Piazza del Campo around which the buildings and streets have been forged. The three hills on which it has been built have had their impact on the plan. Known as the 'brick city' of red, yellow and brown colours, the exceptional enormous cathedral sits on top of one of the hills, dominating the skyline of Siena. It is constructed in two marbles, white and black in horizontal stripes. There is a predominance of brick, hence it is some times described as the rose city. It is a small town by comparison with Florence, Pisa and Lucca. However, despite the compact, friendly atmosphere the buildings and spaces are huge.

The motto above the Camollia Gate reads. -
COR MAGIS TIBI SENI PANDIT
Siena opens its heart even wider to you.

Piazza del Compo is physically in the centre of the basin formed between the three hills and Palazzo Pubblico with its tall tower Torre del Mangia dominating this enormous fan shaped space. The Piazza has brick paving divided into segments by flat stone performing subtle gullies to drain the area and visually giving it a human scale. It is a man-made paved City Park where people sit and lay in the sun. Others gather in groups to talk or promenade around to look at the diners on the Cafe terraces or simply to absorb the wonderful character and atmosphere of this great civic space.

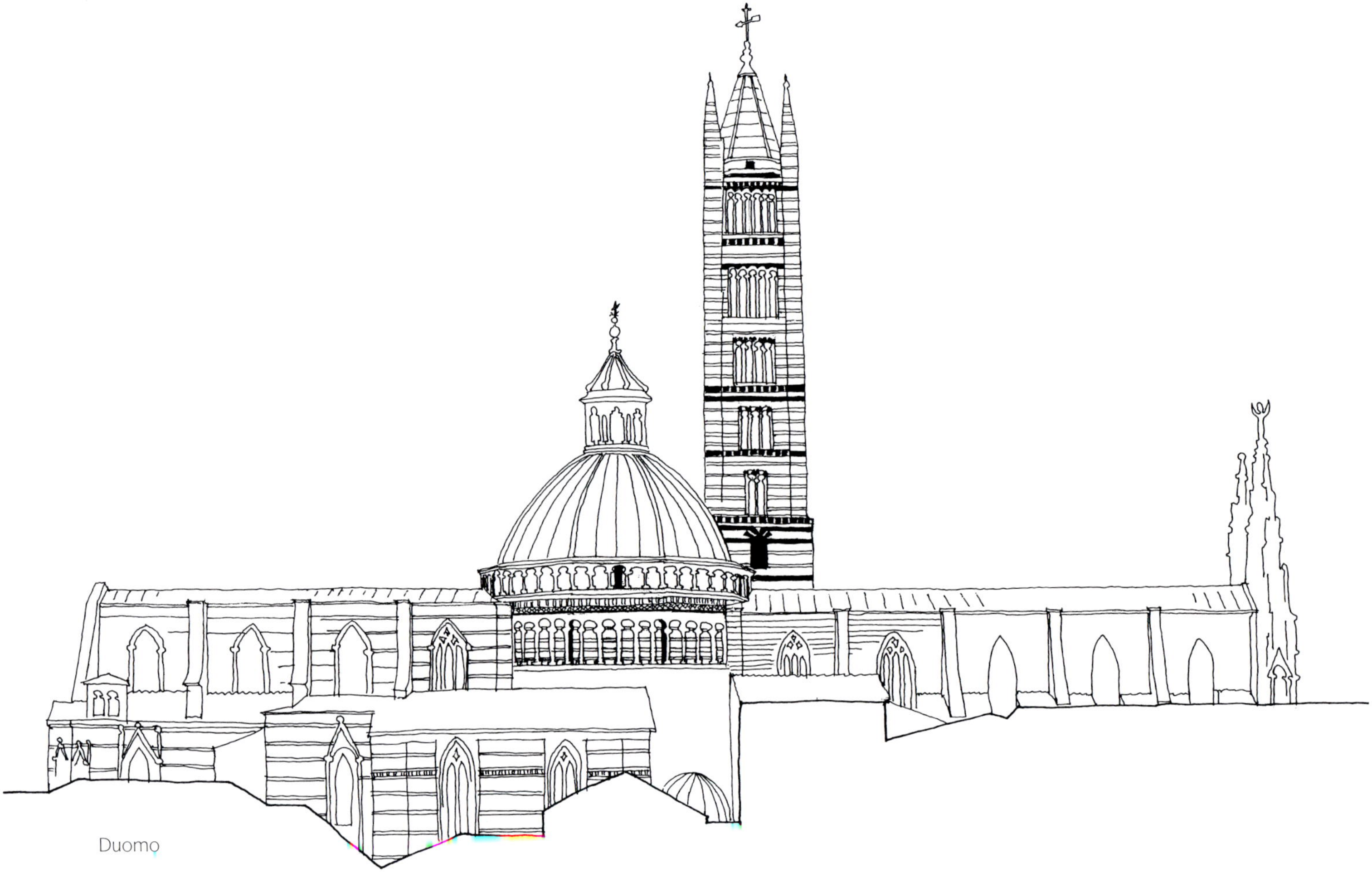

Duomo

Siena is where we experienced the quality of Gothic buildings. Palazzo Pubblico is one such place built at the end of the 13th century with a huge bell tower. It is still the town hall and contains the Museo Civico. Here the original sculptured relief panels from Fonte Gaia, the 15 century masterpiece by Jacopo della Quercia can be admired with copies surrounding the water feature in the Piazza. There are also important works by Lorenzetti and Simone Martini in the Museum.

Twice a year on the 2rd July and 16th August the Piazza is transformed into a horse racetrack where the age old race on bareback horses has occurred since at least 1283. The strong rivalry between the 17 'contrade' or districts of Siena produces a harsh festival of pageantry.

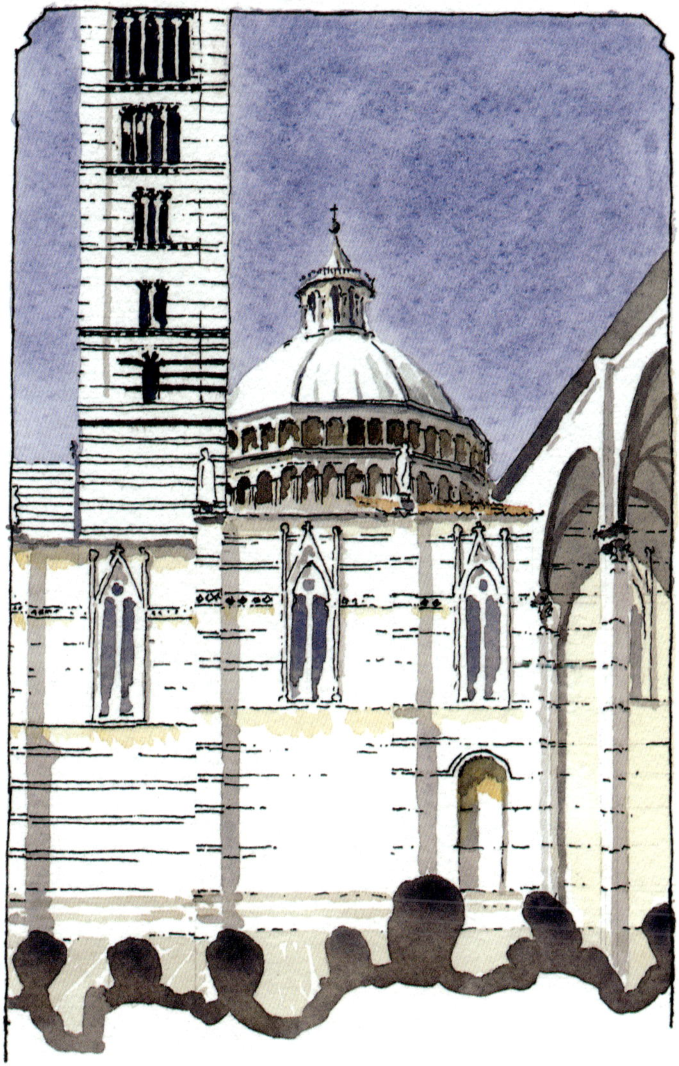

The space for the unfinished nave of the Duomo

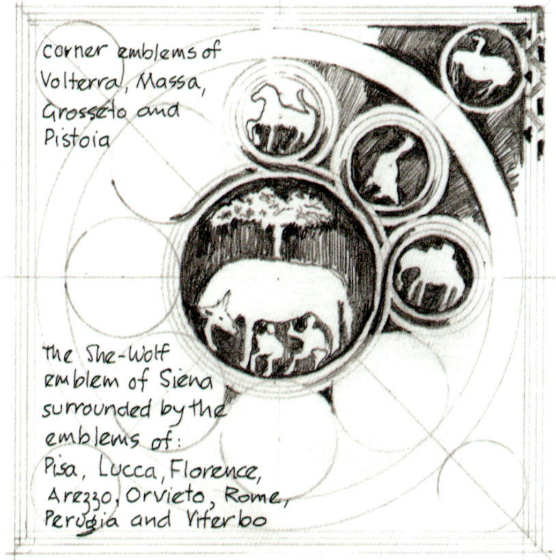

A fraction of the remarkable marble pavement in the Duomo

In marked contrast to the buildings of Siena is the Duomo, faced in white marble with black horizontal stripes. Ambitious plans were produced in 1339 to build a new nave with the object of creating the biggest church in the Christian world. However, the plague killed many of the population and the plans were abandoned. It is possible to visualise the scale from the unfinished end wall, the column bases and the complete Aisle that is now the Museo dell'Opera del Duomo. Without the extension it is still one of the most impressive churches in Italy, situated in an irregular shaped Piazza with the main facade built in two parts, the doors in 1284–97 and the remaining parts in 1382 to 90. An impressive flight of steps rises to the entrance of the duomo. On the opposite side of the Piazza

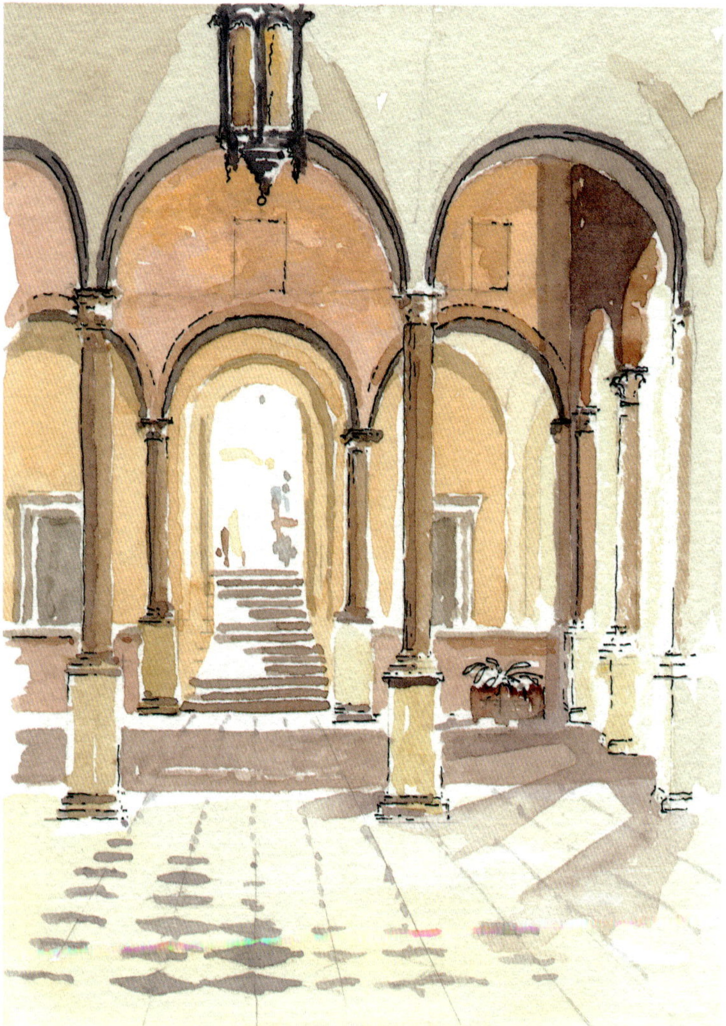

Cloister of Casa di Santa Caterina, patron saint of Siena

is the long façade of the hospital, of Santa Maria della Scala. The black and white marble from nearby quarries is taken into the interior. Examine the inlaid marble floor with remarkably designed paving and the carved panels of the pulpit by Pisano 1265-68. Do not miss the Piccolomini frescoes (1509) in the library portraying the Life of Pope Pius II

It is difficult not to see the huge Gothic barn like church of the San Domenico, started in 1226 where St Catherine of Siena experienced her ecstasies and where Il Sodoma painted the famous frescoes depicting scenes from her life.

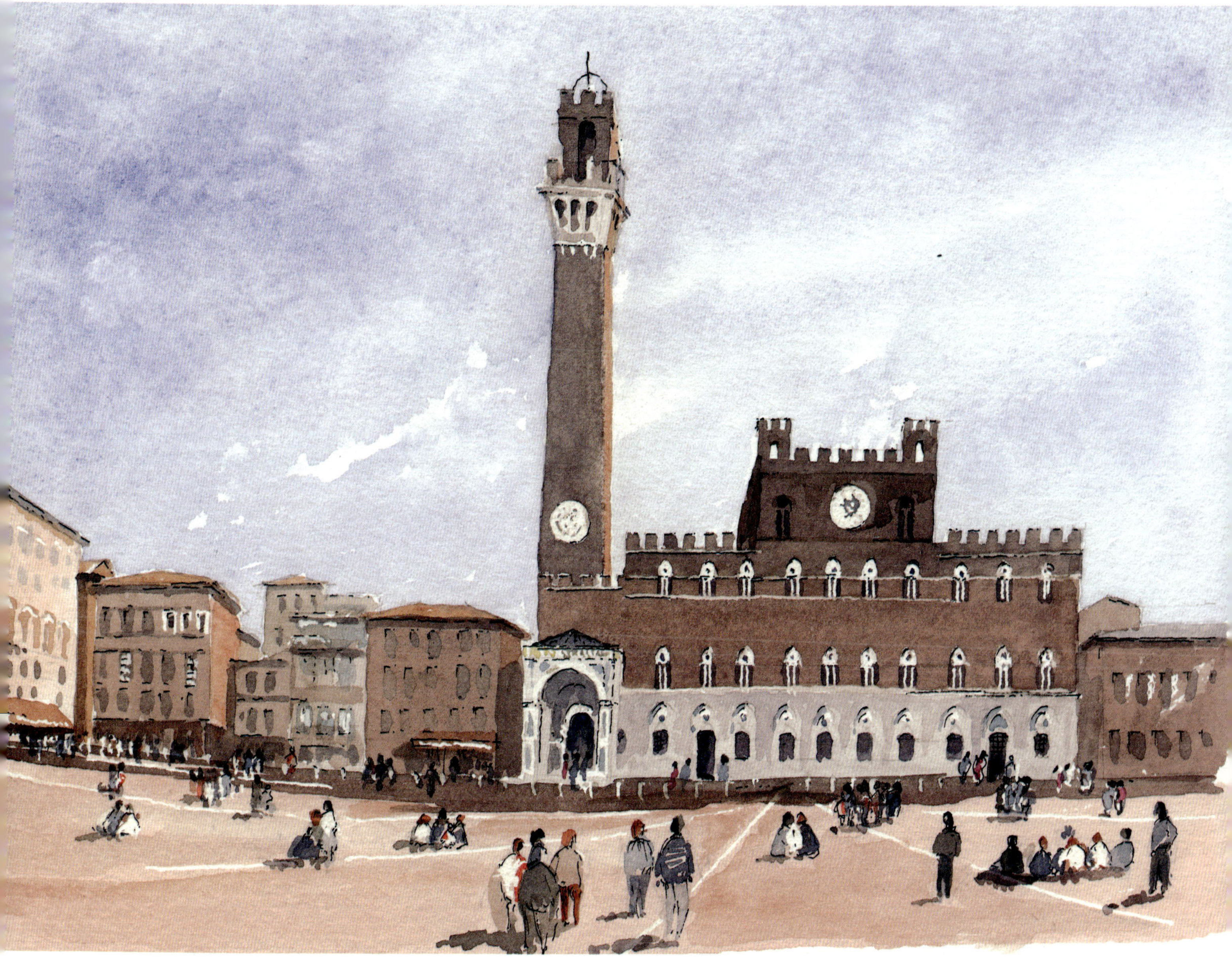

Palazzo Pubblico and Piazza del Campo

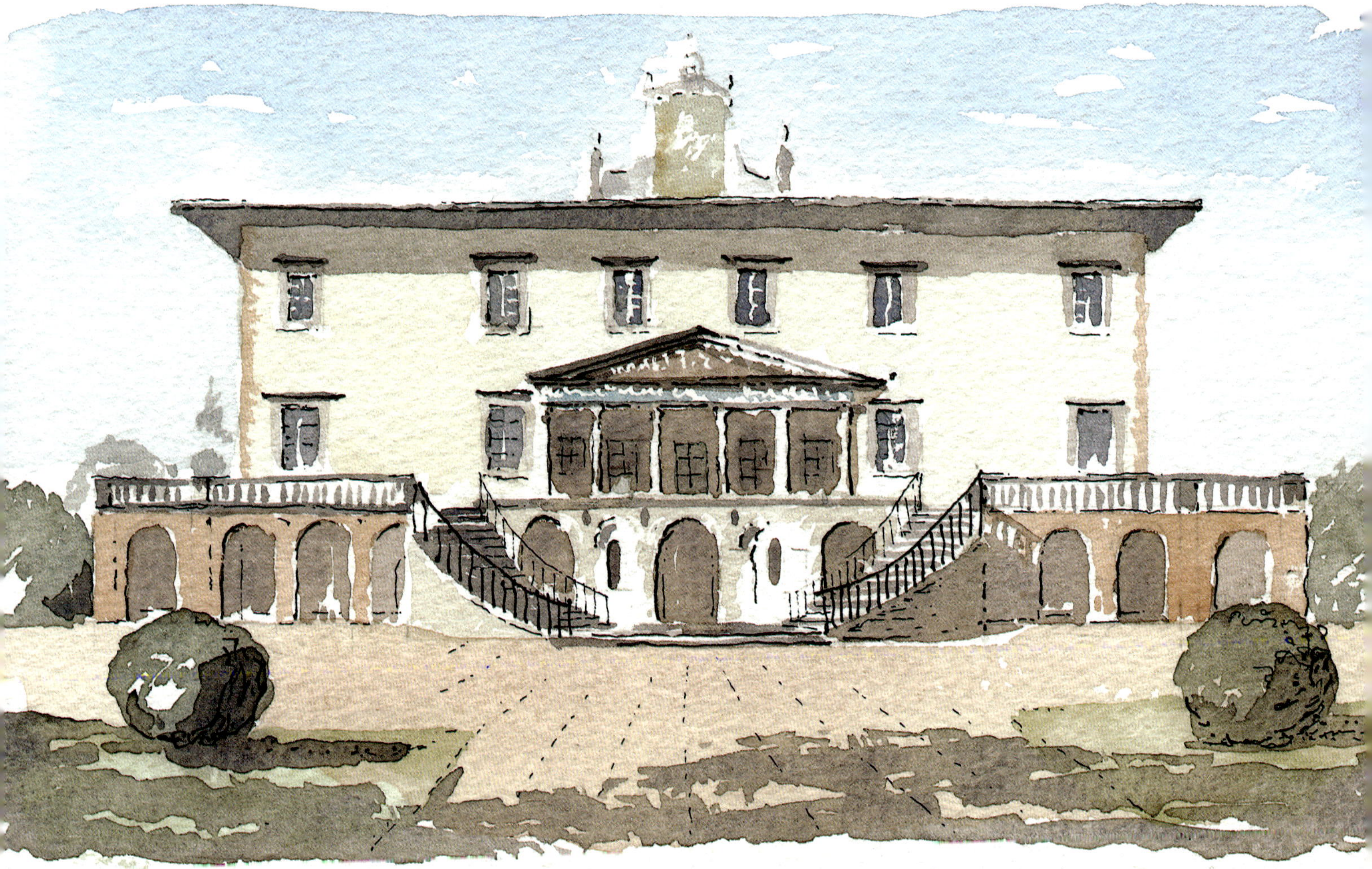

 Medici Villa Poggio a Caiano 1470

Tuscan Villas and Gardens

With the collapse of Imperial Rome where gardens were an essential element of their Villas, it was the monasteries, churches and abbeys that maintained the art of gardening and horticultural knowledge through the medieval period.

The major change in garden design occurred when the Medici, the wealthy humanist banking family, started to build their Villas at Fiesole, Craeggi and Poggio a Caiano. This family counterbalanced the influence of the church and Gardens and villas became a priority for the wealthy. It coincided with the issuing and later publication of a treatise on architecture in 1452 by architect and humanist Leon Battista Alberti of Florence. Attention was focused on classical Rome and the works of Vitruvius.

Saingallo used these principals for the first time in the design of the Medici Villa at Poggio a Caiano, but for the villa and garden it was at Fiesole where the recommendations were implemented. The location was to be on sloping ground taking advantage of the sun and the view with associated thermal movement of cool air over the terraces. Giovanni di Cosimo de Medici, a director of the rich Medicean Bank, an unenlightened patron and art collector challenged Michelozzo to come up with an original design for this superb site at Fiesole with magnificent views of Florence in 1451. The result was a compact house on three levels with main rooms and entrance loggia on the upper level where the terrace was laid out as a parterre and a narrow raised rose bed adjacent to the hill has a path to the Lemon House. A small private terrace at the rear at mid floor level has a large bowl water feature and a fine view over Florence. There are steps down to the long pergola walk and a further flight at right angles to reach the centre of the lower terrace at lower floor level. A small fountain is in the centre flanked by box parterres. Further down the hill are the terraces of the farm. Oranges and lemons

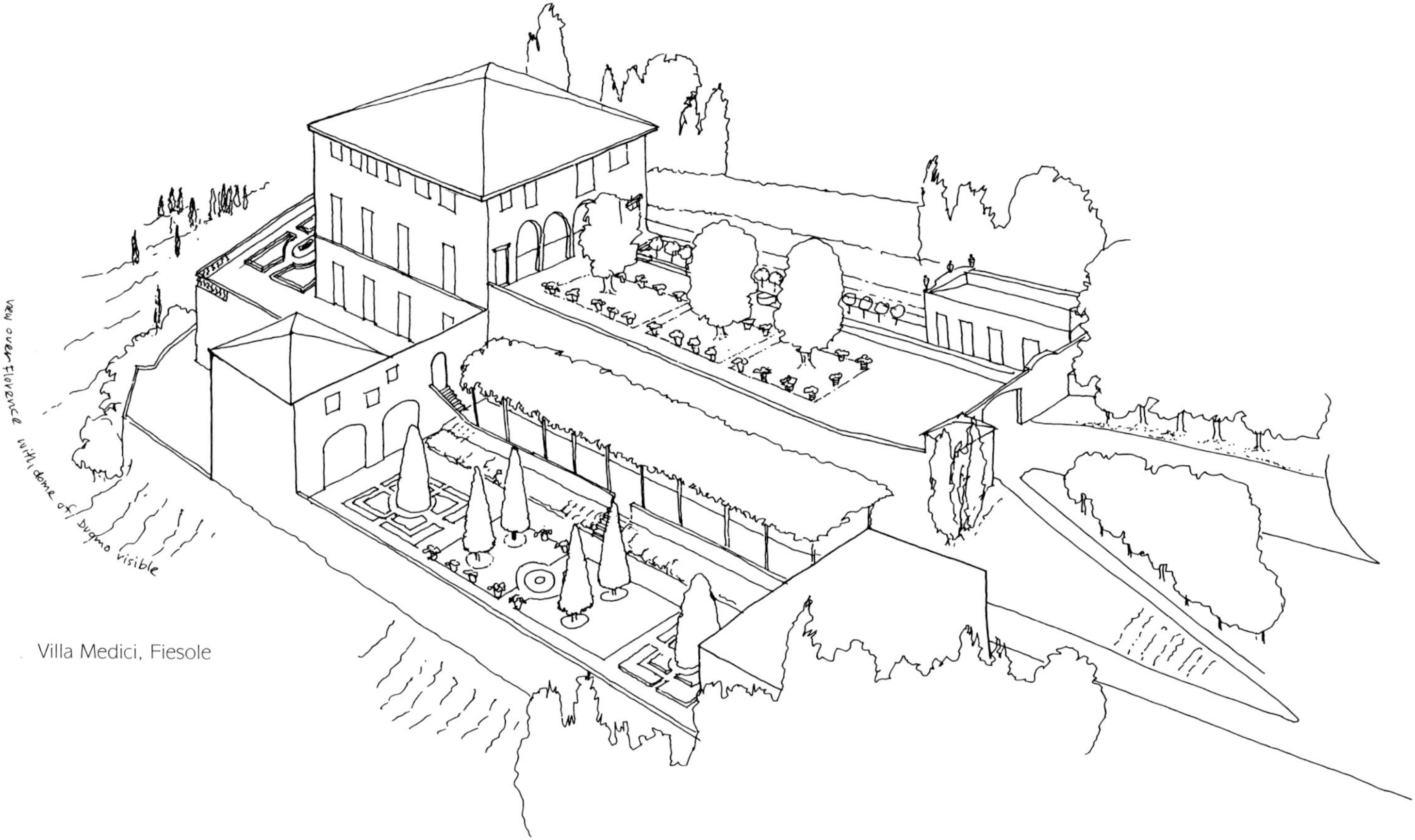

Villa Medici, Fiesole

grown in large decorative terracotta pots were in vogue and provided a contrast to the vegetation outside the garden. By 1469 Lorenzo the Magnificent inherited the villa and one of his frequent visitors wrote poetry of this beautiful place.

One of the other rich banking families of Florence was Luca Pitti who commissioned Brunelleschi, in 1453, to design the Pitti palace. Financial problems forced a sale and Eleanora, wife of Cosimo I de Medici, bought the unfinished palace and the hillside beyond from the Borgoli family. In 1549 Niccolò Tribolo was asked to design the garden to become the Boboli Gardens. The sculpture designer based the layout on the central axis of the palace and in the remains of the stone quarry built the amphitheatre. There were several designers after his death. Cosimo II decided in 1612 to enlarge the

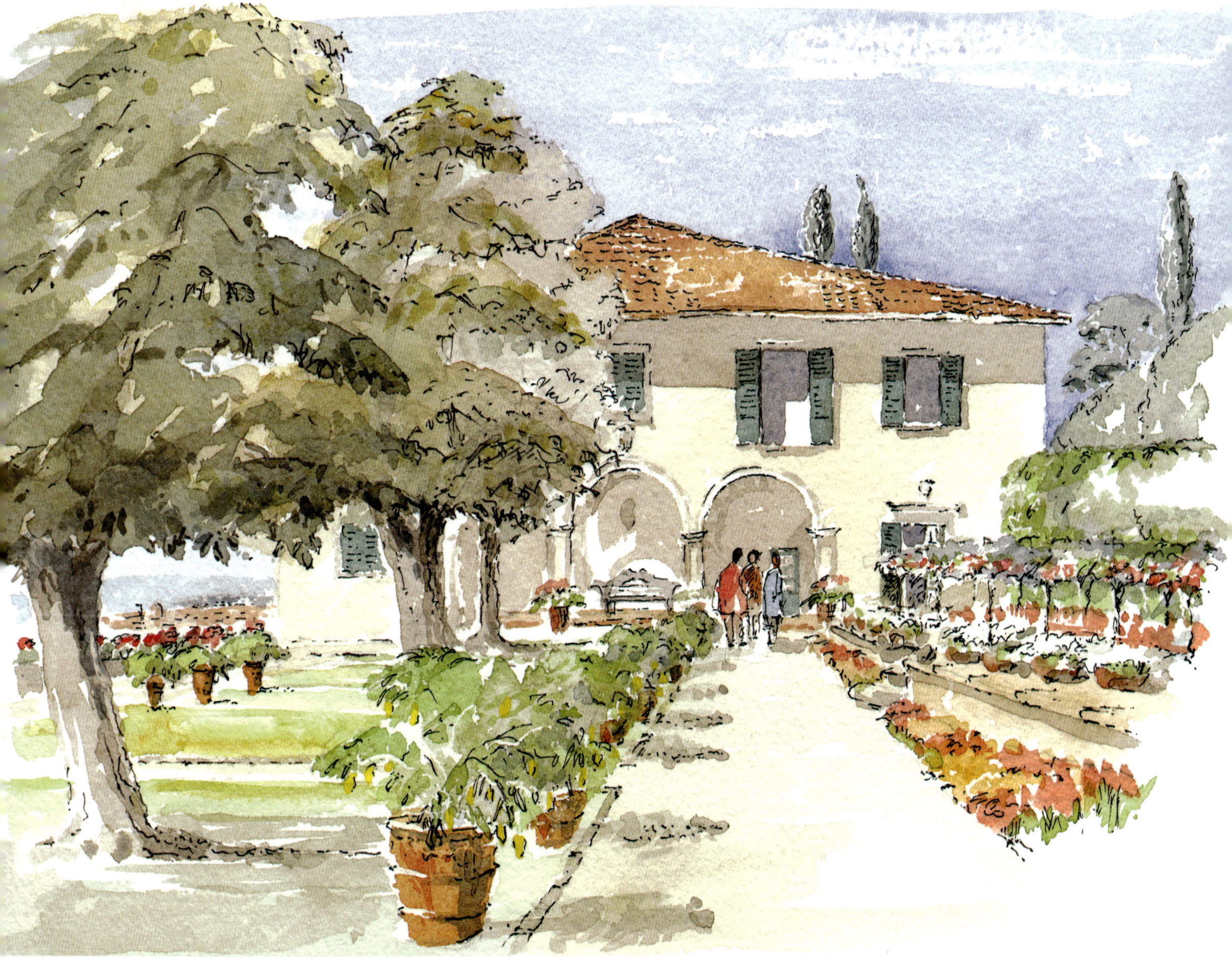

Top garden of the Villa Medici, Fiesole 1451

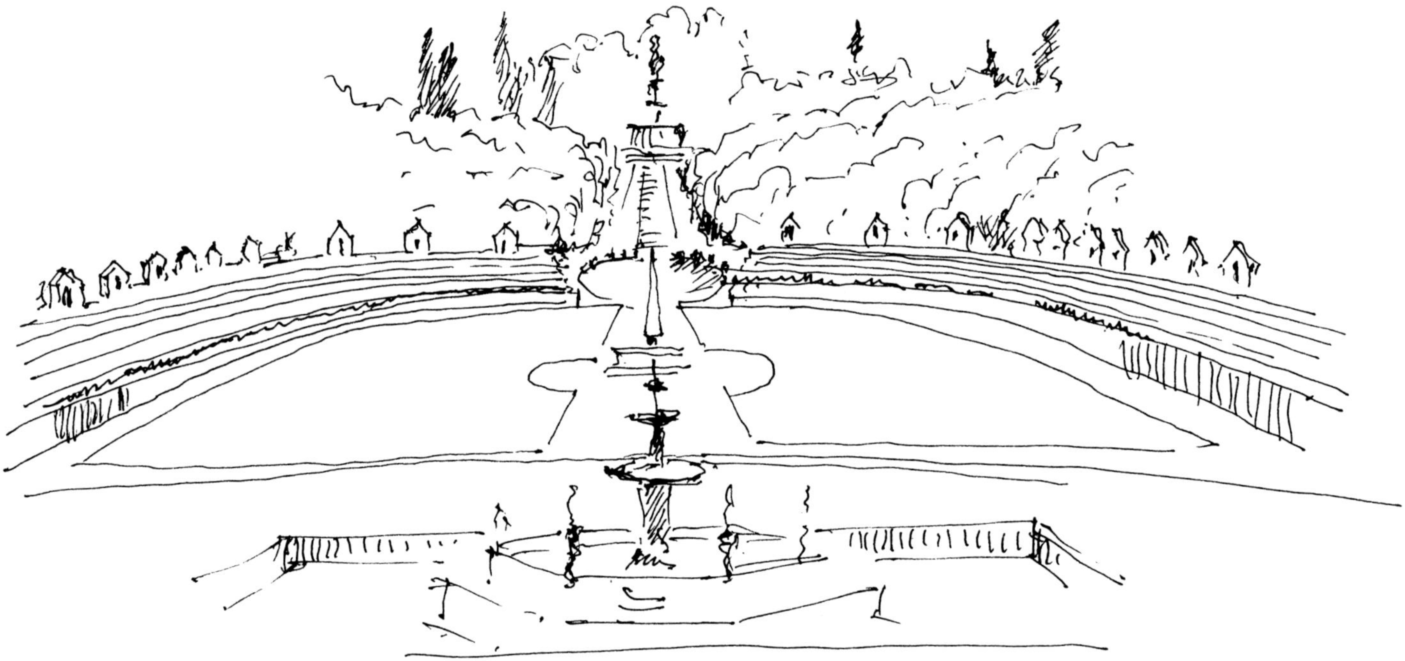

The amphitheatre of the Boboli Gardens seen from the terrace of the Pitti Palace with the Forione Pool in the middle distance and beyond the statue of Abundance

garden. A new axis at an angle from the first was laid out with the Cyprus avenue to the pool of the Isolotto and fountain of Oceanus. There is also the botanical garden, grottoes and the lemonaia to explore. The grotto was an important element of these gardens where designers experimented with a mixture of art in silence - philosophy, art and enchantment were interwoven and form the whole. The lunette of the garden by the Giusto Utens 1599 illustrated the original design of the formal garden before it was extended.

Villa di Castello was by date the first of the Renaissance garden, when in 1537 Cosimo I enlarged the estate using Niccolò Tribolo as its designer. In the centre was a maze of cypress trees surrounded with box hedges enclosing flowerbeds and a large number of statues. Beyond the lemon citrus garden, on

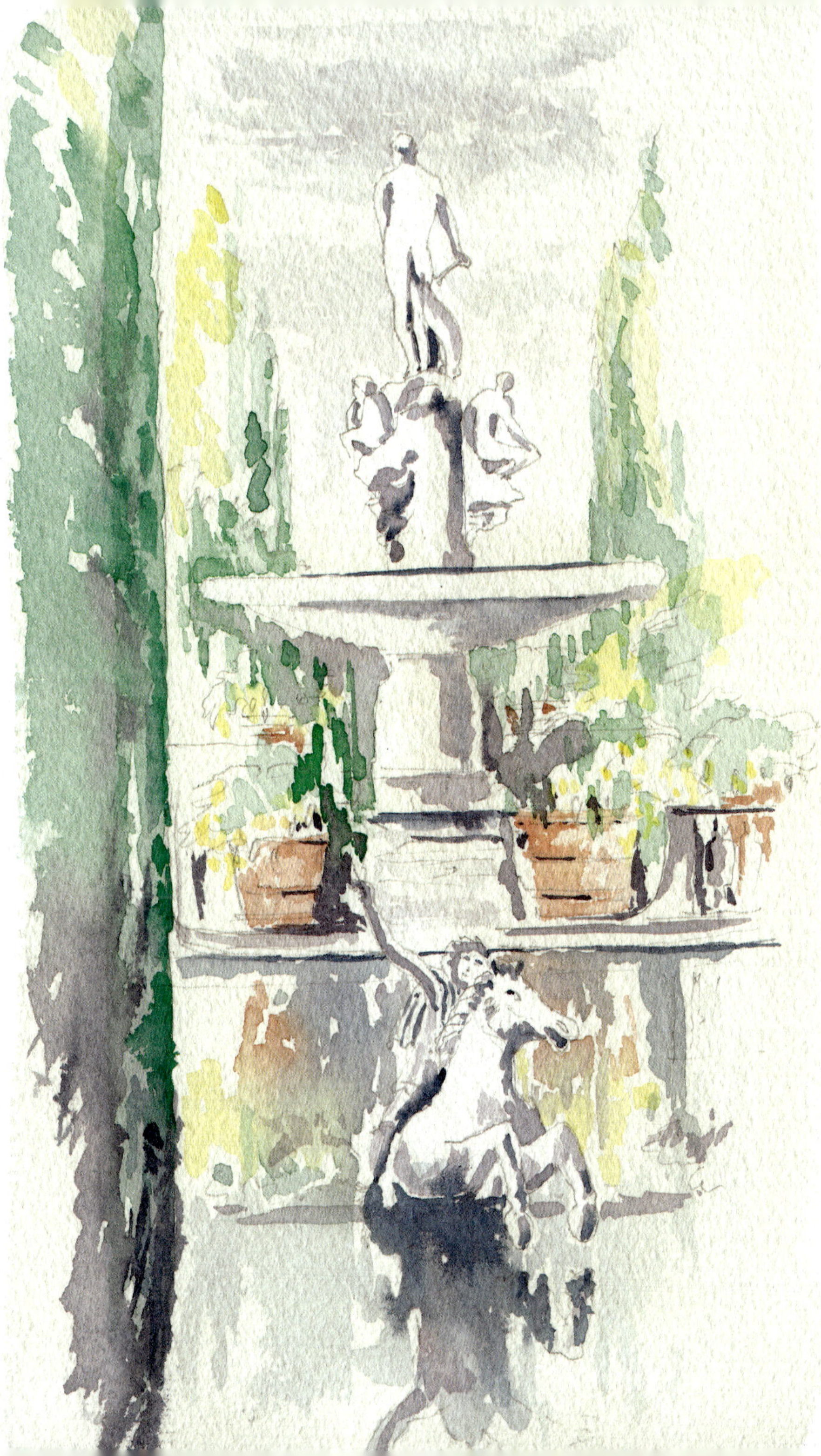

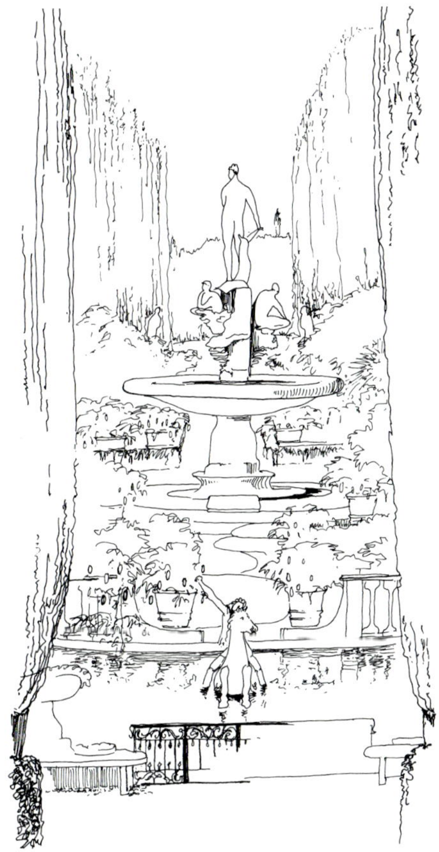

Boboli Gardens, Florence. Pool of the Isolotto dominated by the fountain of Oceanus by Giambologna 1637–41 and Perseus on his horse in the foreground

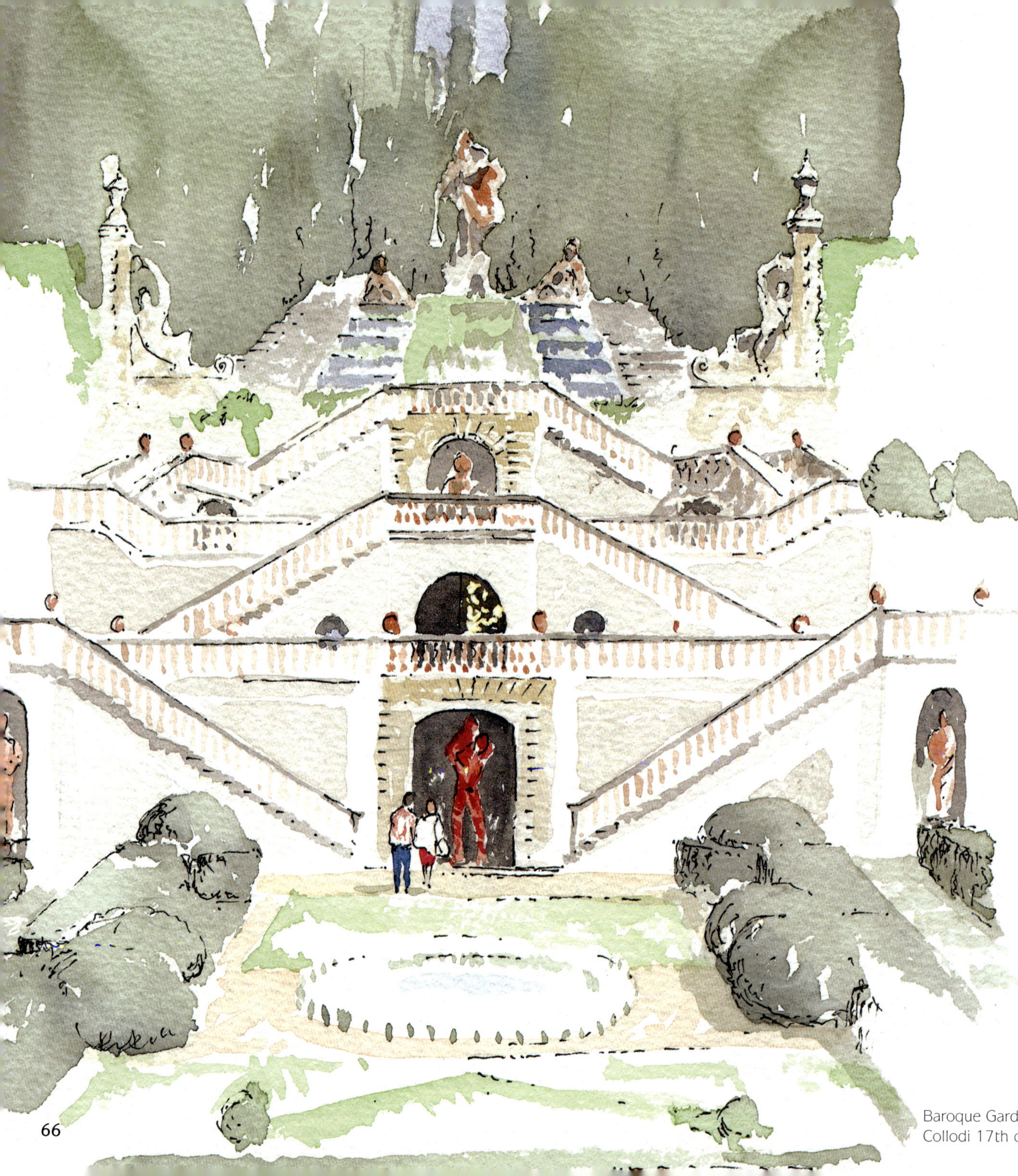

Baroque Garden of Garzoni,
Collodi 17th century

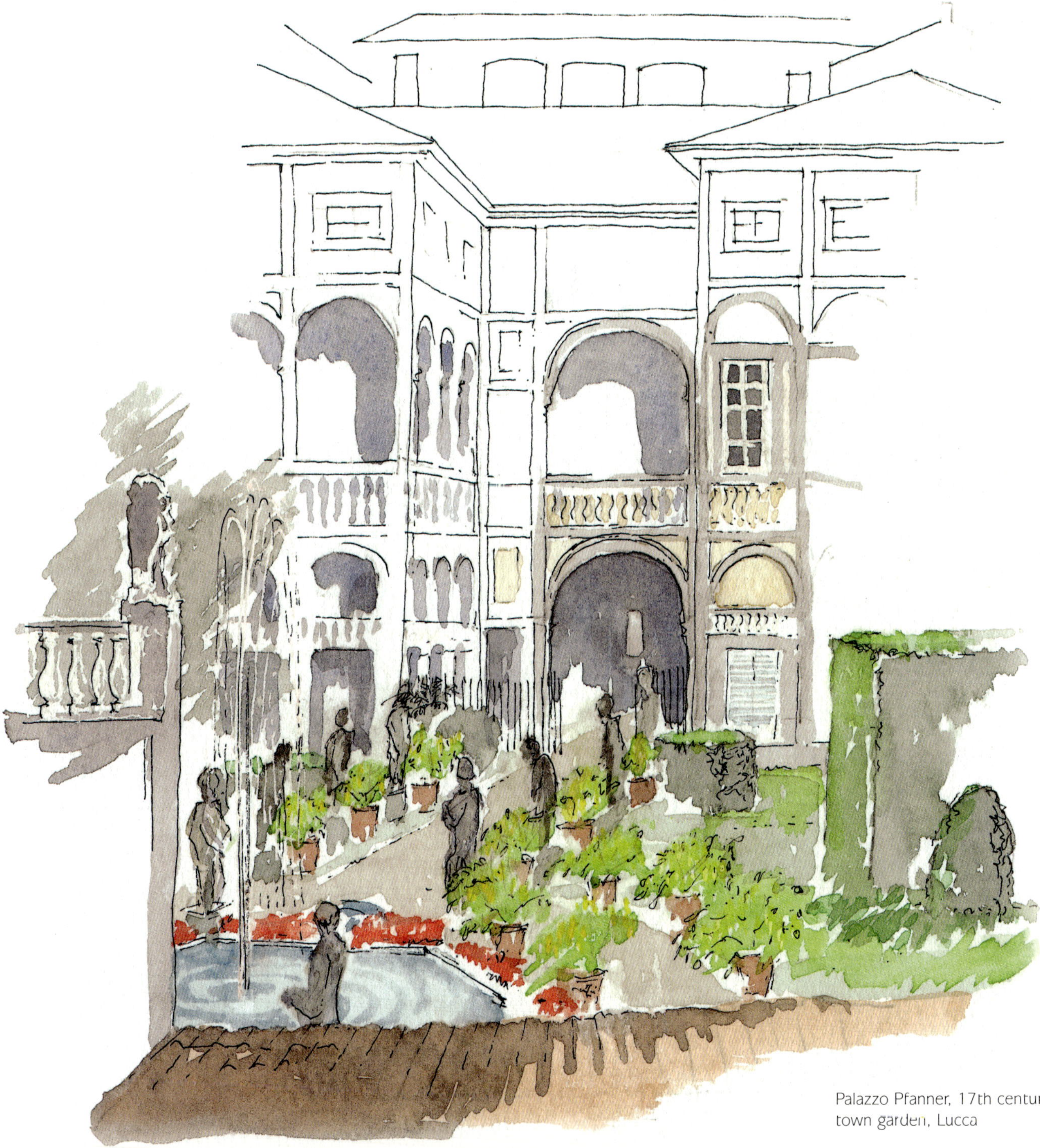

Palazzo Pfanner, 17th century
town garden, Lucca

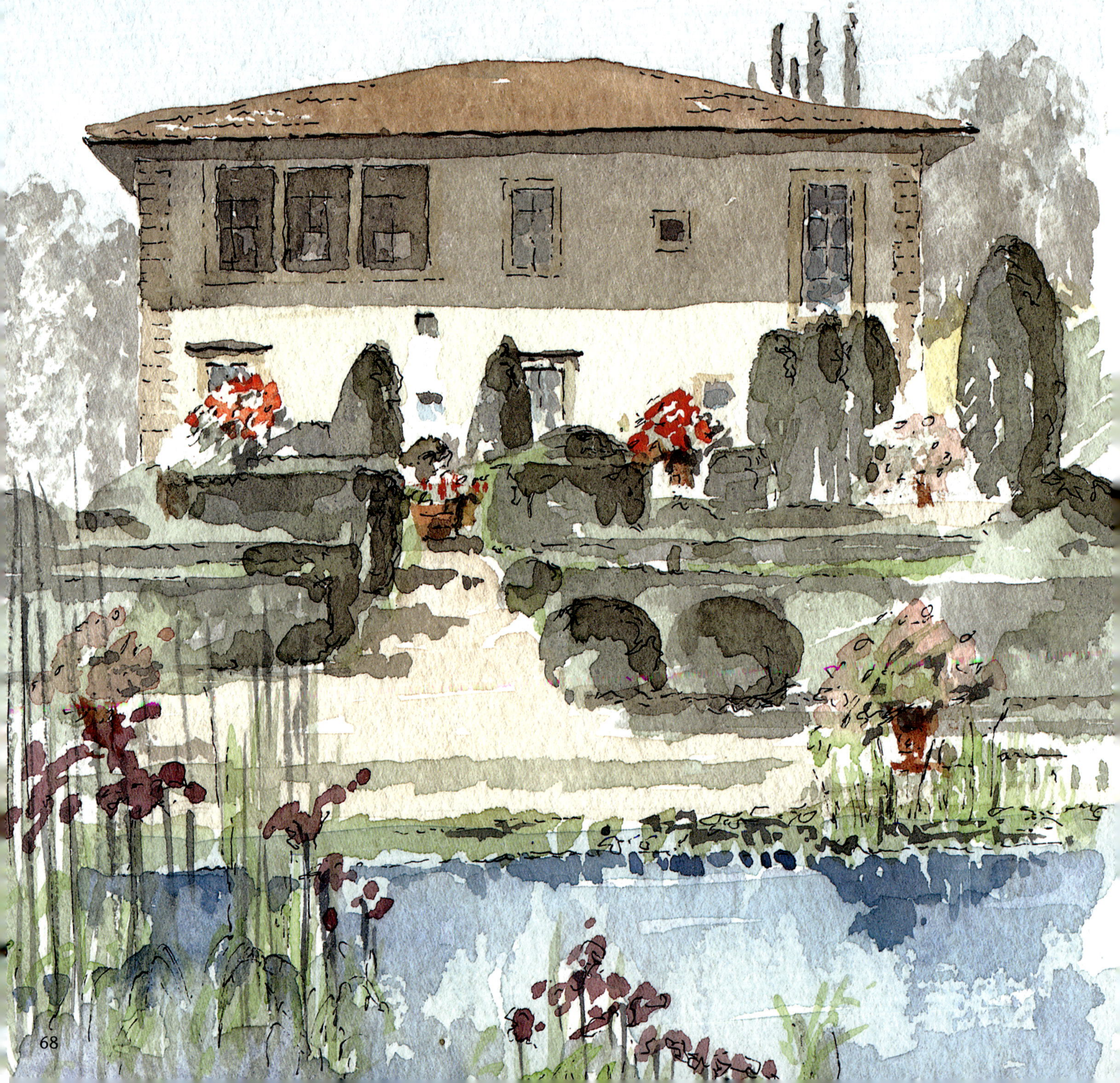

Villa Mansi, Segromigno. 17th century and later partially transformed into an English Landscape Garden

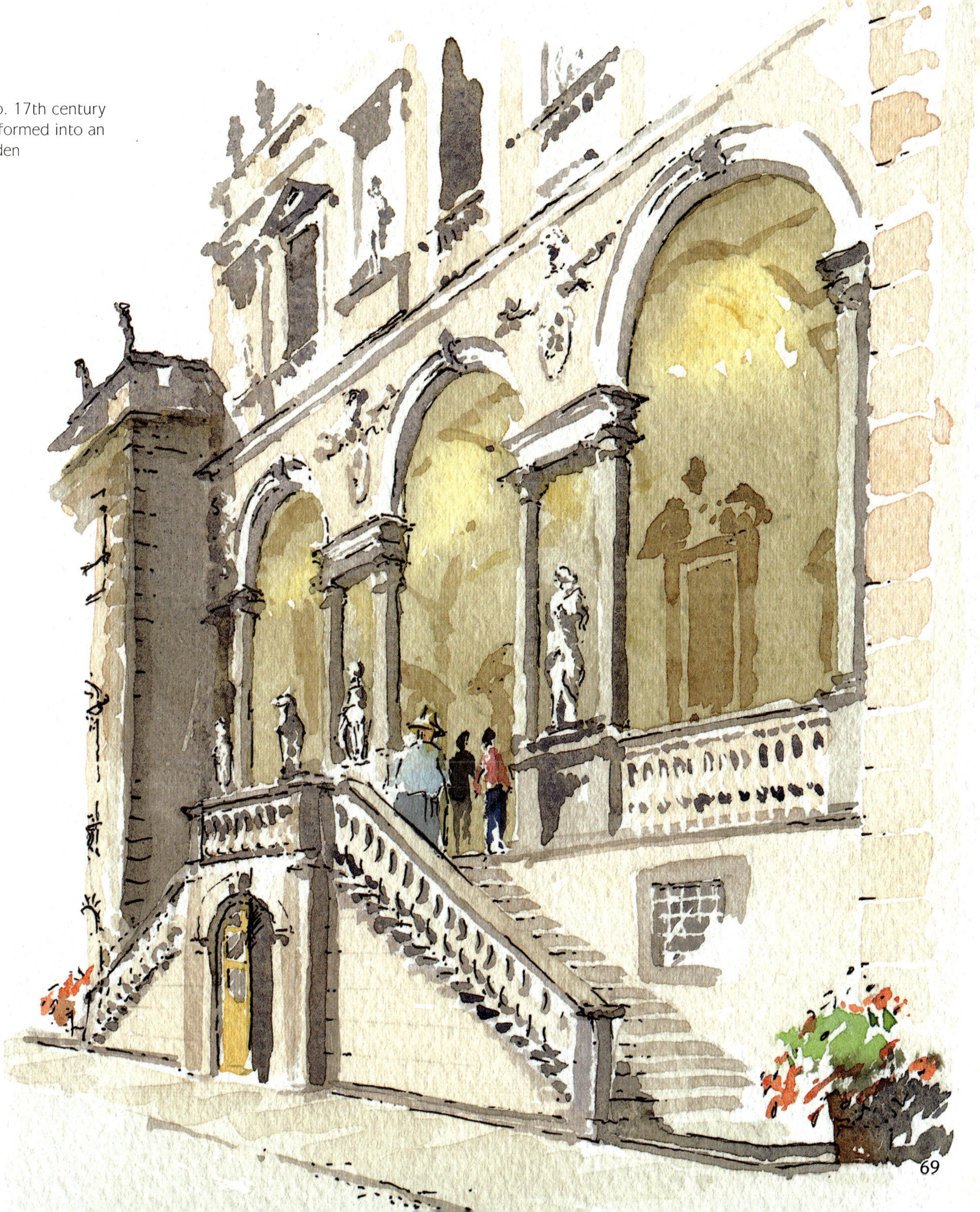

Villa Gamberaia, Settignano

'Scultura Flottanye Celle' 1990. Lake with floating forms and kinetic fountains by Marta Pan from Budapest. Villa Celle

the main axis of the garden is the grotto of animals, where an allegory of the Medicean world can be found. Further away is the fountain of Fioenza 1785 to 1788 and the English wood of the 19th century. Originally the garden had a large collection of exotic plants.

News of these exciting new gardens spread rapidly. The number of prints, engravings and the lunette, a type of aerial view of the Villas and Gardens were readily available, reinforcing the influence of garden design outside Italy. They were taken back by travellers on the Grand Tour to various parts of Europe. John Evelyn, a prolific diarist of the 17th century, was eagerly read in England describing not only his travels in Italy but also the gardens. Writers from many different countries conveyed the same message.

In the late 17th century and early 18th century the gardens changed and interest focused on the architectural layout where perspective played a key role. From this emerged the Baroque garden of Villa Garzoni and Villa Gamberaia.

One can then trace the influence of these gardens on Western Europe and the return of new ideas to Tuscany. Le Nôtre of Versailles fame visited the garden in the 17th century and put forward some sketch ideas that transformed the garden around the Villa into a landscape park. The only remains of the 16th century is a small sunken floral garden with its nymphaeum.

At the Villa Mansi, only the water garden of the Baroque garden remains. The main garden was transformed into an English Park in the 19th century.

Continual change has taken place at Villa Marlia. First a 16th century garden followed by a Baroque design and then Napoleon's sister Elisa Baciocchi created a romantic Park. The present owner has added a 20th century modern garden inspired by an Islamic water garden.

Comparatively recently Giuliano Gori purchased Villa Celle near Pistoia, a Baroque Villa with 25 hectares of English landscape Park. Art collectors with connections to important 20th century artists decided to make a series of ambitious commissions. Artists from near and far were invited to visit and select a space to create a unique piece for the chosen site. The result is a remarkable collection of unique works of the present time, held together by the landscape of the Park.

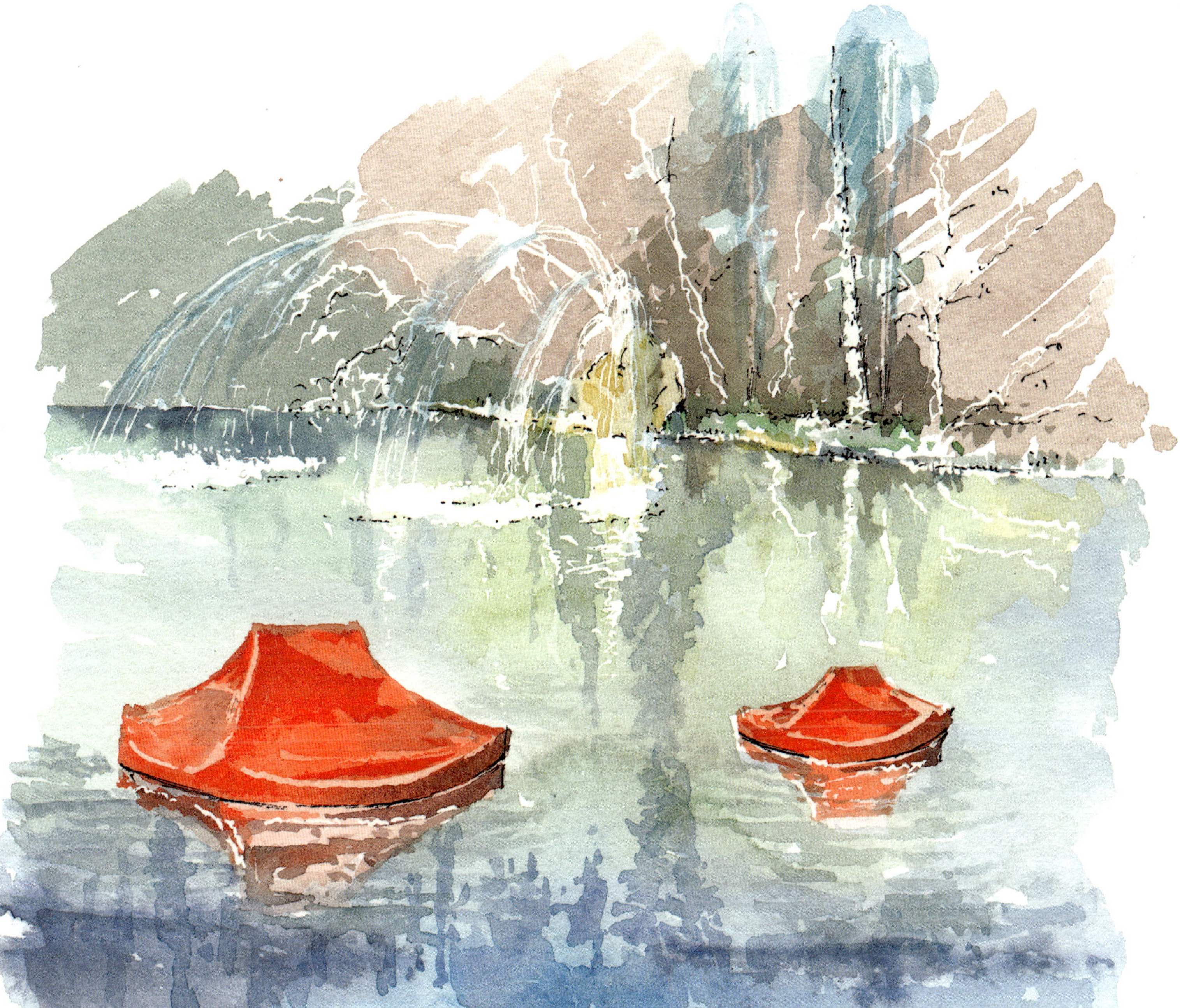

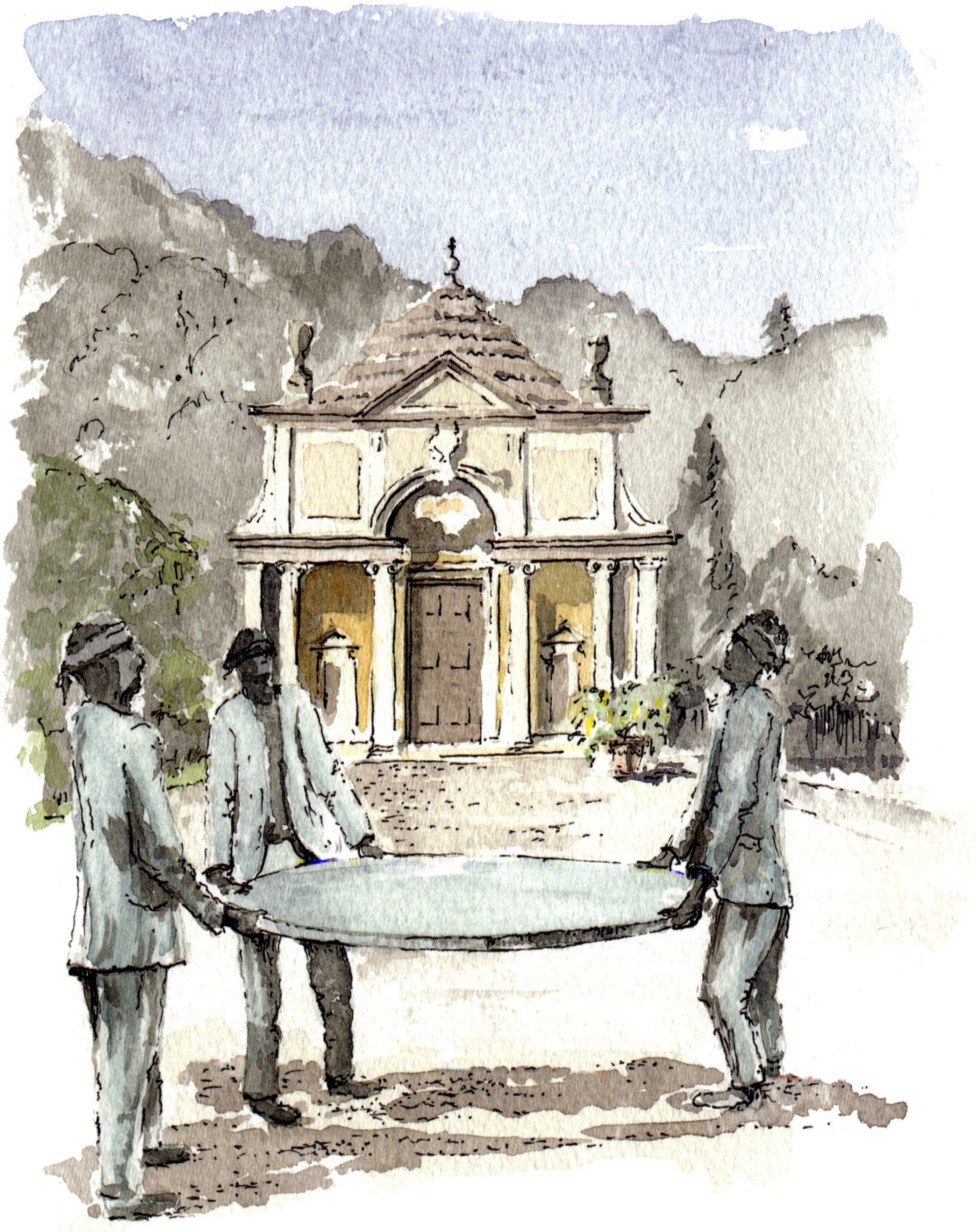

Villa Celle near Pistoia. Three figures with disc/table top in bronze

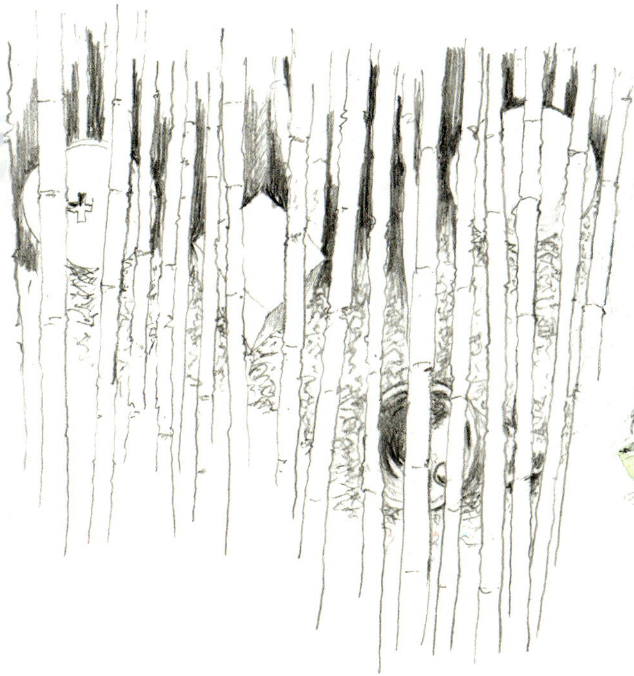

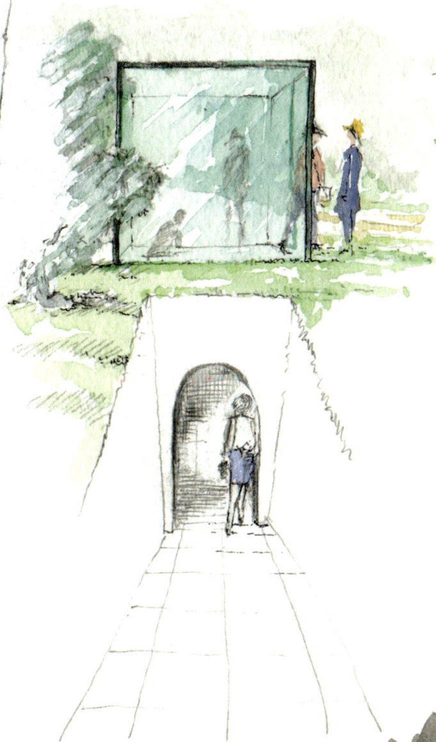

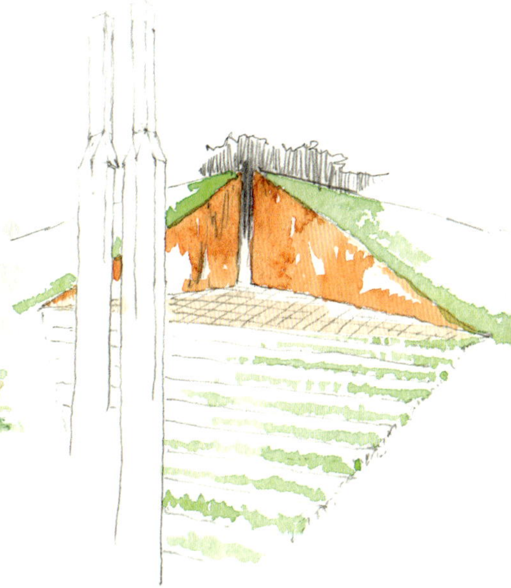

A small selection of the many permanent outdoor installations

White marble forms in a bamboo grove

'My hole in the sky' 1985-89 by Bukichi Inoue from Japan. Starting from a small paved area down an open corridor into the earth and exit by a curved white marble staircase into a glass cube at ground level

Celle Theatre Space 1992 by Beverly Pepper from New York

'Open Field Vertical Elevation 1982 by Richard Serra from San Francisco

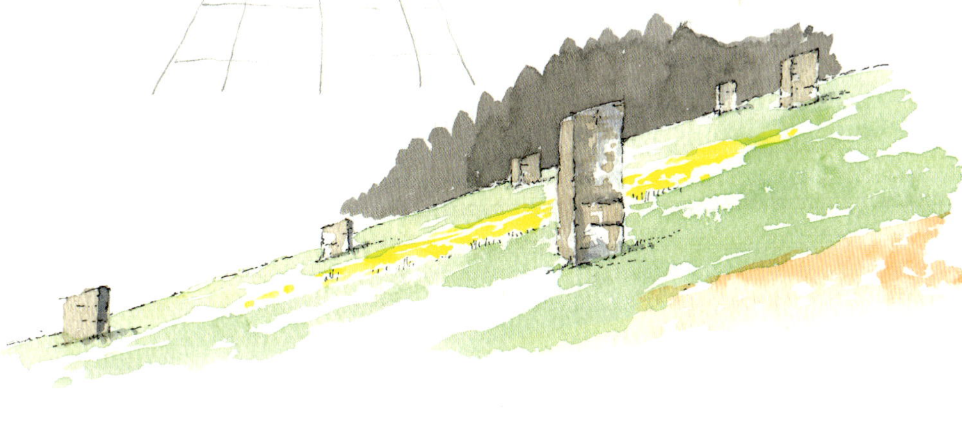

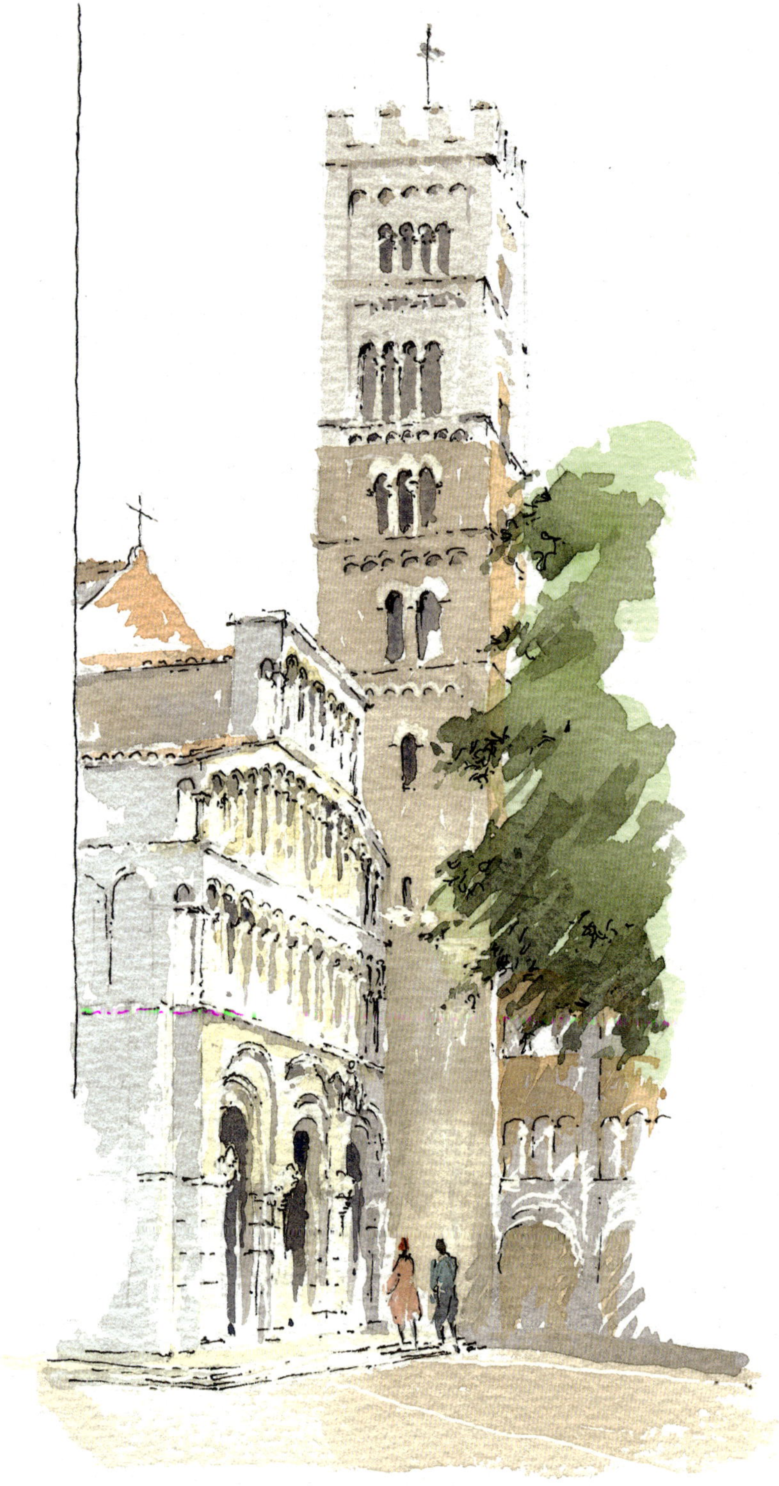

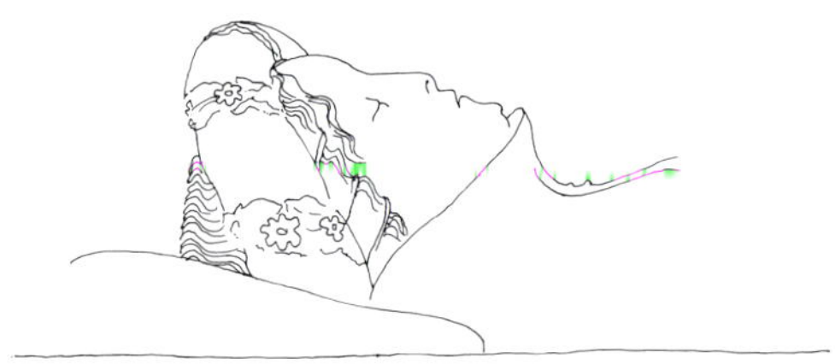

Marble tomb of Ilaria del
Carretto in the Duomo

Duomo of San Martino

Lucca and the north

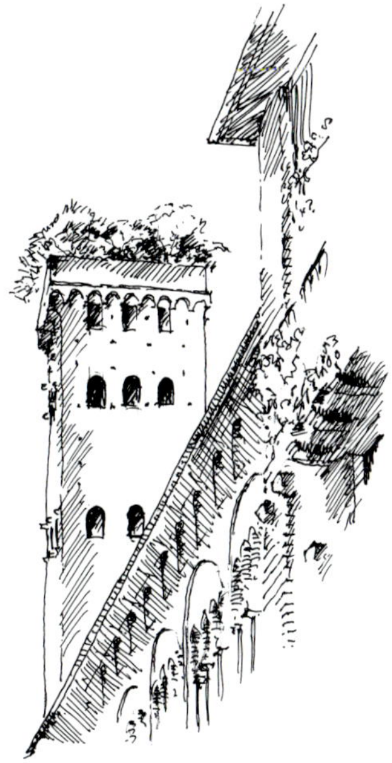

Medieval Torre dei Guinigi

There is no better way to absorb the atmosphere of Lucca than to join the locals in the early evening, at 'passeggiata' time, when the inhabitants stroll past shops and cafés to meet friends before dinner.

Lucca, for many, is the most enchanting and hence their favourite city of Tuscany. It is compact and enclosed by the massive complete town walls but is made friendly by the green slopes and mature trees. The main entry to the city is through St Peter's gate. The Romans laid out the city on a grid in 180 BC. The old amphitheatre is now an oval Piazza del Mercato and the outline of original Roman arches can be seen in the outer walls of the ochre-washed medieval buildings. It reached its peak in the 14th century due to the flourishing silk industry, when many of the palaces, houses and churches were built.

The massive brick enclosing walls built between 1504 and 1645 have never had to be used for defensive purposes. A superb high level linear park with forest trees encloses the city, giving opportunities to walk round at high level to pick out streets and buildings to explore later. It is possible to see into the fine formal garden of Palazzo Pfanner 1667. The Giardino Botanico laid out in the 1820 includes a good collection of plants from Tuscany. Giacomo Puccini was born here in 1858 and so was Luigi Boccherini.

Still to this day it is a medieval town with narrow streets and relatively small piazza. The Duomo, a Romanesque building of the 11th to 13th century was rebuilt in the Gothic style in the next century. The campanile was originally a defensive tower in 1060. When it became part of the Duomo in 1261 two upper tiers were added resulting in an asymmetrical balance with the façade, unequal arches at

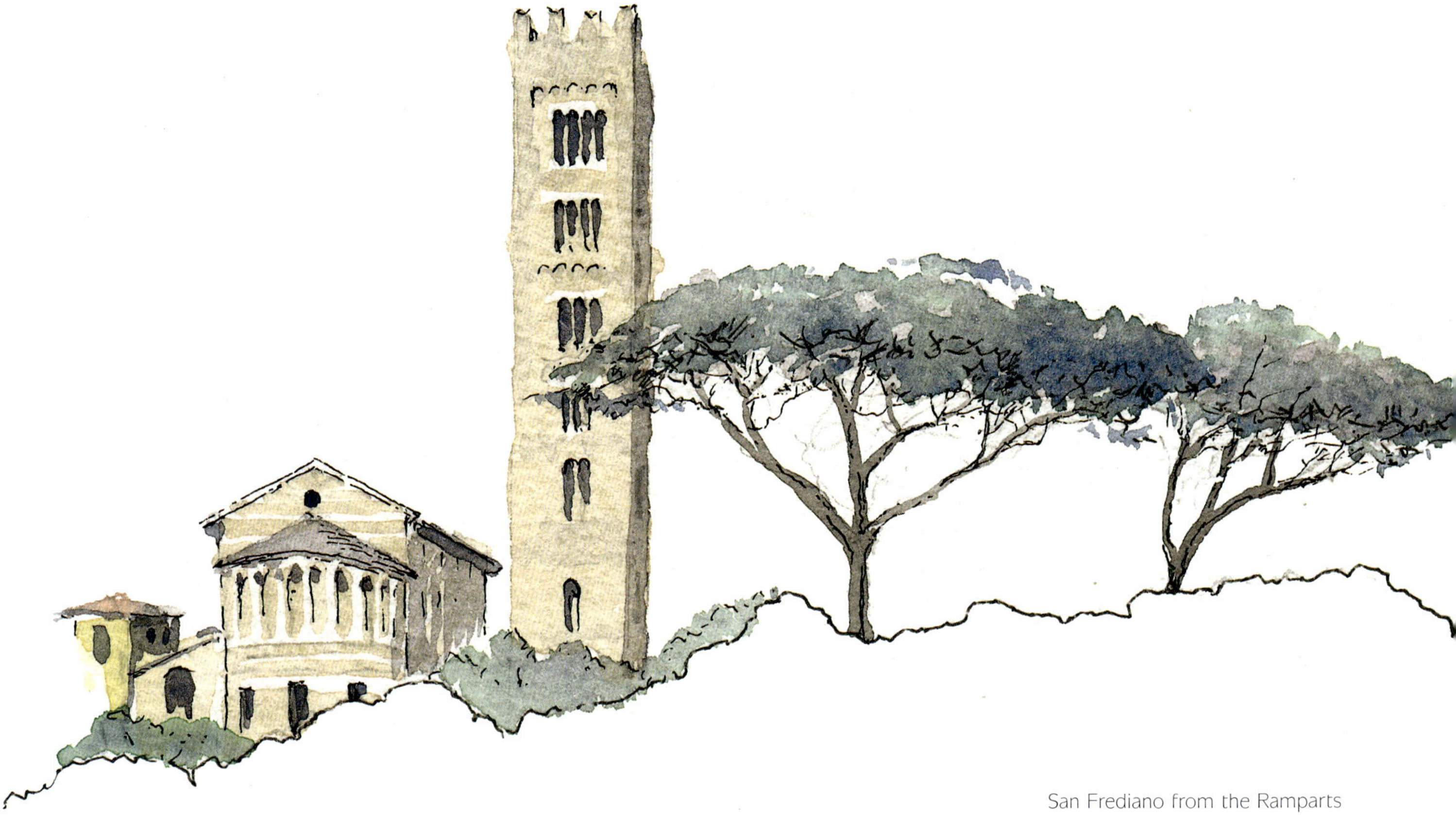

San Frediano from the Ramparts

ground level and the typical three-tier colonnaded gable above. On the outside is a sculpture of St Martin but this is a copy for security reasons and the original 13th century work is inside the cathedral. One of the finest Italian funereal carvings is to be found on the tomb of Ilaria del Carretto 1405–6 a beautiful white marble work by Jacopo della Quercia.

Two further fine churches are the San Michele in Foro with a striking 13th century facade surmounted by a large statue of St. Michael slaying the dragon and two musician angels on each side. San Frediano is the largest Romanesque Church with a fine 12th century carved relief font. Via Guinigi is dominated by the medieval tower of the same name that sprouts oak trees on top.

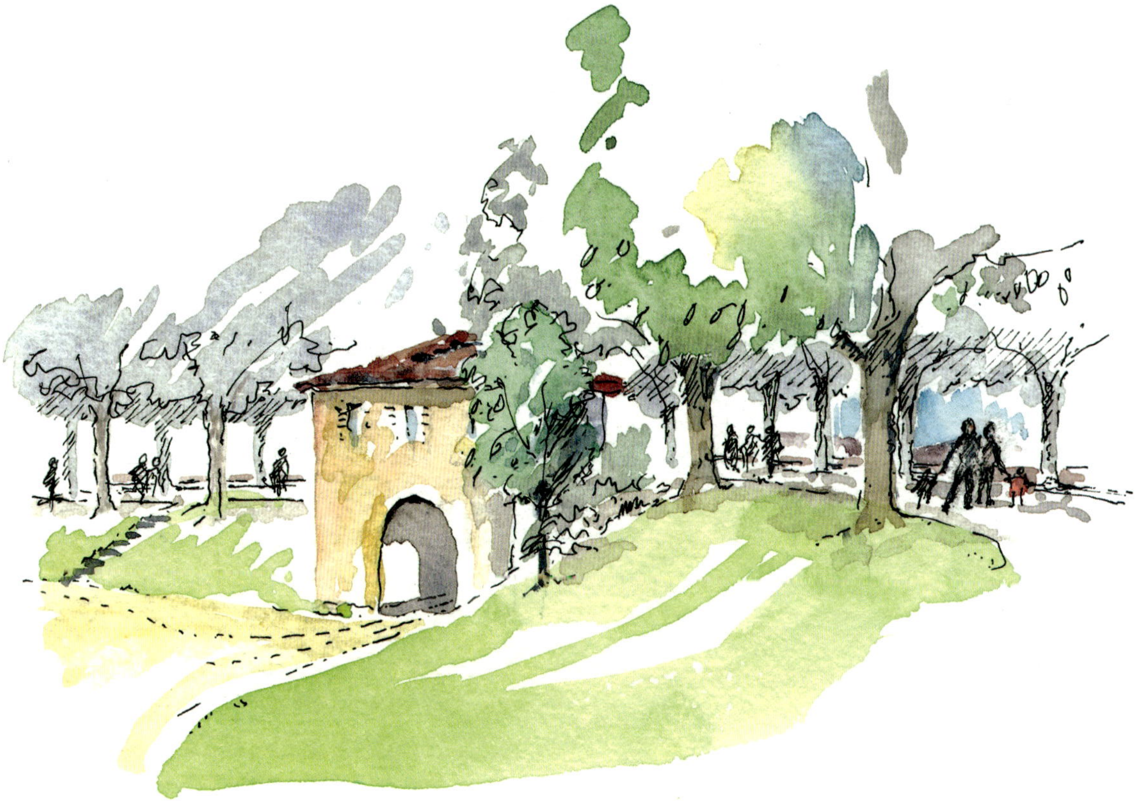

Tree lined walk on the Ramparts

Lucca for most of its history was independent of Pisa and Florence. Napoleon occupied the city in the 1805. He gave the republic to his sister, Elisa Baciocchi and later to Marie Louise, his widow. Both were well received by the people. In 1847 it was sold to Leopold II of Tuscany.

Henry James described it as 'Overflowing with everything that makes for ease, for plenty, for beauty, for interest and good example!'

The lasting visual image is of a lively urban place with tall buildings in narrow streets opening onto a variety of piazzas. Of warm brickwork, occasional soft colour grey stonework and painted stucco in light Tuscan red, pink, ochre, terracotta and light green. The town within the walls are for people and bicycles only.

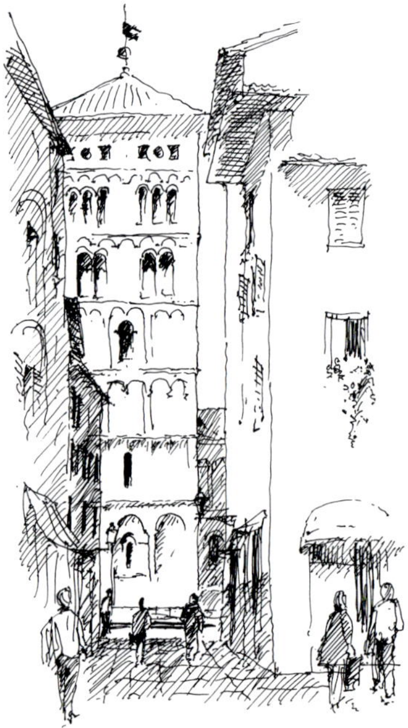

Torre dei San Michele

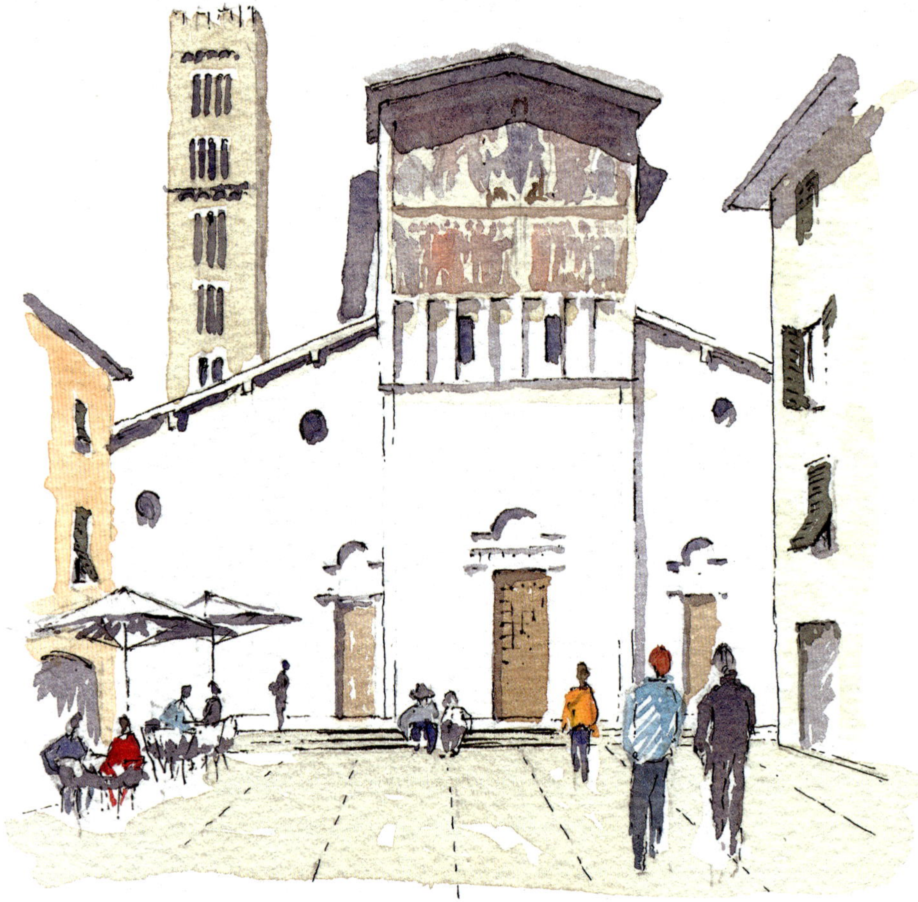

San Frediano from the Piazza

Tuscany north of Lucca is in marked contrast to the rolling hills and valleys of the South, comprising the mountain ranges of Alpi Apuane and Garfagnana leaving a narrow coastal strip. Travelling north is the striking 12th Century Bridge, Ponto della Maddalena or Devils Bridge. Olive groves and chestnut woods soon give way to pines on the high mountain where the famous quarries of Carrara are located. These have provided superb material from Roman times onwards, a favourite marble of Michelangelo and which are still in demand by Henry Moore and other 20th century sculptors.

Less interesting to me was Bagni di Lucca, a shadow of its former past when it was a favourite spa of such people as Elisa Bonaparte Baciocchi, Byron, Brownings, Shelley and Heine. However on the slopes of the Serchio Valley is to be found the beautiful small town of Barga. Explore the fine Romanesque Duomo. Inside you will see a superb 12th century marble pulpit supported by red columns resting on lions and a man in a squatting position. The low relief carved panels depicts the life of Mary and Christ.

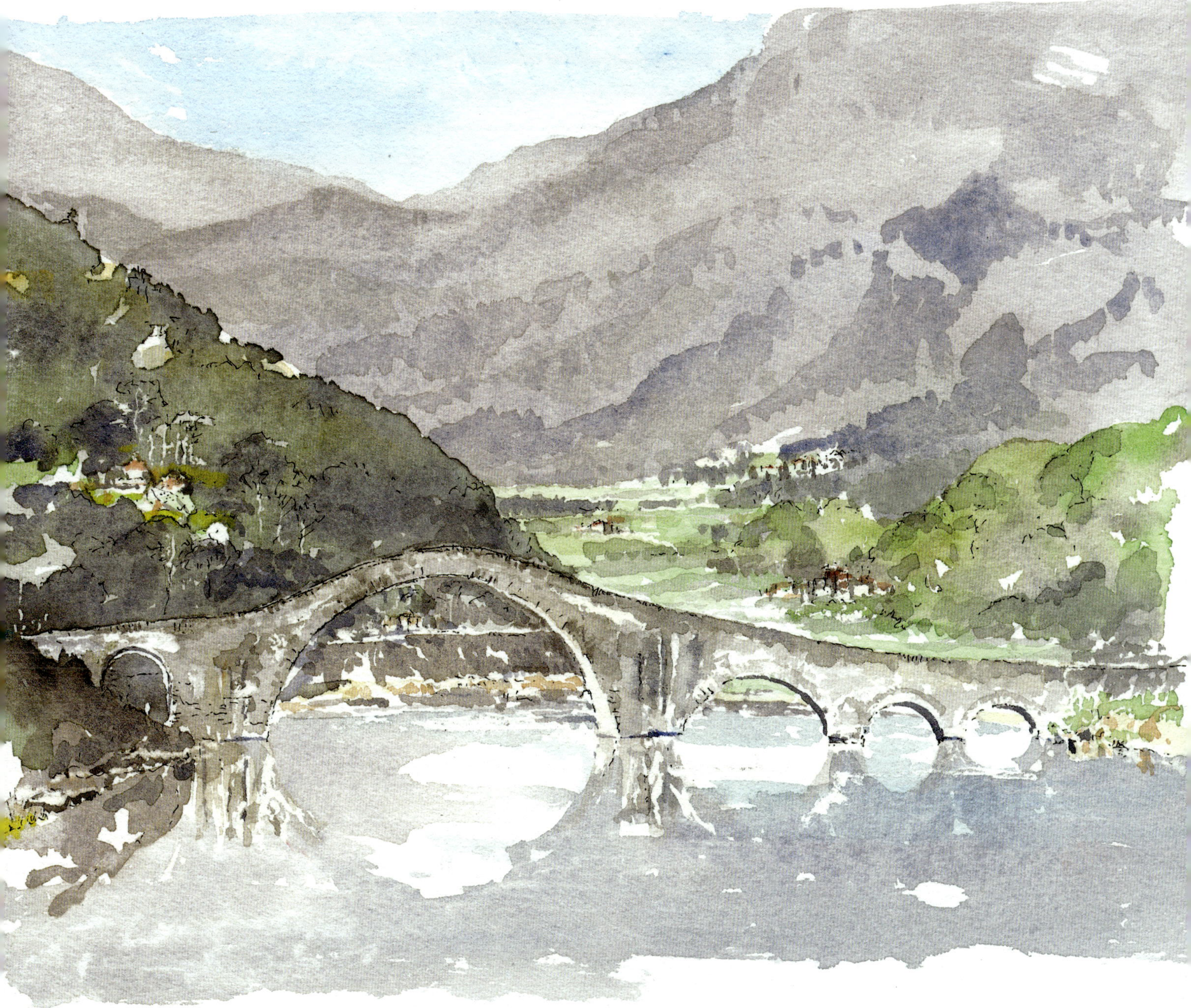

Ponto della Maddalena or Devils Bridge
ncar Borgo a Mozzano

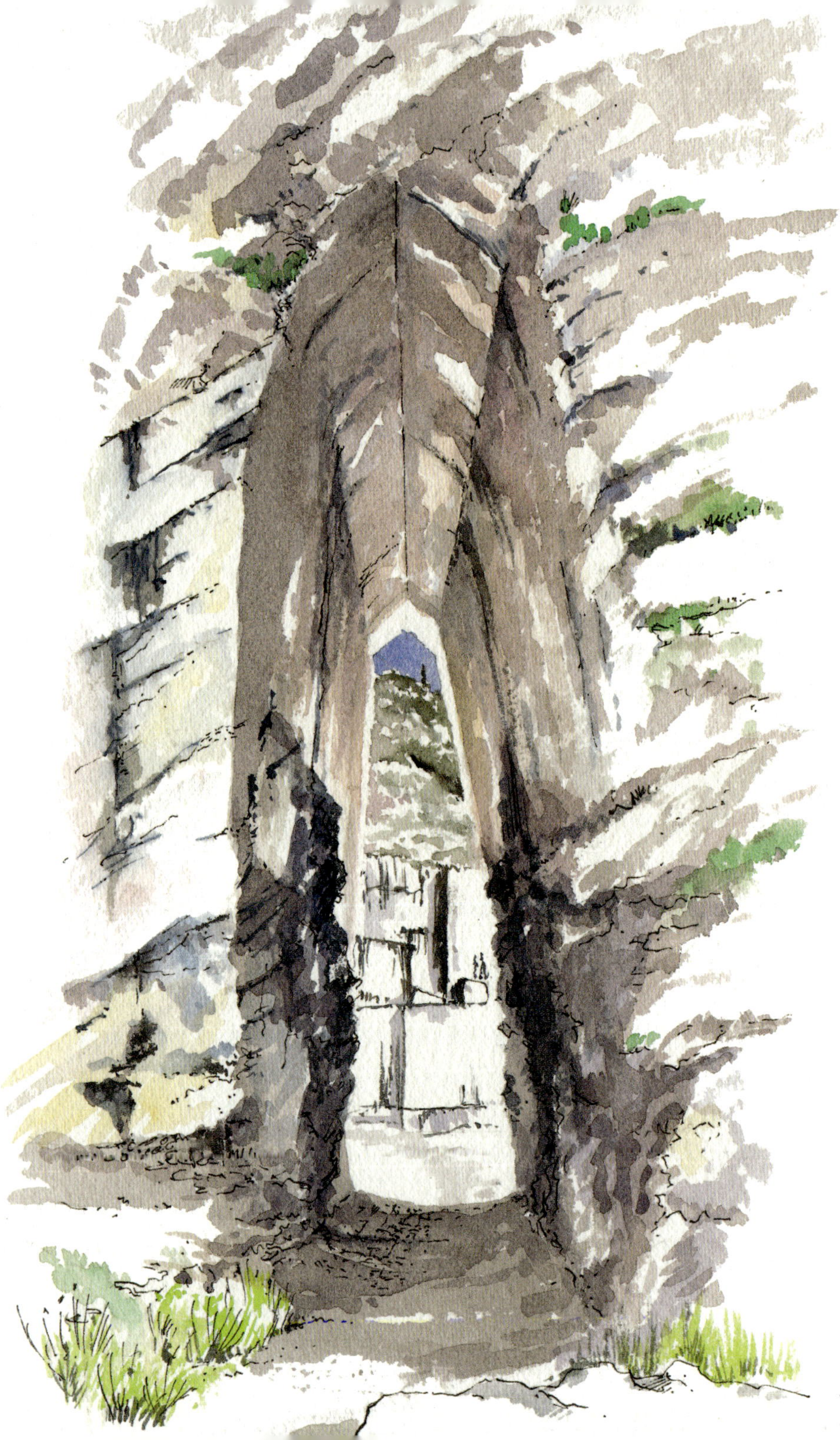

Abandoned marble quarry of Carrara

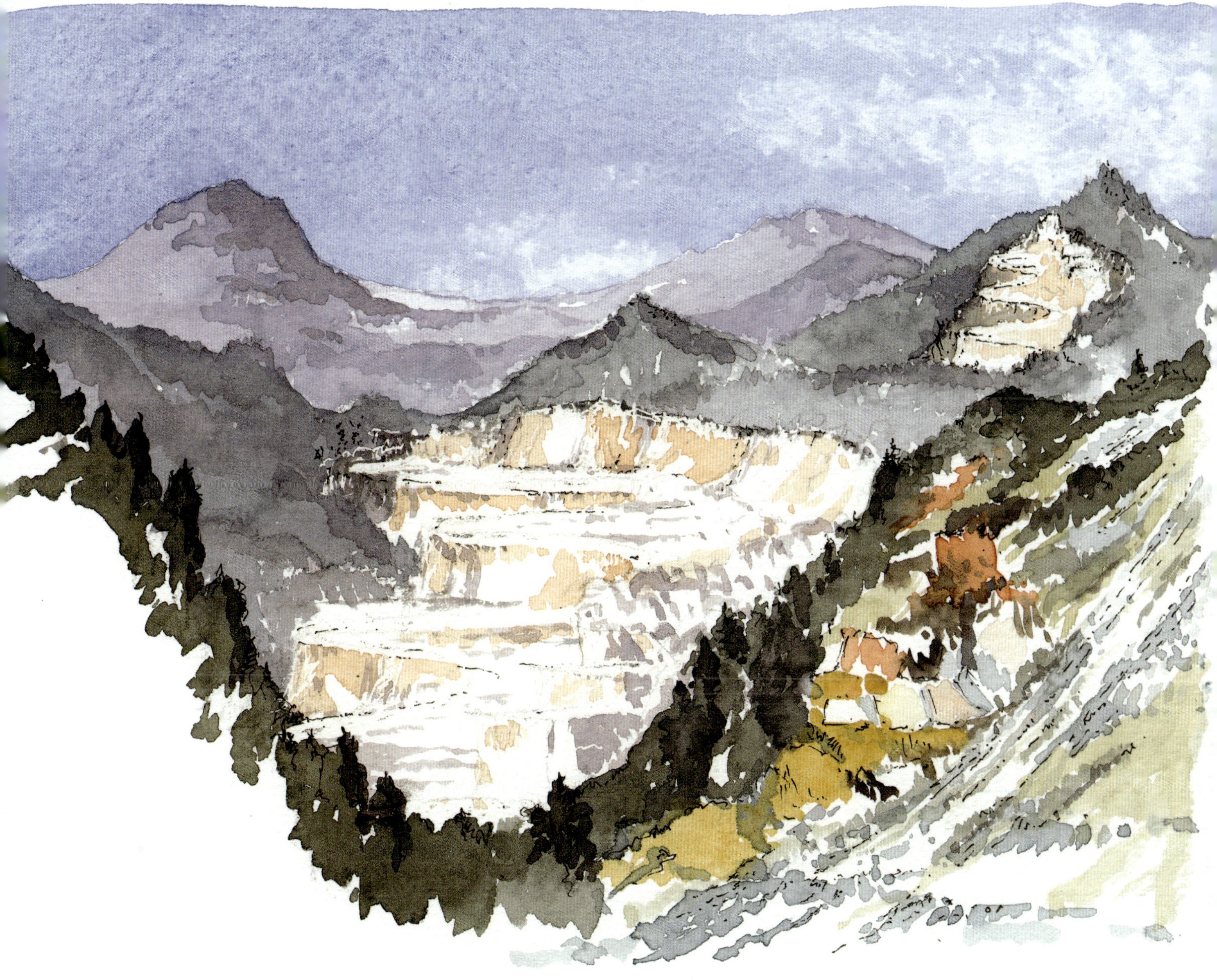

Marble quarries on the hills of Carrara

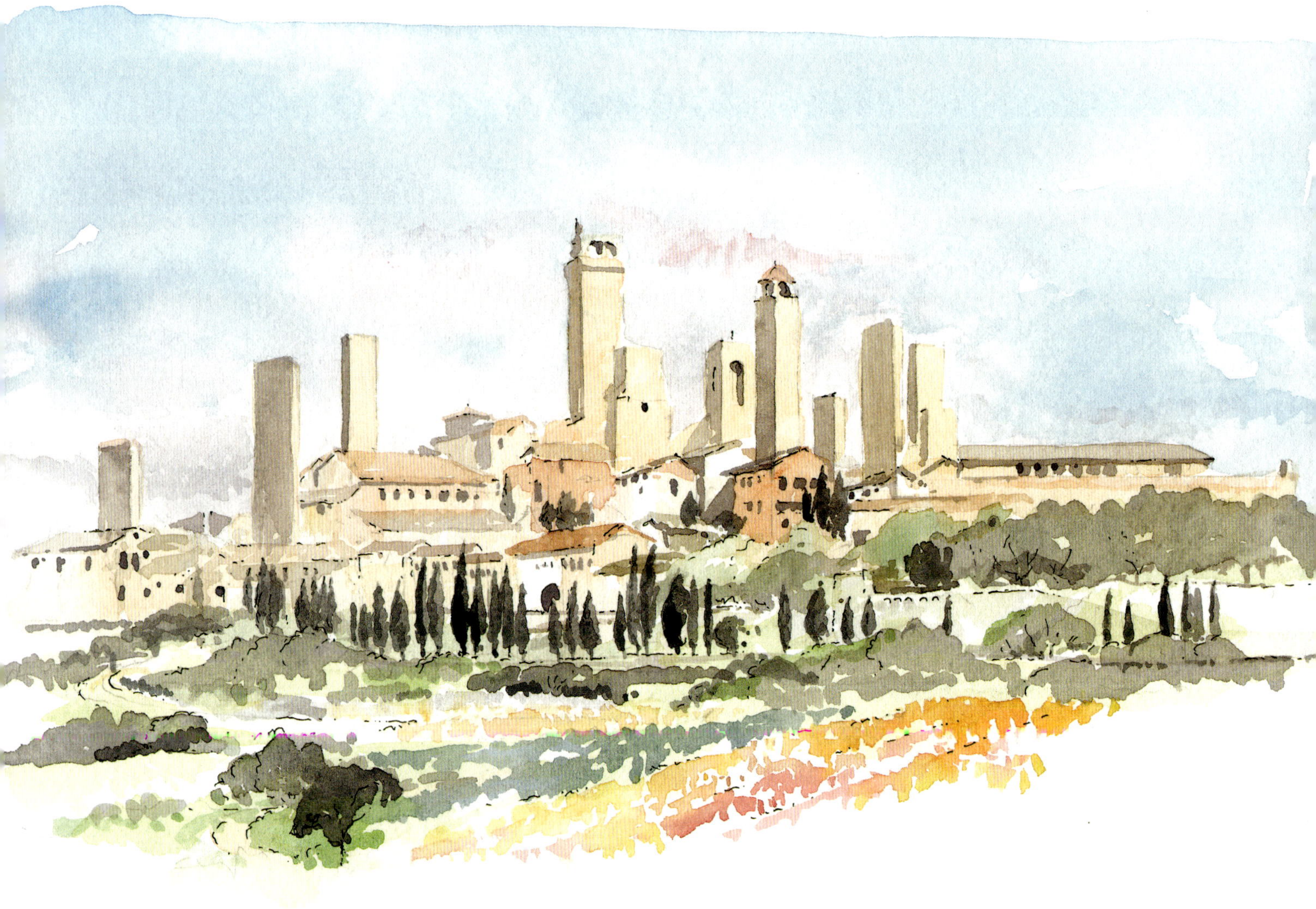

A view the pilgrims may have seen, San Gimignano

Volterra, San Gimignano, Monteriggioni, Colle di Val d'Elsa and San Galgano

There are four contrasting and remarkable hill towns in central Tuscany. The oldest with Etruscan roots is Volterra, originally called Velathri. It has preserved some of the original town layout and artefacts, important in the Iron Age. The powerful Roman fortification had a population of 25000 people and like many cities of this period was situated on the high plateau. The Museo Etrusco Guarnacci has an important collection of the Etruscan works including 'Evening shadow' and alabaster urns of the second and first century's BC. Also to be found is the impressive Roman theatre.

San Gimignano is a medieval hilltop town on the pilgrim route from northern Europe to Rome. The pilgrims would have seen the towers through the rolling hills in the area and would have entered through one of the five gates. Interesting narrow streets lead to the interlocking paved urban spaces of Piazza Luigi Pecori and Piazza del Duomo. The oldest tower may be part of Palazzo Vecchio del Podestà. Look above the shop fronts to see the beauty of the medieval buildings. The windowless towers are a tantalising challenge to the artist and photographer. How does one capture the atmosphere and visual experience when visiting this well-preserved medieval town? To enter the Romanesque Church of Collegiata one is surprised by the blue and white striped aisle, deep blue vaulted roof with gold stars and famous fresco scenes from the Bible. The Rocca or fortress built in 1353 provides superb views of the towers and the countryside in which the town is set.

By comparison Monteriggioni is a town on the crest of the hill enclosed by a wall with fourteen towers. Surprisingly it was built ten years before it became a garrison town in 1213. It was to protect Siena from the armies of Florence. Dante in his 'Inferno' described the town as a 'ring-shaped citadel' and as giants standing in a moat. A large Piazza is found within the walls where small-scale buildings are dominated by the space.

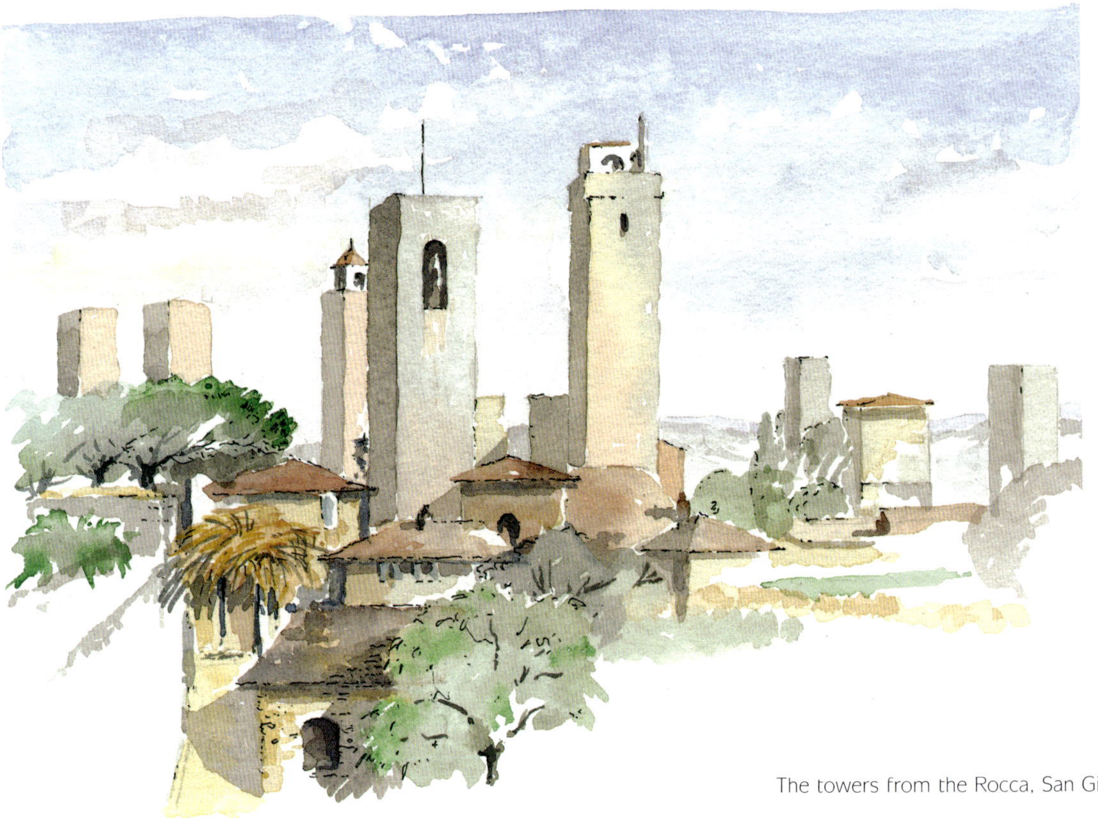

The towers from the Rocca, San Gimignano

It is interesting to find such variety in these towns, no more so than in Colle di Val d'Elsa. The lower town by the river is heavily industrialised but go to the old town Colle Alta that is at the top of the hill. The concept for the upper town is a surprisingly formal, medieval mannerist design of distinction. The Renaissance palaces contrast with the other hilltop towns. The archeological museum has a good collection of the Etruscan and Roman objects found in Val d'Elsa. From the distance a striking silhouette is present.

A great ruin can be seen across the field in front of San Galgano between Massa Marittima and Siena. It can be seen through the mist or in bright sunlight. The monks left a formidable structure: an impressive ruin of the Romanesque Gothic abbey 1224–1288 by Cistercian monks to a design inspired by the mother

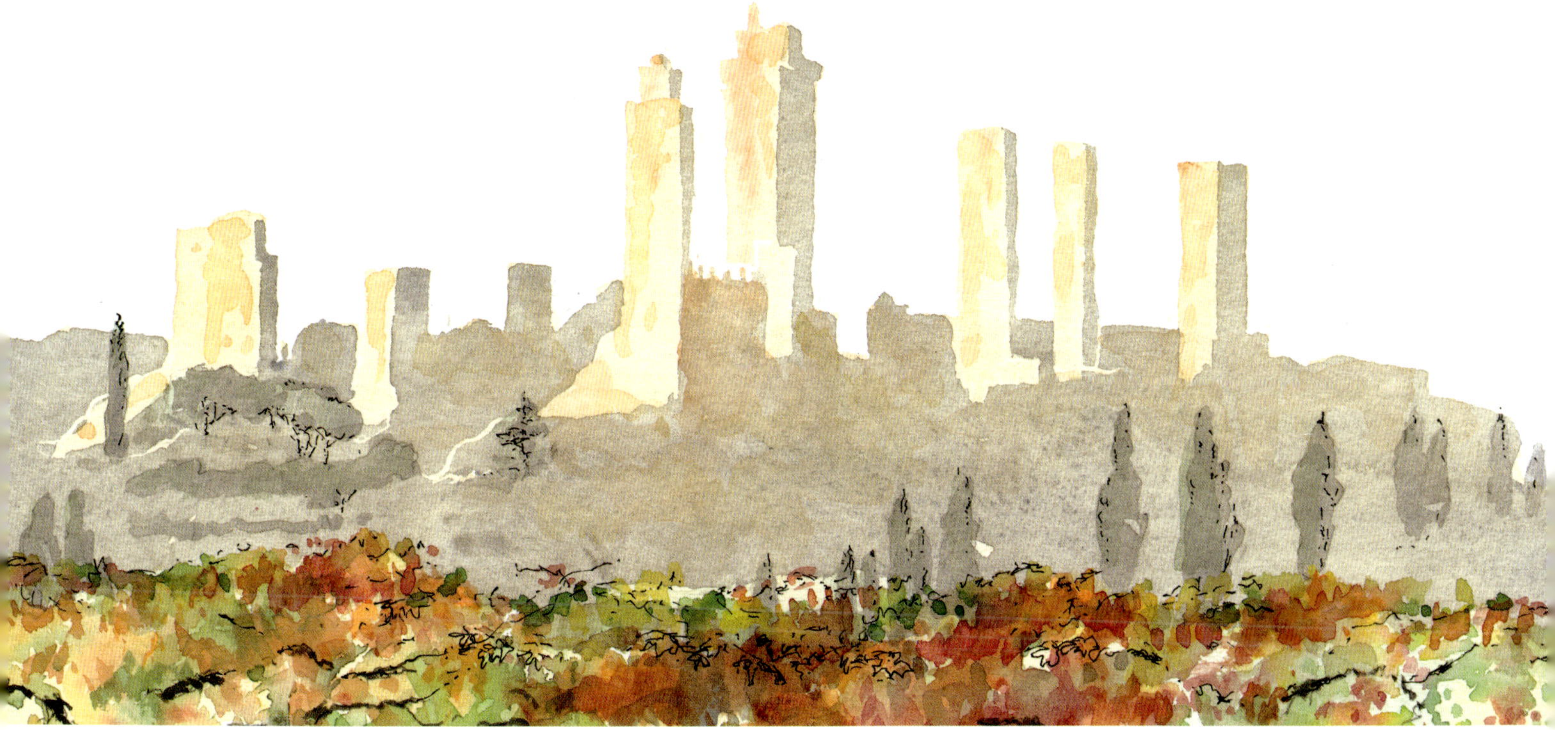

San Gimignano

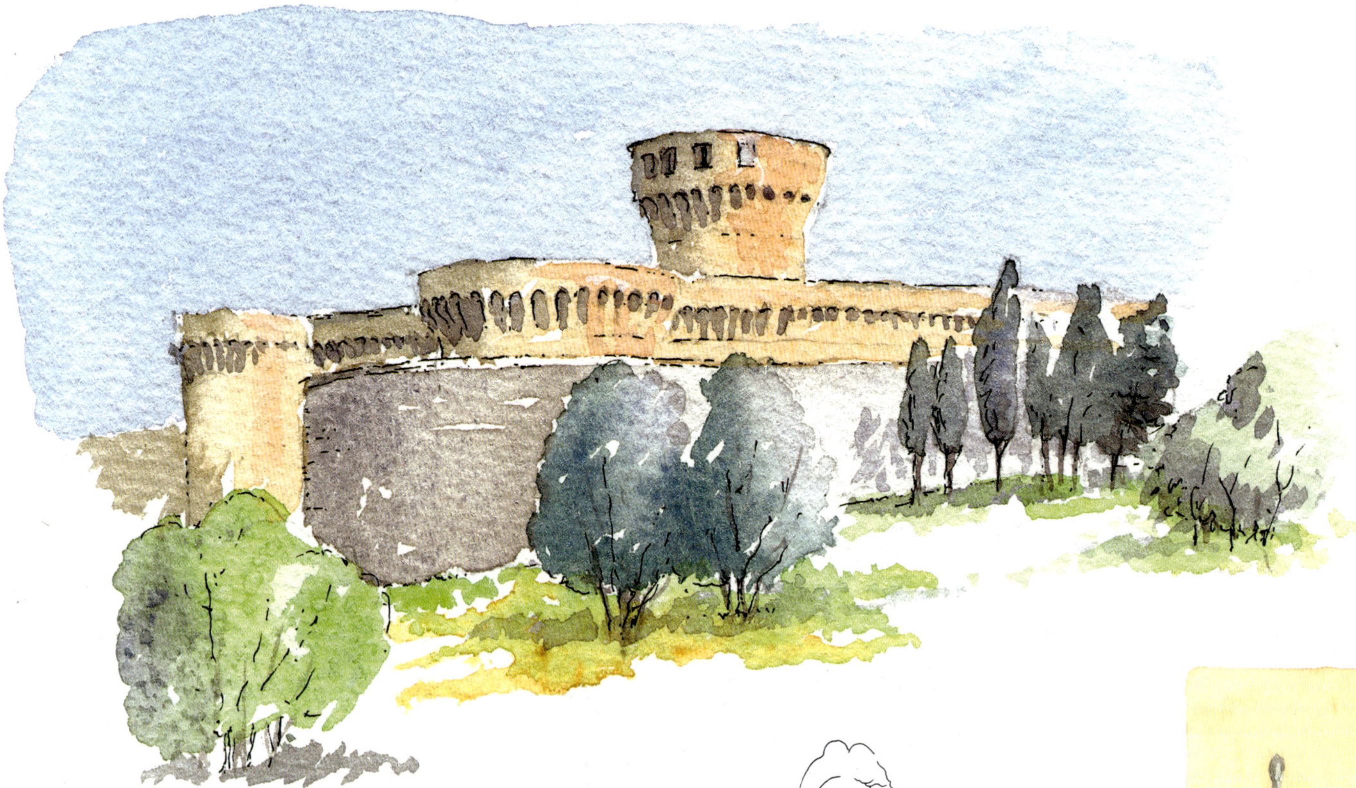

Fortification of Volterra

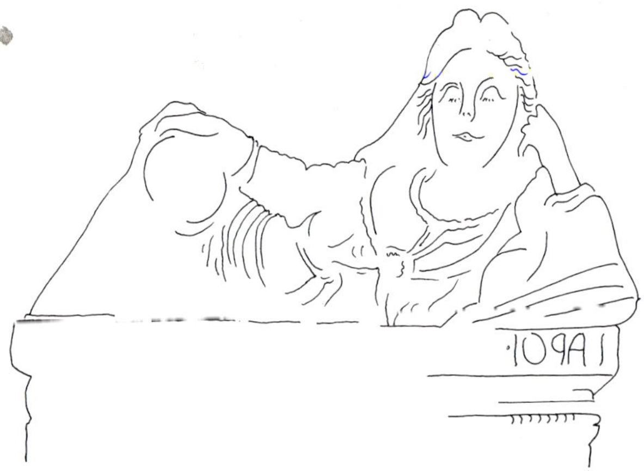

Alabaster urn
Museo Etrusco Guarnacci

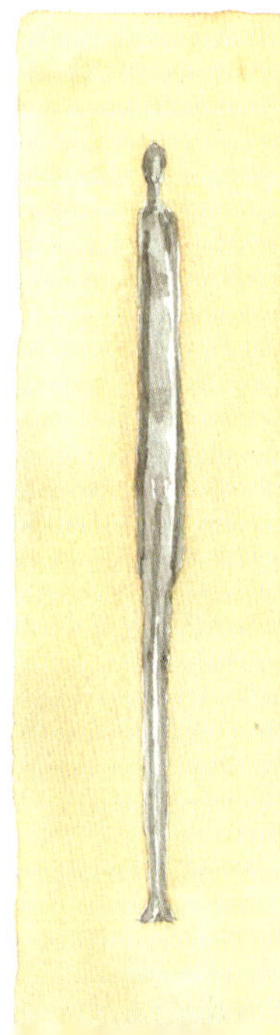

'Evening Shadow',

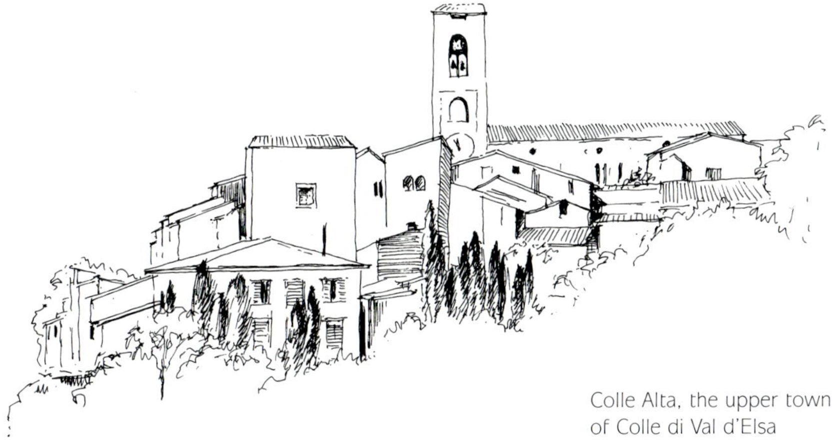

Colle Alta, the upper town
of Colle di Val d'Elsa

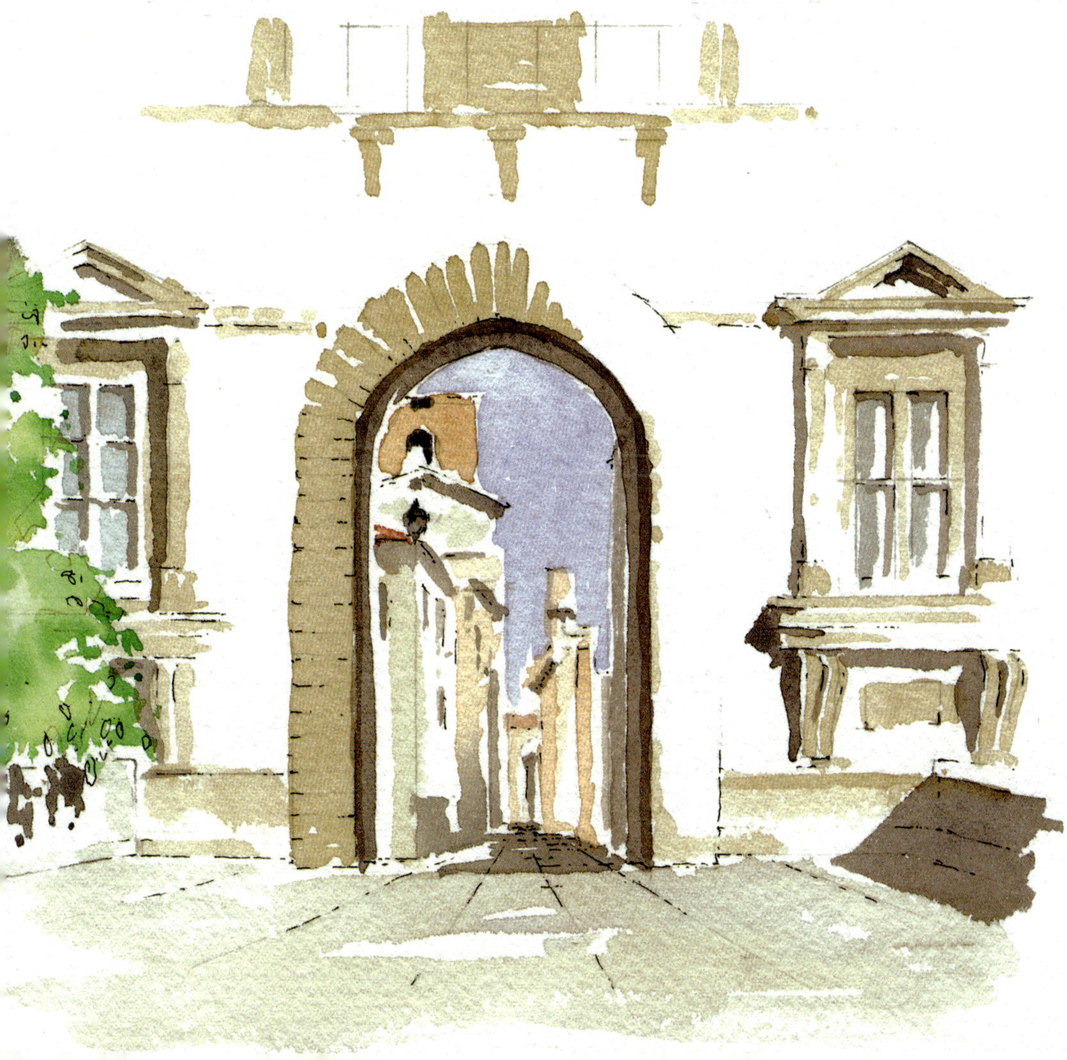

Palazzo Campana, Colle Alta

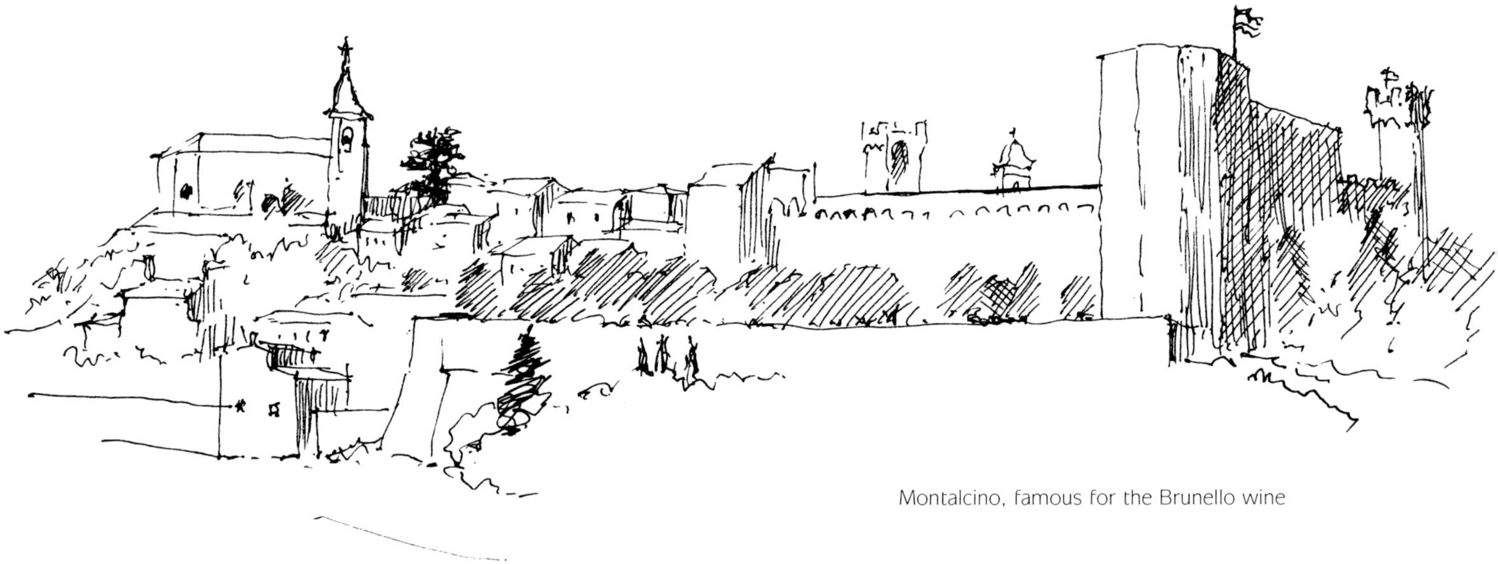

Montalcino, famous for the Brunello wine

church of Citeaux in Burgundy France, that was to influence future Gothic churches in Tuscany. The beautiful ruin challenges the viewer to visualise this great building. It was connected to a community of Mount of Olive Benedictine nuns in a beautiful circular Romanesque oratory which can be visited on the nearby hilltop.

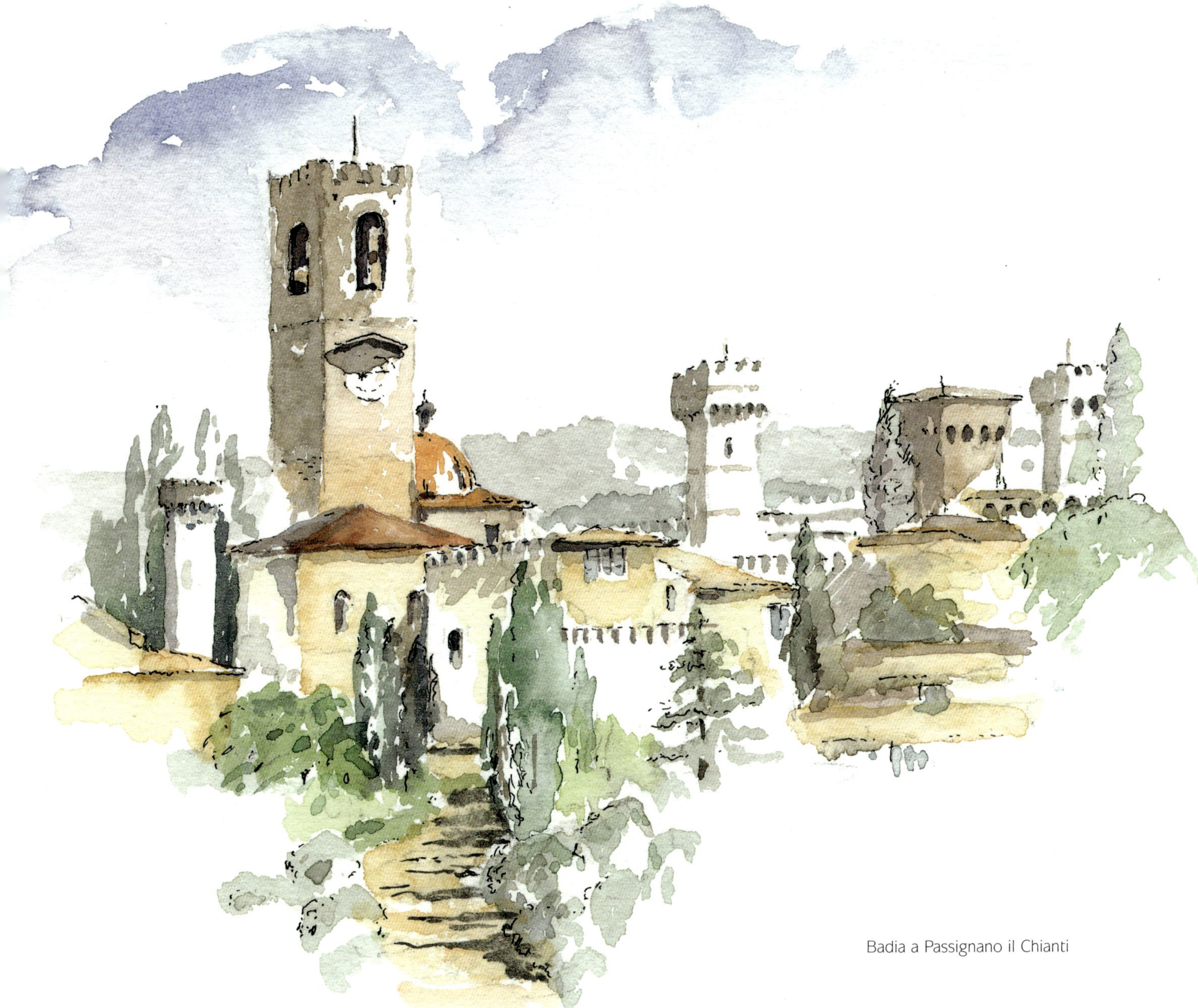

Badia a Passignano il Chianti

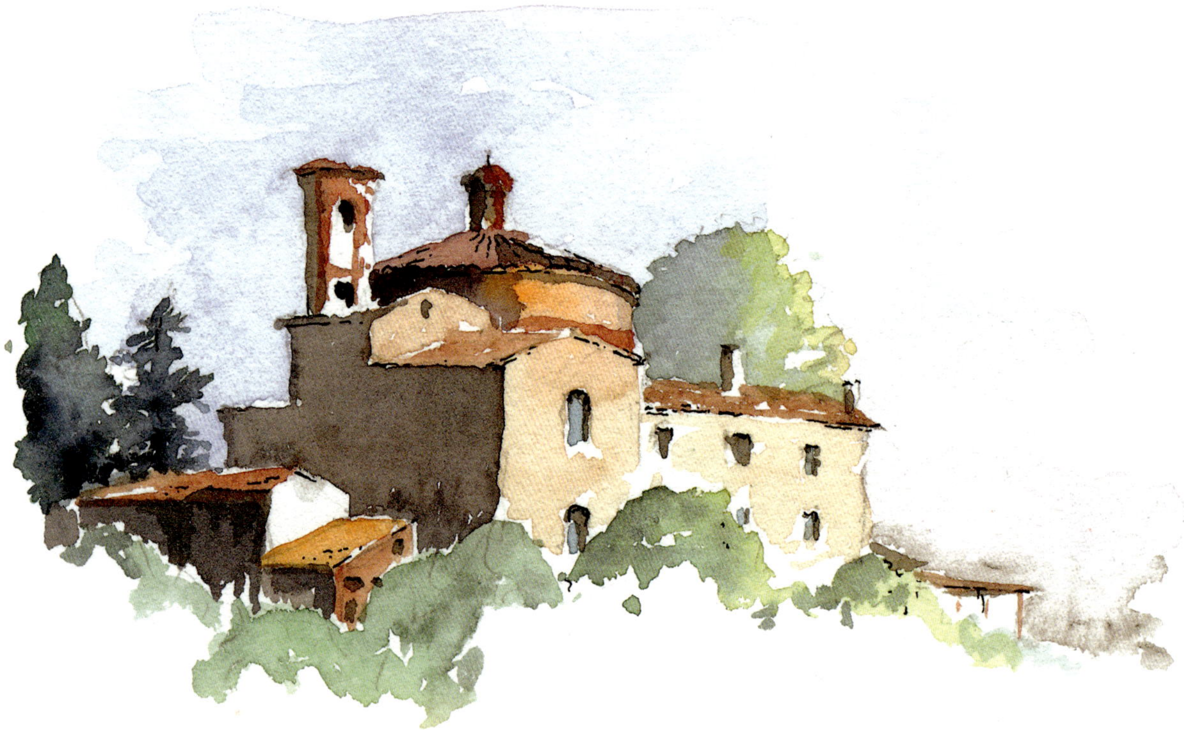

Romanesque oratory near San Galgano

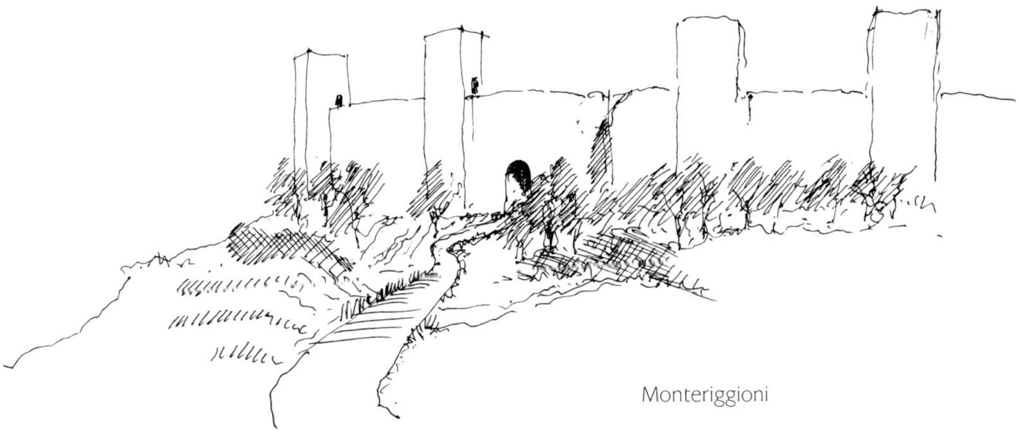

Monteriggioni

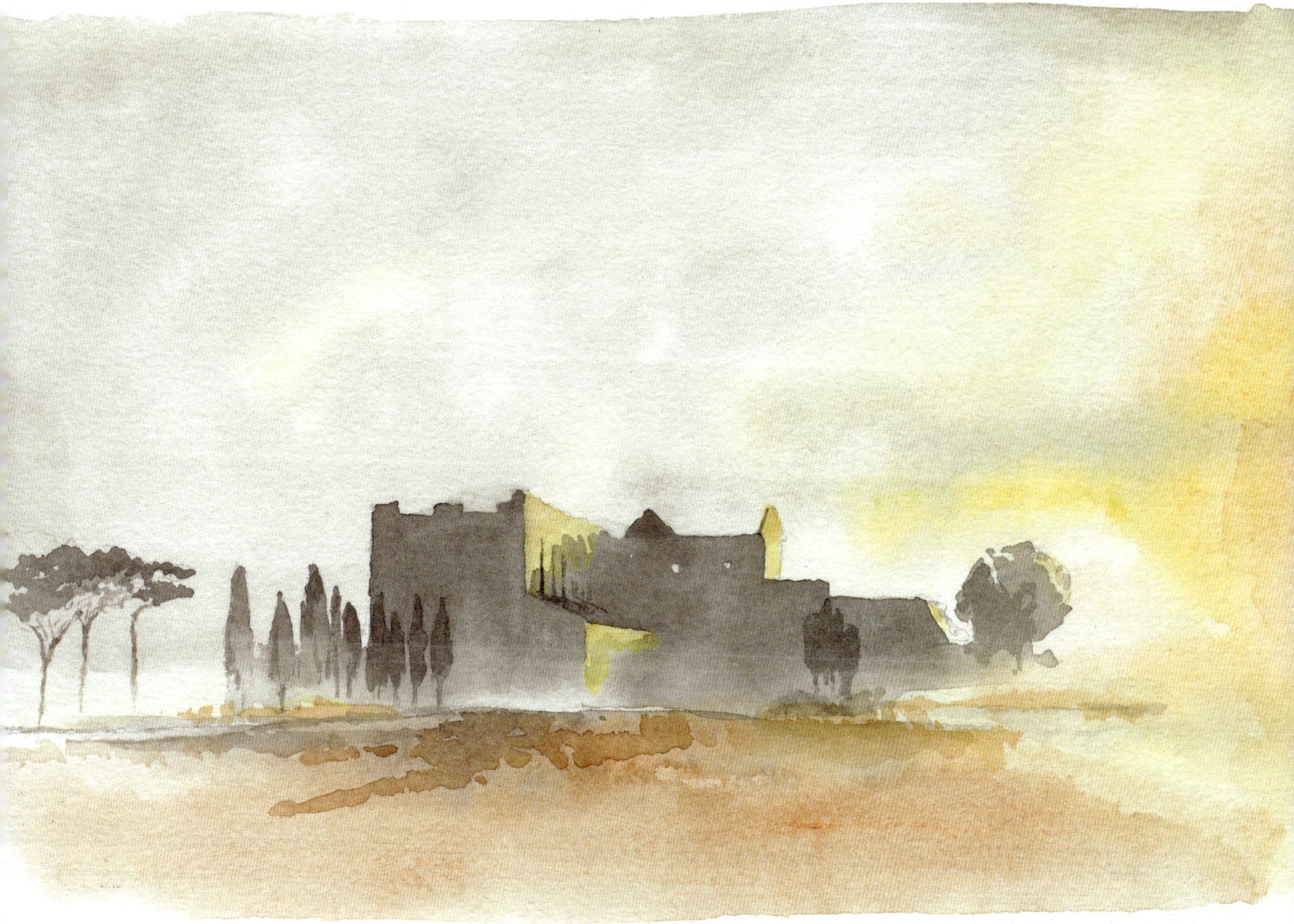

San Galgano in the early morning

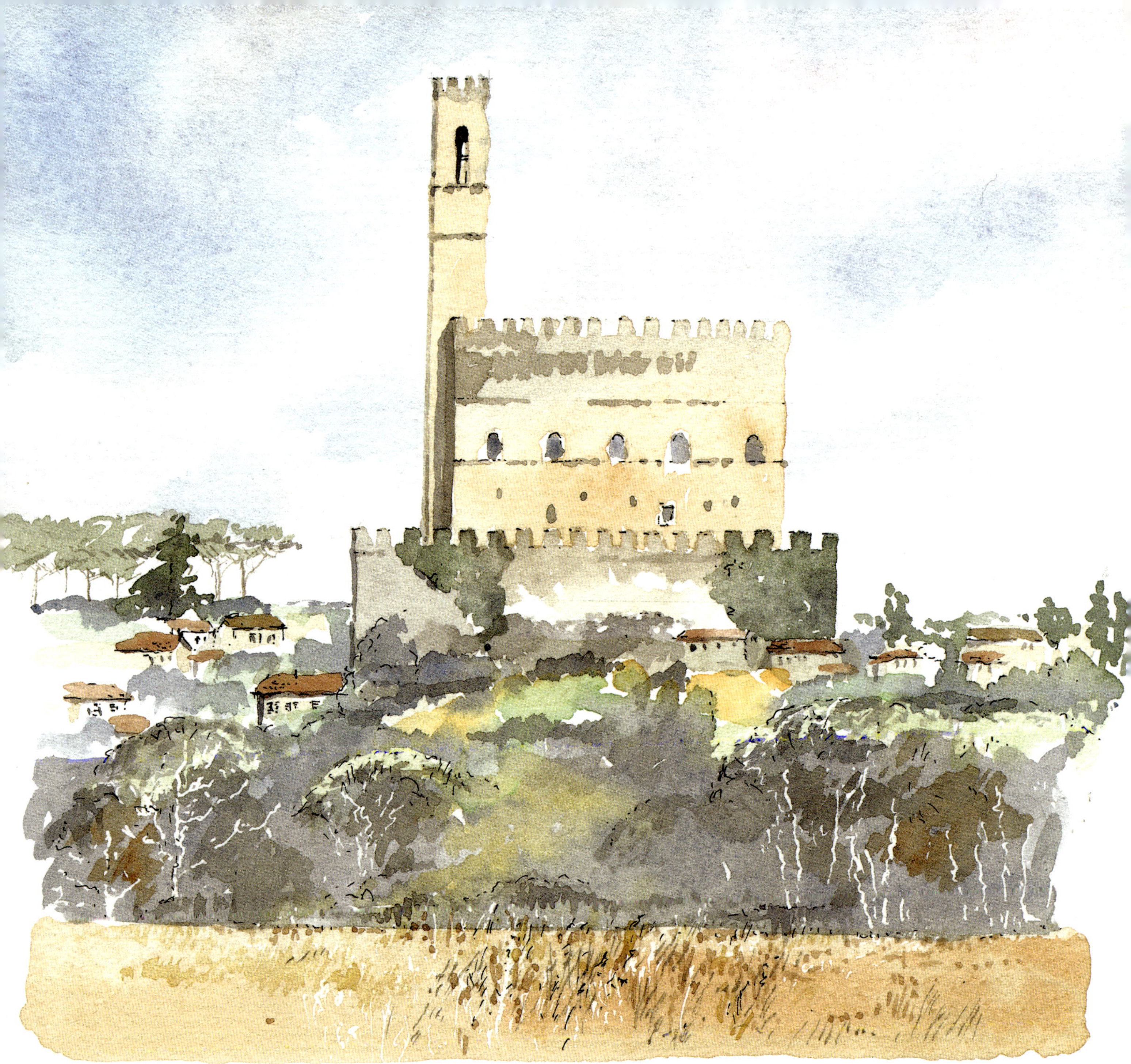

Poppi Castle

Arezzo and neighbouring towns

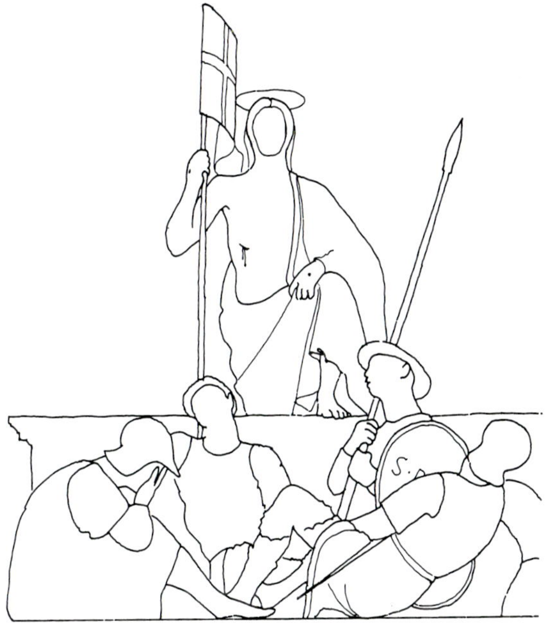

Outline of 'The Resurrection', Sansepolcro by Piero della Francesca

Following the Arno from Florence along the Pratomagno to Arezzo.

Arezzo with Etruscan origins became an important city in Roman times and was the centre for producing the 'Aretine Vase' that was made from high-quality red glazed pottery. Giorgio Vasari, a significant painter and art historian, was born here in 1511 and designed the Loggia in Piazza Grande. The church of San Francesco contains the fantastic frescoes by Piero della Francesca. The legends of the true cross 1452–66 produced one of the great fresco series. In the church of San Domenico is a fine crucifix dating from 1265 over the main altar by Cimabue.

The main focus of attention for me, however, is the work of a remarkable painter Piero della Francesca who was born nearby in Sansepolcro. He was to influence the art of the west 1416 to 92. Veneziano, Masaccio and Uccello taught him. However, it was his individual genius that changed the art world, through the composition, colour and the clarity of his paintings. The impact of seeing the original paintings for the first time left a permanent impression on me. A stunning picture is 'The Resurrection' where Christ has a foot on the tomb and the disciples are asleep. No other picture has moved me more. It can be seen in the Museo Civico in Sansepolcro.

Northwards to Poppi on the edge of the Arno Valley in the Casentino where the massive castle can be seen from considerable distance. It was built in the 13th century for the Count Guidi and is in perfect condition with a fine atrium staircase space. The castle is used as the town hall and the library of the Great Hall still has the original painted decoration. In the upper town, attractive arcade streets are found below the castle.

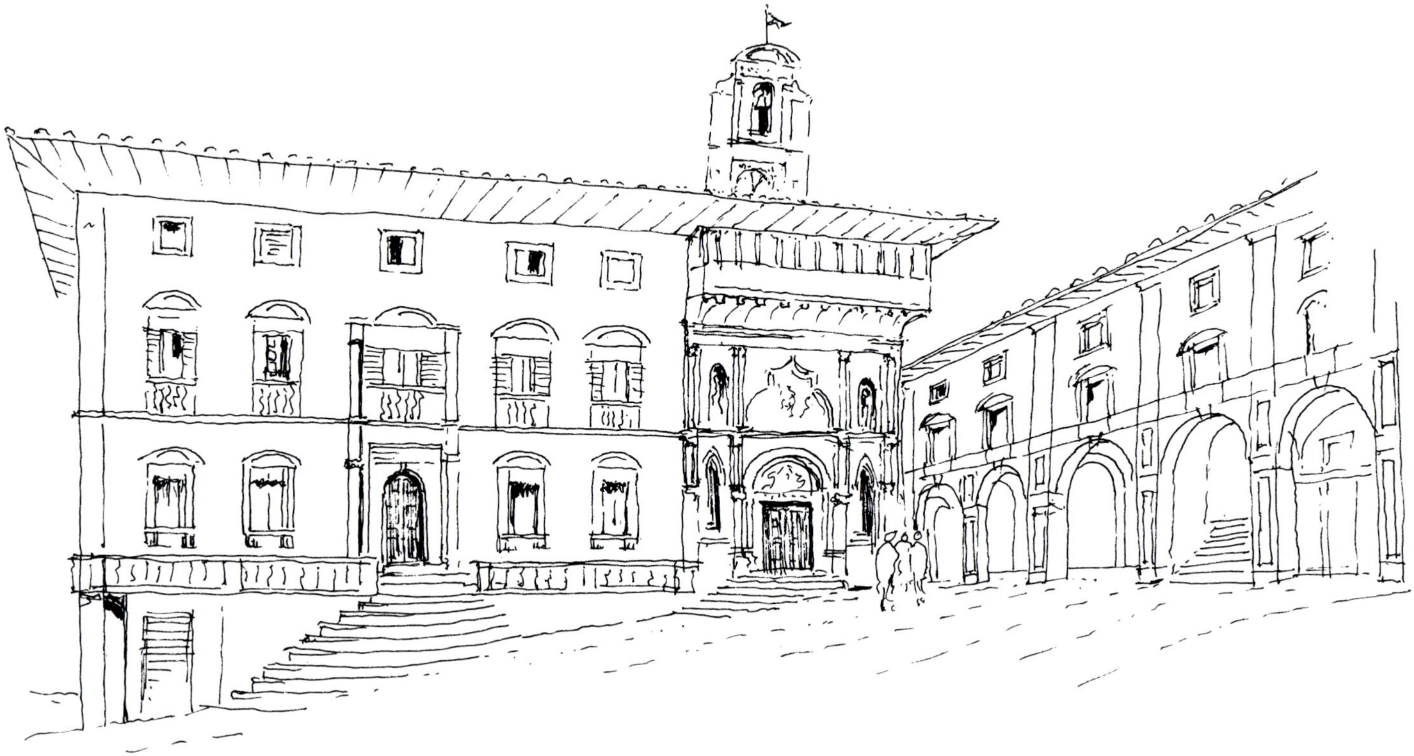

Piazza Grande, Arezzo

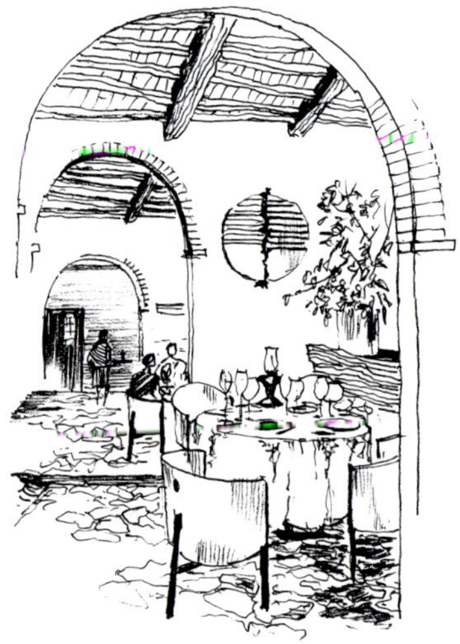

Le Antiche Sera, Sogna near Ambra is special. A mediaeval Borgo restored and converted into a Restaurant with four suites. Delicious food, interesting modern art and the furniture designed by Philippe Starck. There was a warm welcome from the owners Loretta, Vicenzo and daughter Barbara with the young chef Luca.

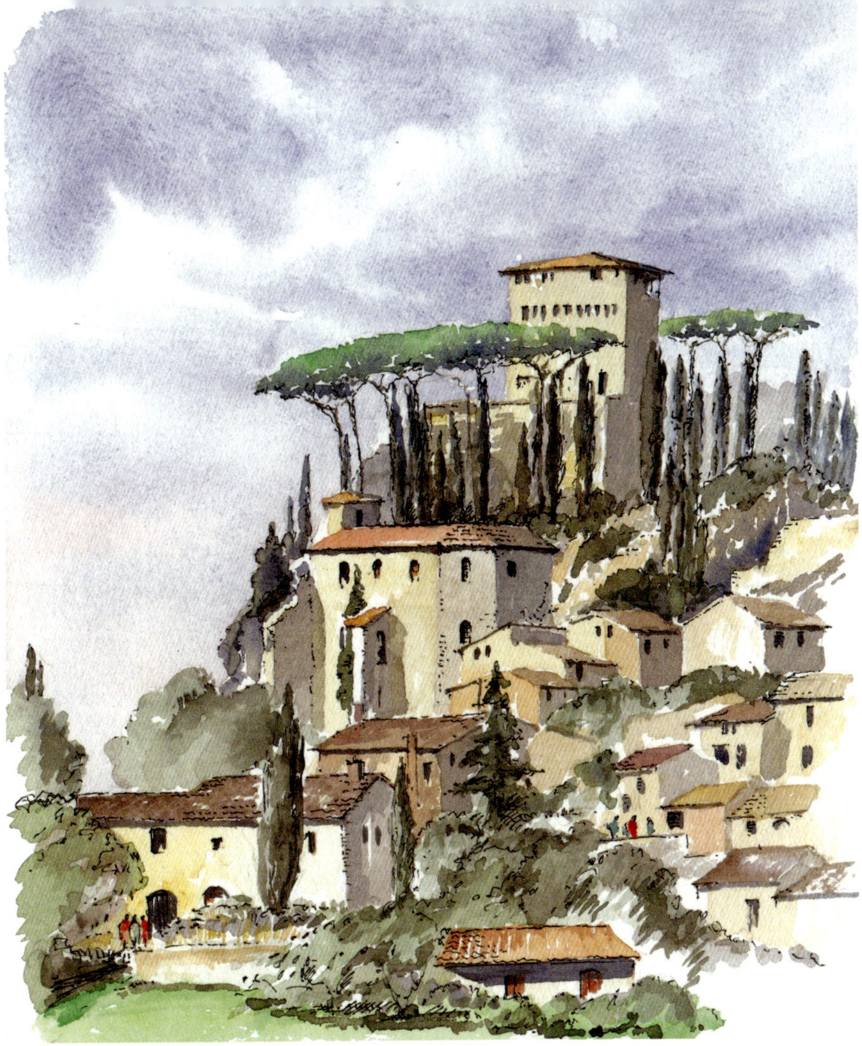

Cortona

Cortona is one of the oldest cities in Tuscany, situated in an elevated position high on the mountain ridge, and was an obvious place for the Etruscans to build. The town stonewalls contain Etruscan remains to this day. It also attracted the Romans but now it is the medieval town that impresses with its twisting streets and first floors overhanging the buildings. There are extensive views over the vineyards of the Chiana valley. The jewel in the crown amongst many must be Museo Diocesano with the Annunciation and the Madonna, two of the best works of Fra Angelico. Examine the eye contact between God and the Virgin Mary. Also look at the work of Pietro Lorenzetti 1280–1348 and Luca Signorelli 1441–1523. Palazzo Comunale is a powerful building of the 13th century. Etruscan, Roman and other fine artefacts can be found in the Museo dell'Accademia Etrusca.

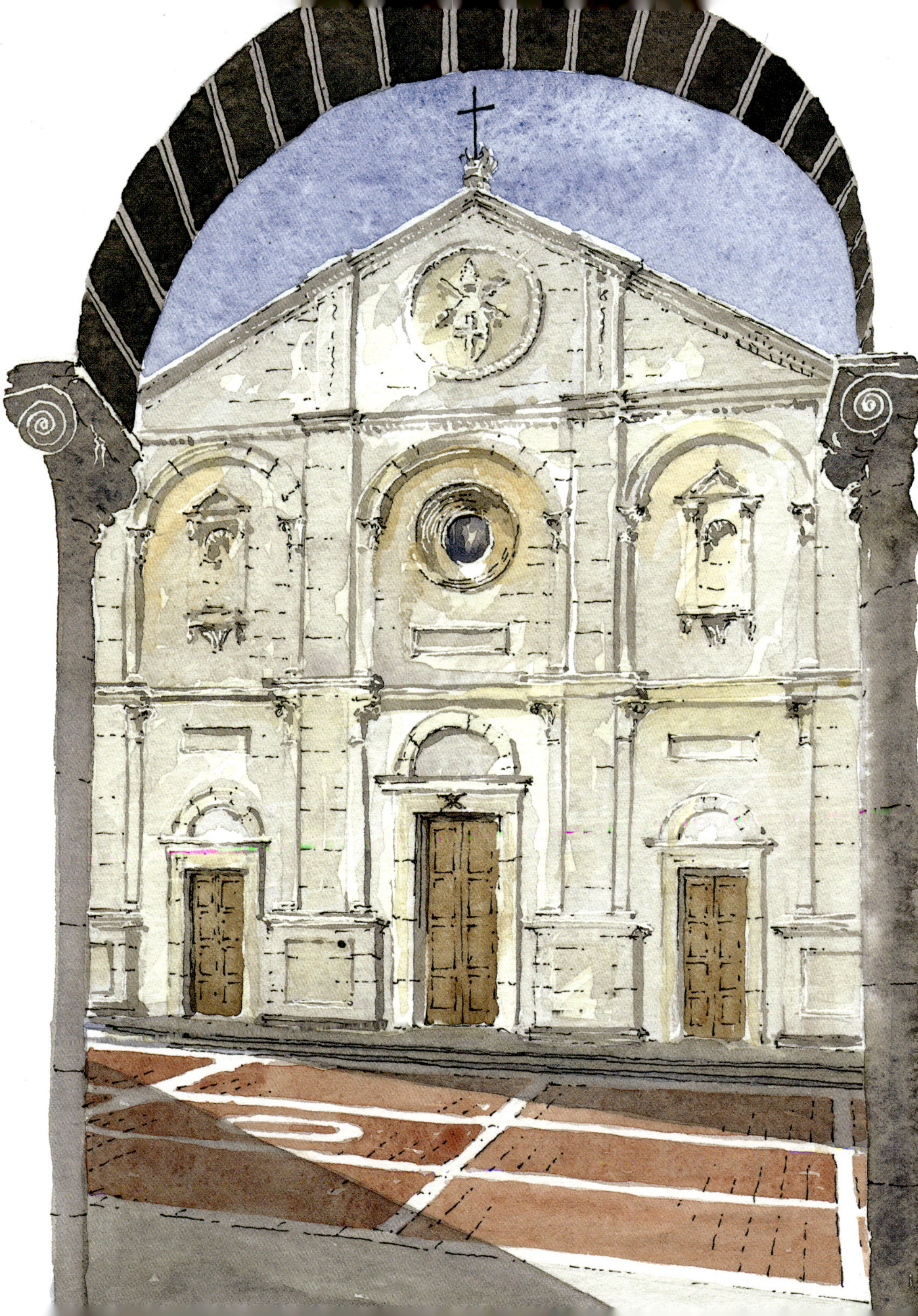

Duomo from the Loggia,
Piazza Pio II, Pienza

Pienza, Montepulciano and the south

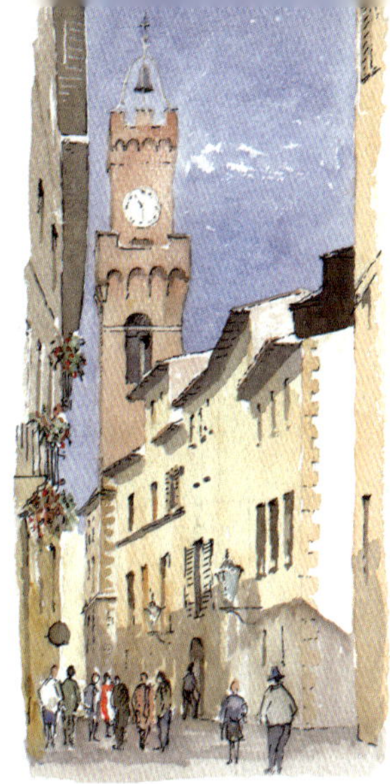

Via Rosselino and tower of Palazzo Pubblico, Pienza

Two distinct landscapes, excluding the coastal strip, are found in southern Tuscany. Firstly there are the beautiful rolling hills covered by vineyards and pasture, with many hilltop towns like Pienza and Montepulciano. Then further south near the Umbria border in the land of the Tufa, two visually different stunning small towns are to be found, Sorano and Pitigliano.

The hills provided the founders of Pienza with a superb view over the Orcia and Asso valleys. An outstanding architect from Florence who had been a pupil of Leon Battista Alberti, namely Bernardo Rossellino, put forward in 1459 an enlightened plan to convert the village into a magnificent town at the request of Pope Pius II who was born in the village. It is a model renaissance town but only the centre was completed, comprising a new Piazza Pio II where beautifully designed paving forms a perfect setting for the Palazzo Comunale and its open Loggia at ground floor level. To complete the enclosing of the space is the Bishop's Palace and end wall of the Duomo, creating a wonderful sense of place. There is also a fine Palazzo Piccolomini near by. Superb views can be seen from the wall built around the town and the wall from the outside provides the continual visual foundation seen from the south.

In contrast is the wine town of Montalcino situated on the top of the hill, an imposing 14th century Fortress that dominates the skyline and towers over the vineyard covered landscape. One of the great Italian wines is Brunello di Montalcino is made exclusively from the Brunello grape on the outskirts of the town.

Not far away is a very holy place. This was my first impression when entering the Abbey Church of Sant'Antimo set in the beautiful olive and cyprus tree Tuscan landscape. It is a Romanesque Abbey founded in the 9th century reaching its peak in the 12th century. A magnificent minimalist austere

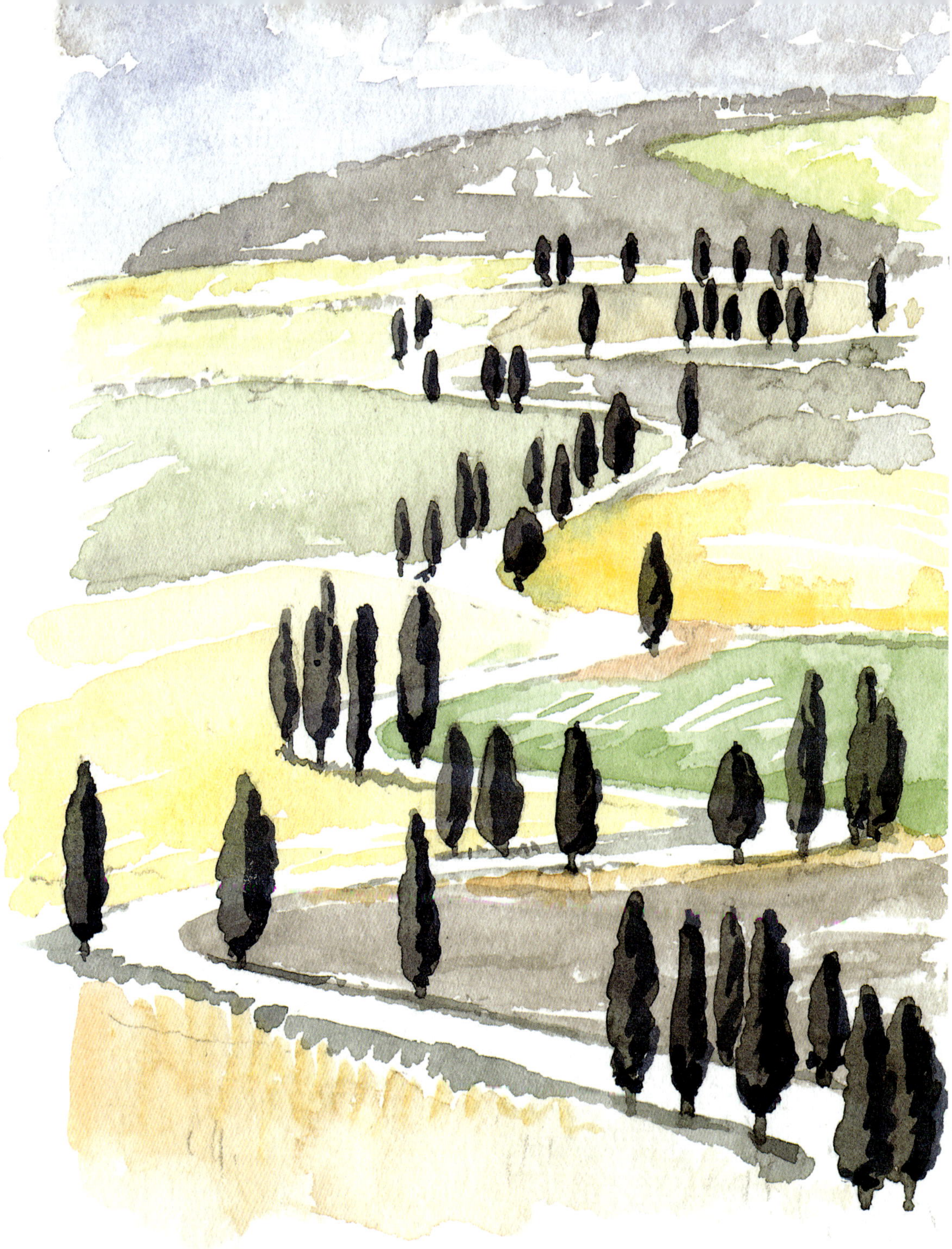

 Beautiful Tuscan landscape in the Val d'Orcia

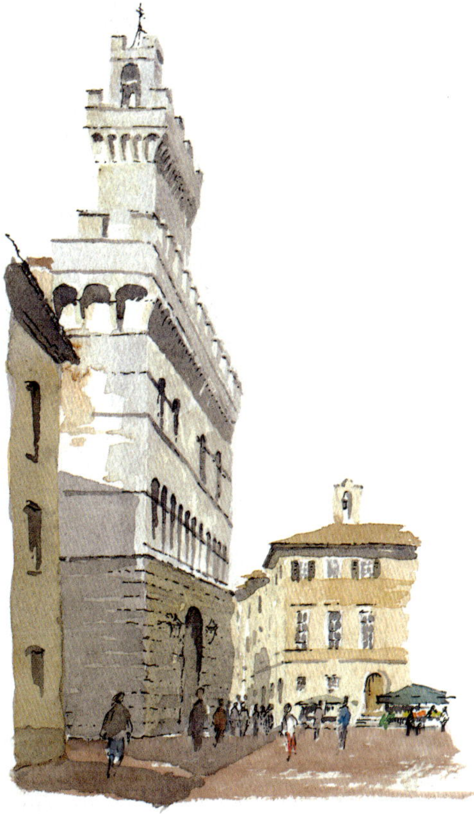

Palazzo Comunale, Piazza Grande, Montepulciano

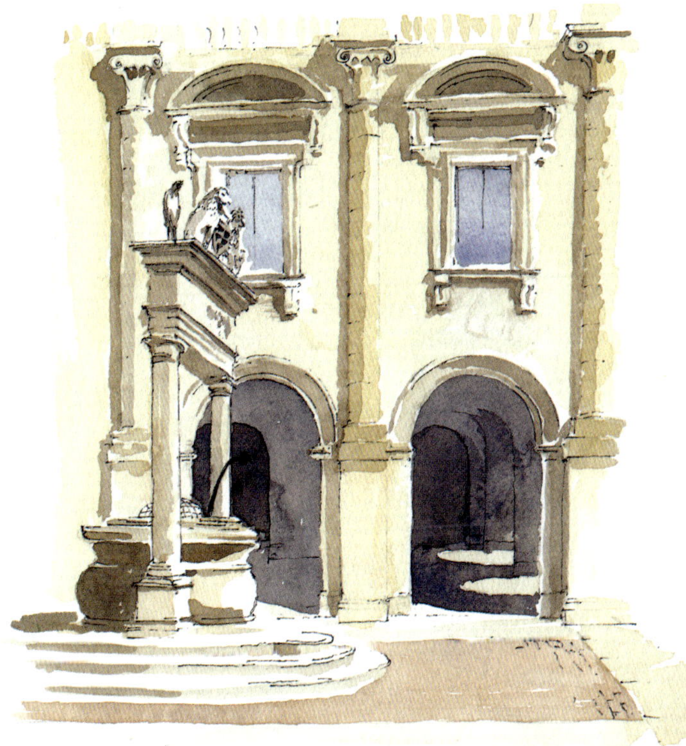

Renaissance well attributed to Vecchio in front of Palazzo Nobili

interior in creamy travertine is a perfect setting for the 'Gregorian Chant' simple melodies to the words of the Psalms, sung by the Augustinian monks.

On a narrow limestone ridge is the site of Montepulciano, a long thin town with the Piazza Grande in the centre of an irregular sloping space. Dominated by the massive Palazzo Comunale, the Gothic town hall is still in use today and has superb panoramic views from the rooftop. On the north side is Palazzo Nobili-Tarugi and opposite is the Duomo of the 16 &17th century, visually a little disappointing. A picturesque well is beautifully situated in the square. Savour the robust red wine – Vino Nobile di Montepulciano in the Piazza wine cellars.

The surprise is to find San Biagio situated below the town, a magnificent pilgrim church perched on a grass platform below the city wall. It is a gem of a Romanesque building of 1518.

In the very southern part of Tuscany are two beautiful and very different towns giving the appearance of growing out of the Tufa rock. Sorano, built and carved out of the rock, was developed

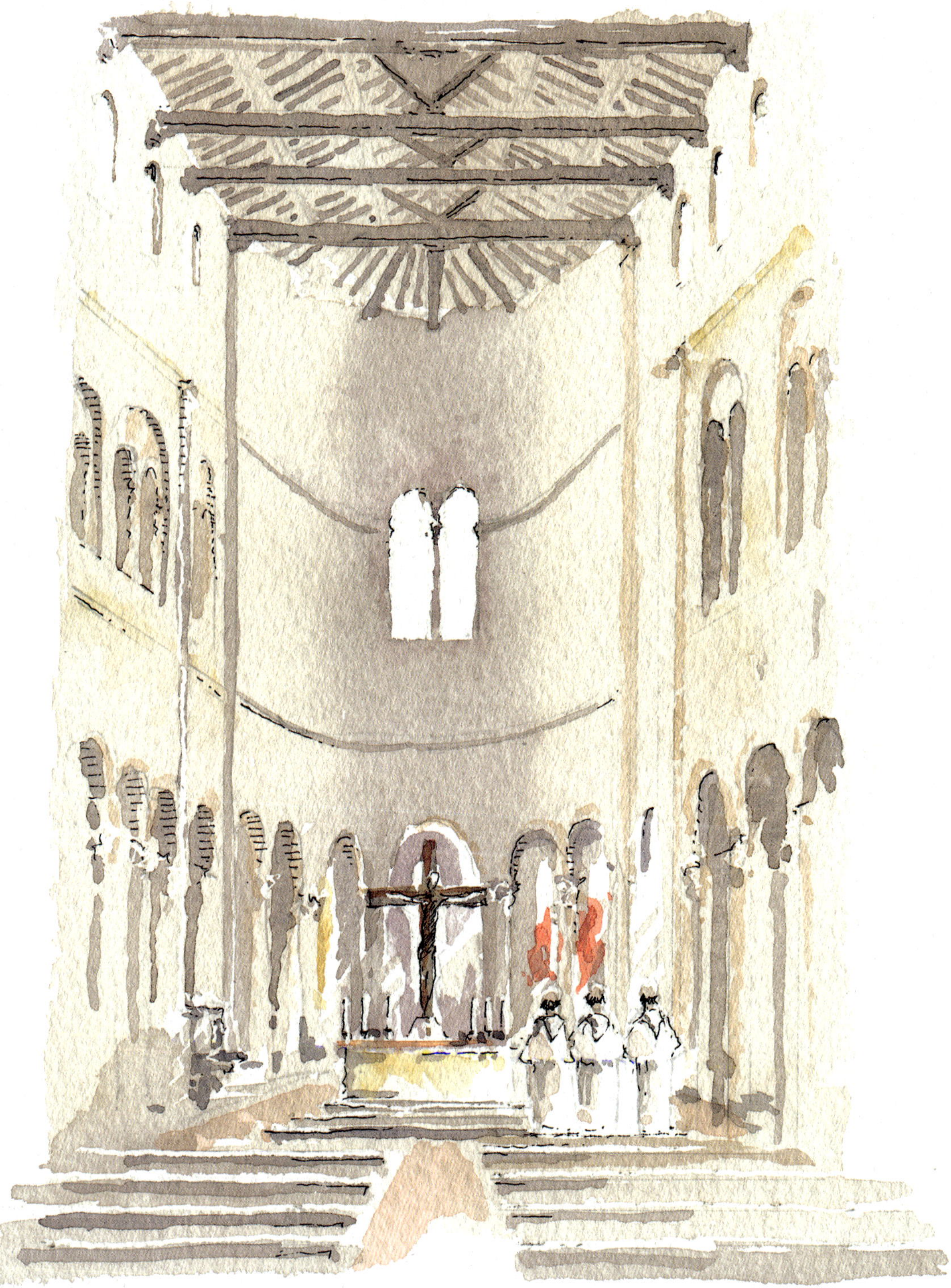

Abbey Church of Sant'Antimo

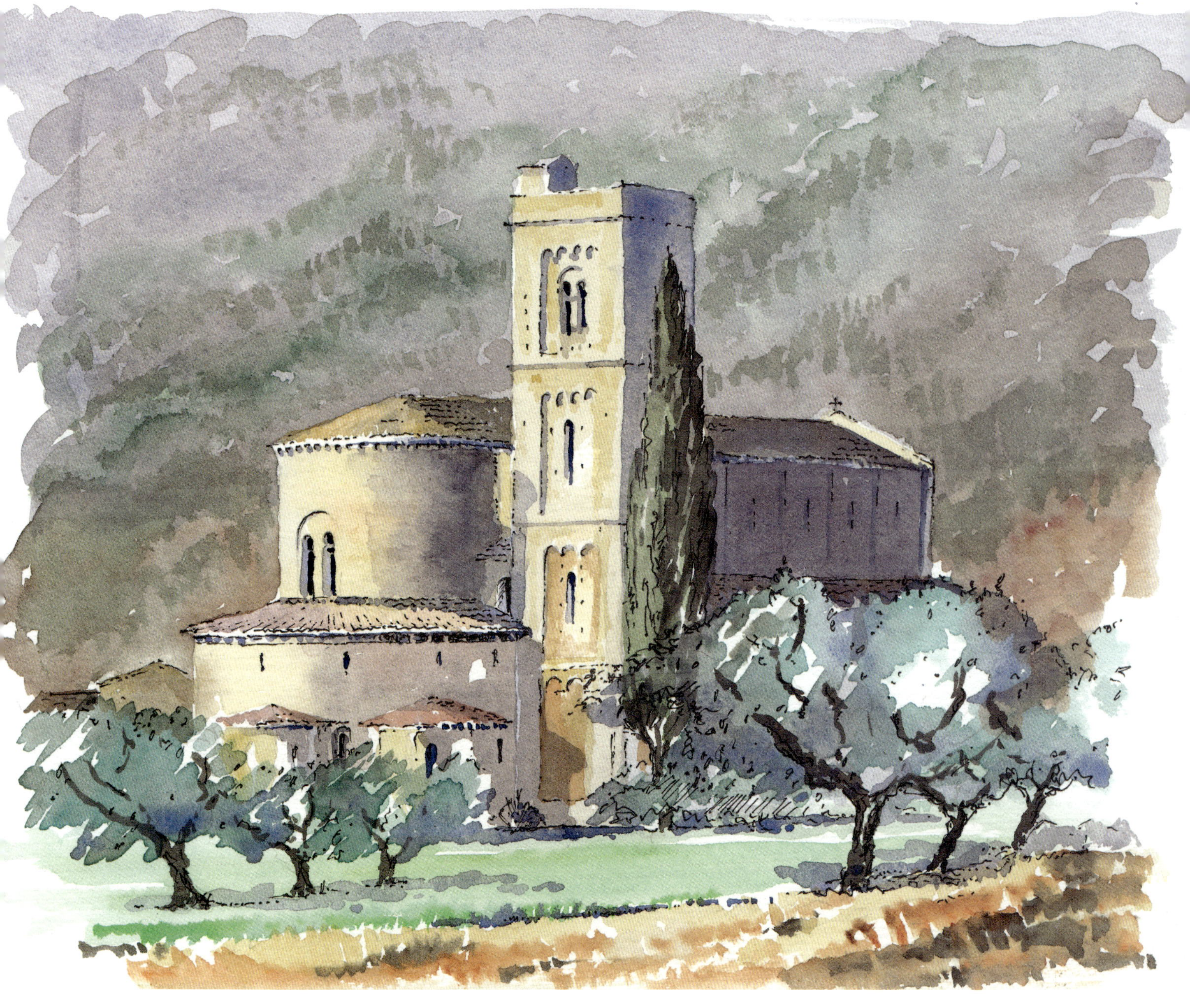

Abbey Church of Sant'Antimo

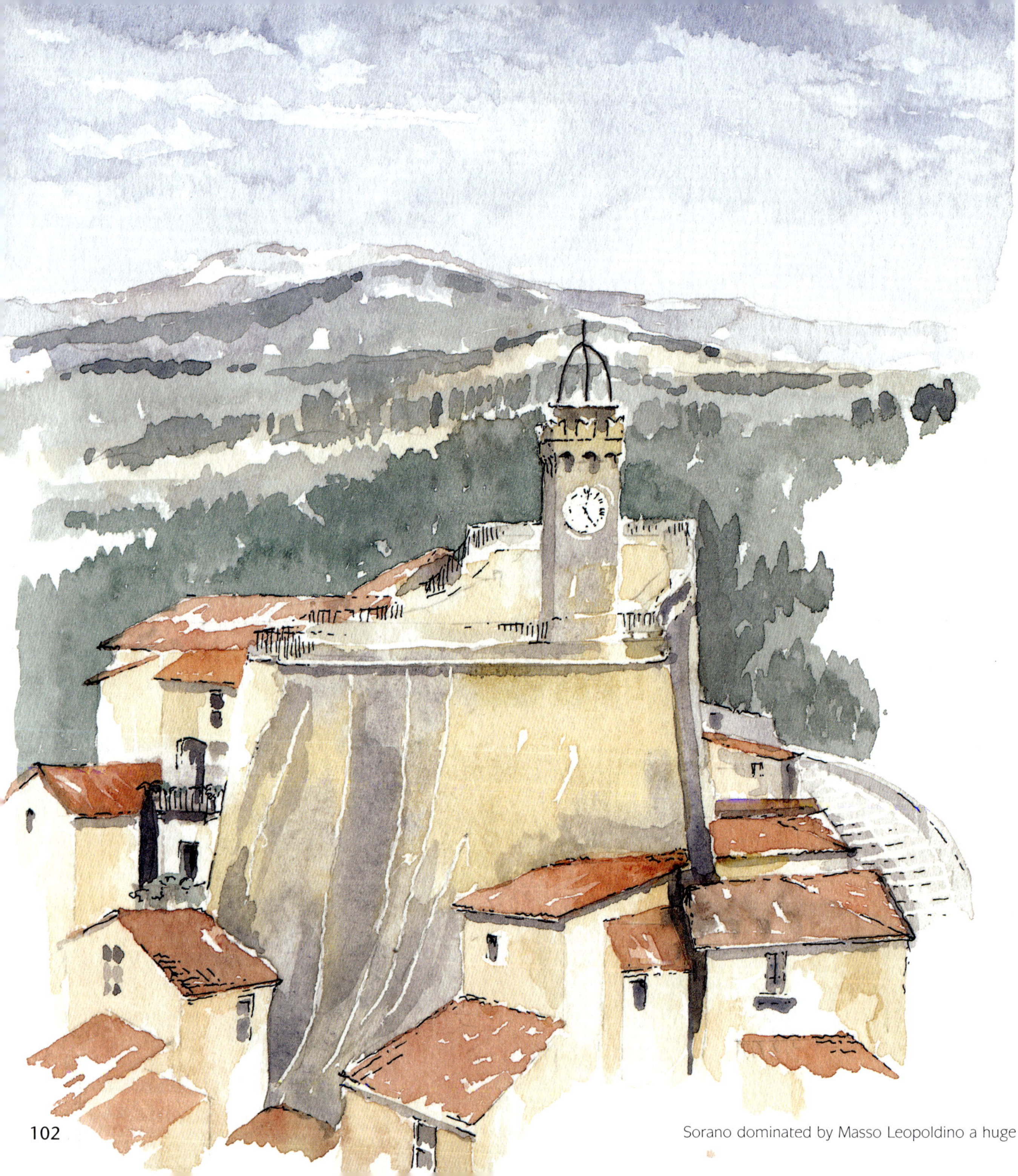

Sorano dominated by Masso Leopoldino a huge natural tufa bluff

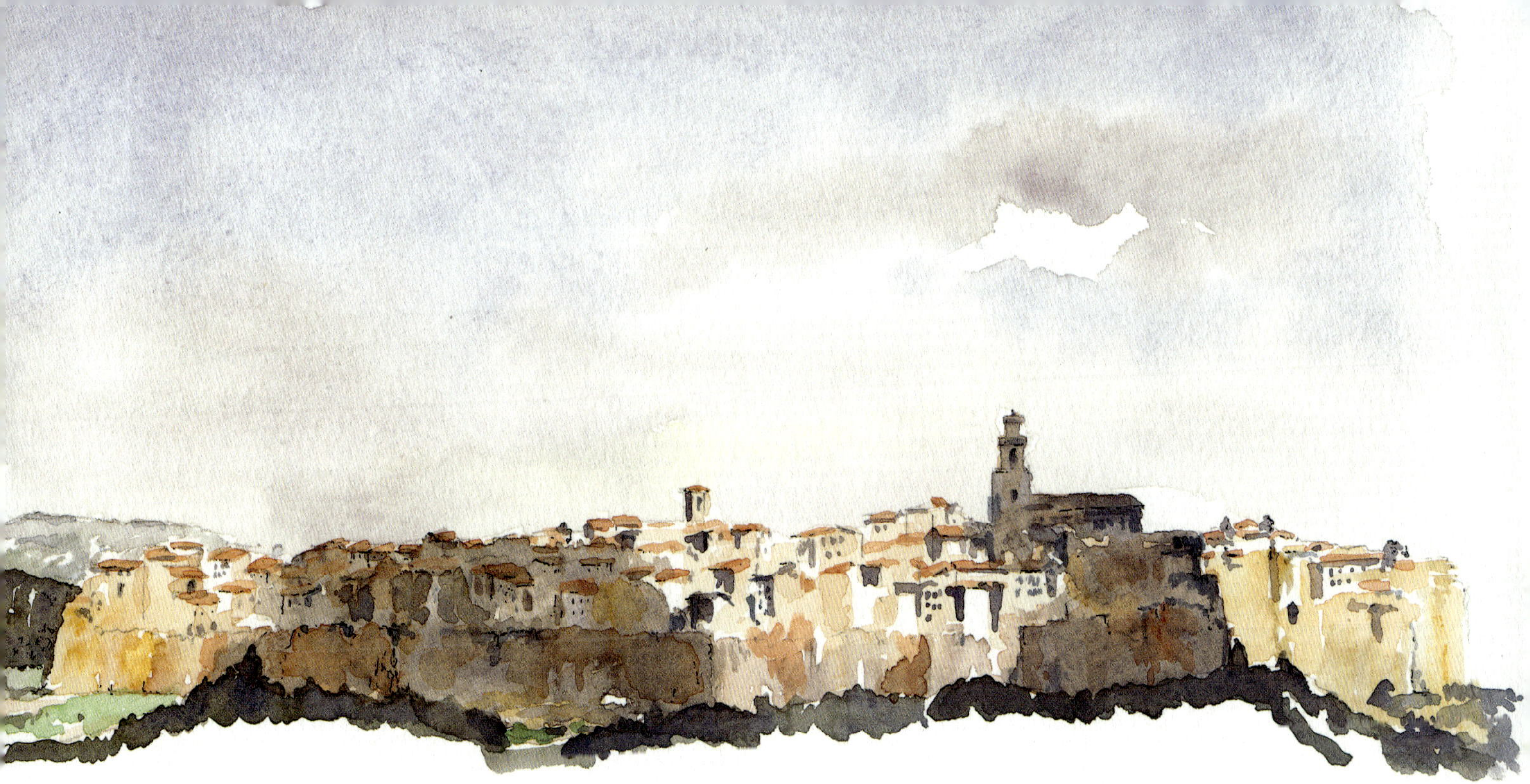

Pitigliano

from the ancient roadways cut deep into the rock by the Etruscans and later built to an impressive height giving the town a huge scale. Sorano became a unique medieval town dominated by Masso Leopoldino: an example of great courage to exploit the huge tufa bluff with a sheer drop to the river Leute. The flattened top forms the Piazza with the clock tower. Explore the narrow streets and stairways between the tightly packed houses.

A little distance south is the other town, Pitigliano that also grows out of the rock. It is on the main road and therefore better known. The plan of the town is linear with Etruscan foundations on the Tufa. The Michelin Green Guide explains the nickname for the town. 'Pitigliano was given the nickname little Jerusalem because of its medieval appearance and thriving Jewish community, who settled here in the second half of the 16th century. The old synagogue and unleavened bread oven can still be seen in the village'.

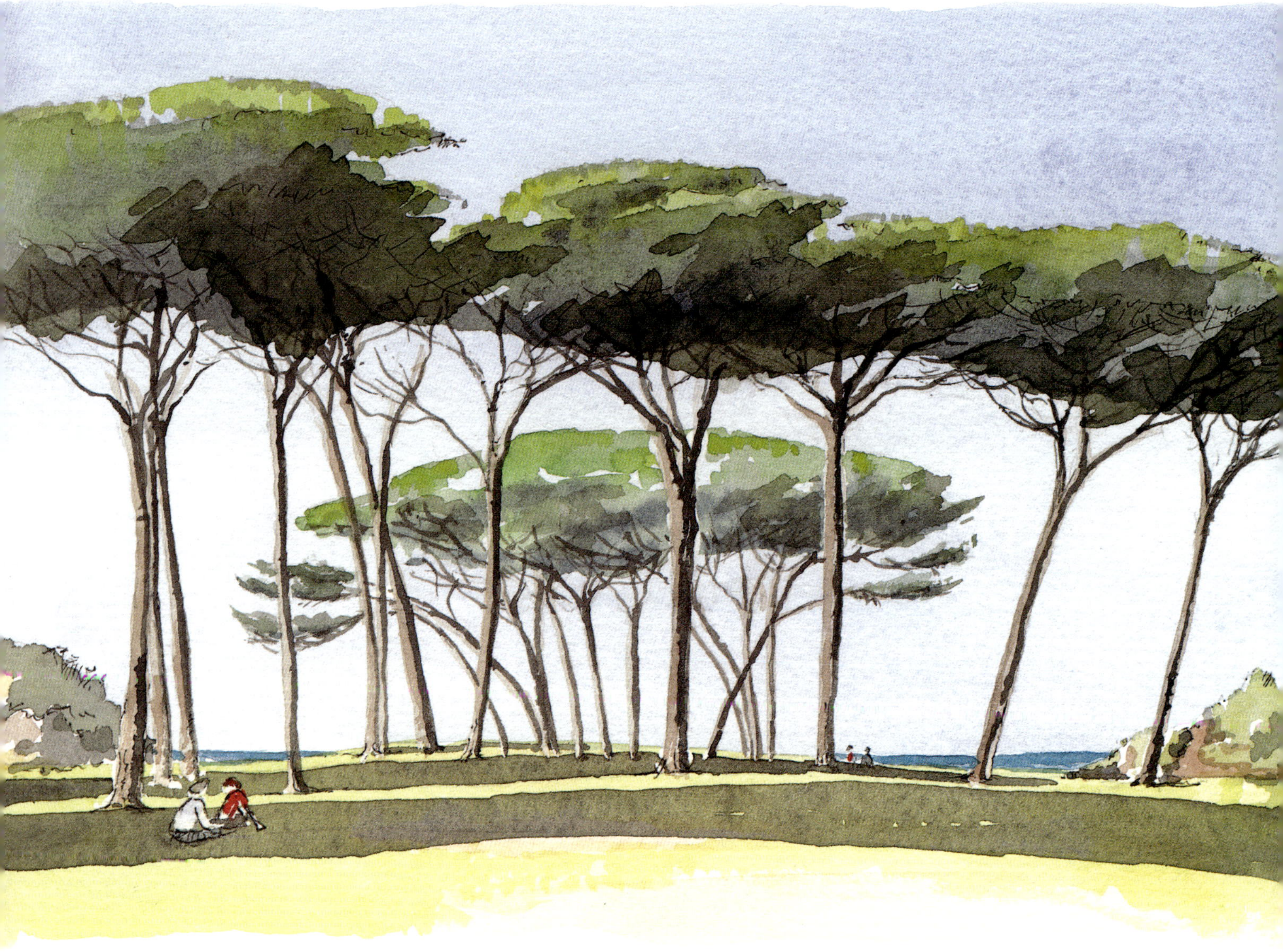

Spectacular group of Umbrella pines (Pinus pinea) in Baratti Bay

The Tuscan Coast

It is perhaps difficult to visualise that a great area of Tuscany was marsh and that Pisa was on the coast in Roman times. Recently the British Consultant Ground Engineer who was working to stabilise The Leaning Tower of Pisa proved this and his theory that this building was built on sea shale.

The Romans were the first to cultivate the marshes of the Maremma, but the area went into decline until the 18th century when drainage schemes brought the land back into cultivation.

There is much natural flora and fauna to be found including wild boar. Cowboys raise the long horned white cattle and it is a spectacle to see them working the herds in the Maremma.

The coastline has a long history exploited by the Etruscans and Romans. Both were great maritime powers. Many communities were established along the coast. In the southern area of the Maremma the Etruscans gained their wealth from mineral resources found in Tuscany. Little remains of these fascinating people except tombs and artefacts found in them. In the south on the coast there is Baratti and Populonia – beautiful bays where the Etruscans founded the Gulf of Baratti. It was breathtaking to suddenly come upon the most stunning picturesque view of umbrella pines on a very green grass slope with golden sand and deep blue sea beyond in perfect sunlight. Hence no surprise to find the scene was the picture post card icon of the area. Etruscan tombs are near the beach and a necropolis in the woods, evidence of an important settlement that has disappeared.

Further south is Orbetello, once a small Spanish town situated near two tidal lagoons.

The island of Elba is where Napoleon was exiled for nine months after the fall of Paris in 1840. A beautiful place to explore the wild and varied landscapes.

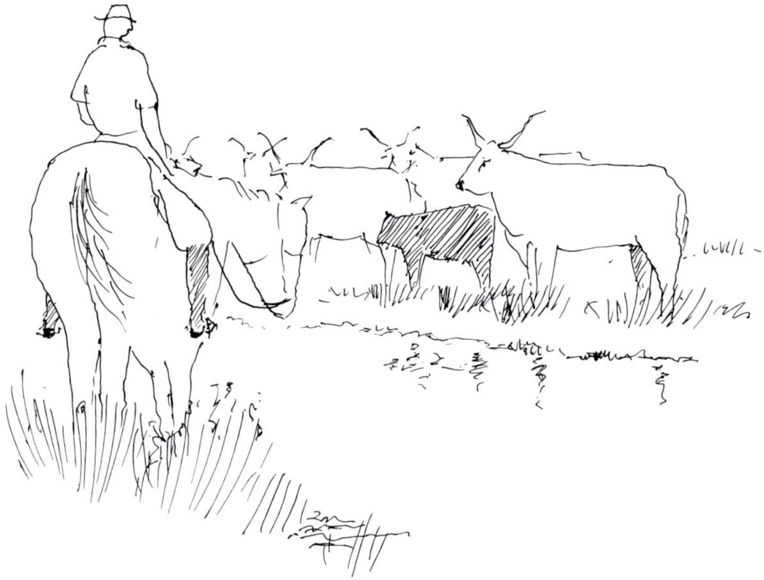

Cowboy with long horned white cattle, Maremma

In central Tuscany on the coast is Livorno, which replaced Pisa as the principal port when the sea receded. A modern city, however it was the massive brickwork of Fortezza Vecchia, the Old Fortress that fascinated me. It stands as a powerful statement of ports engineering from the 1590s and became the 'Port of the Medici family'. From 1607–21 the English marine engineer Sir Robert Dudley built the sea wall to protect the harbour and in 1608 it was declared a free port. It flourished as Jews, Protestants, Arabs and Turkish traders used it as their base without prosecution.

The coast north of Pisa is frequented by the wealthy from Florence, Milan, Pisa and Lucca. In the 1920s there were elegant beaches abounding with 'Art Nouveau' buildings, few remain but the style has been preserved in Margherita Theatre and the Balena bathing establishments. Puccini had a house Torre del Lago Puccini where he said his 'second favourite instrument' was his gun for shooting wildfowl in the reed-fringed lake that is now a nature reserve for rare birds and migrants.

Every summer in August there is a Festival of Puccini's Operas performed outdoors on the lakeside.

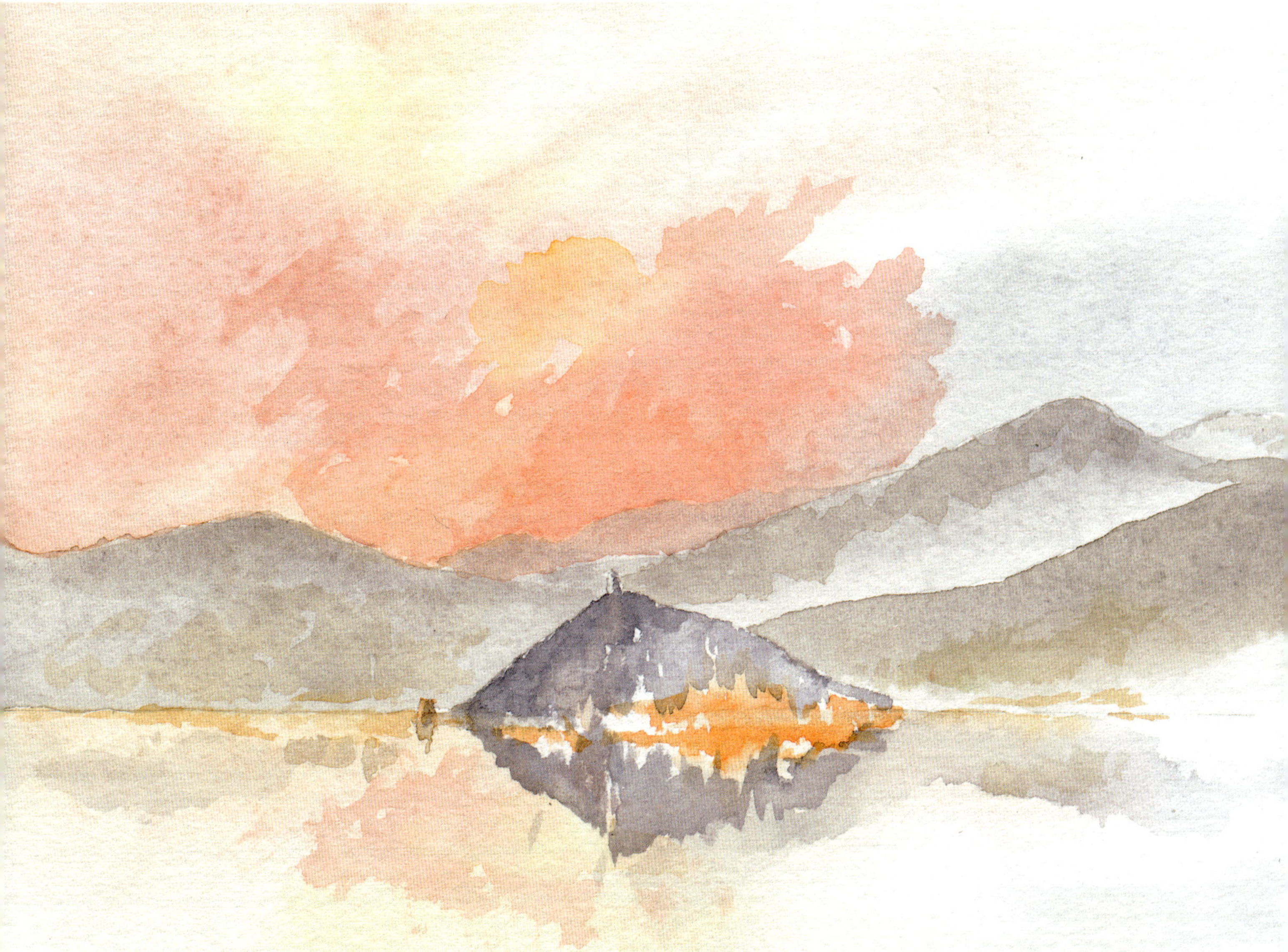

Islands of the Arcipelago Toscano at sunset

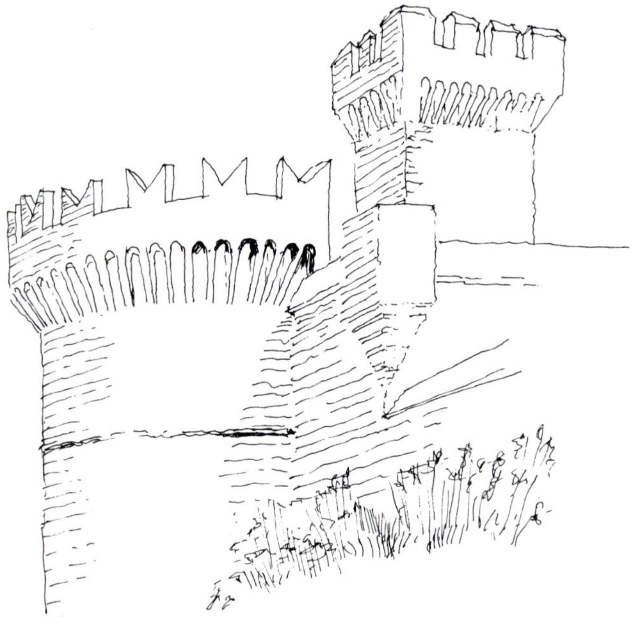

Mediaeval Castle, Populonia

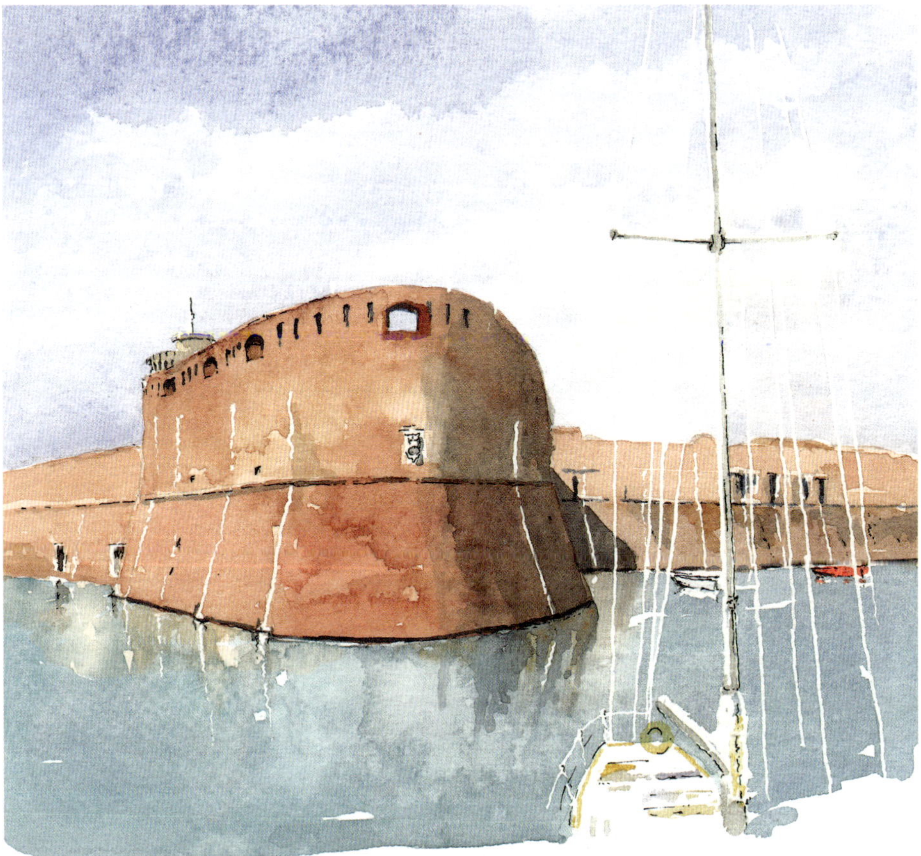

Livorno

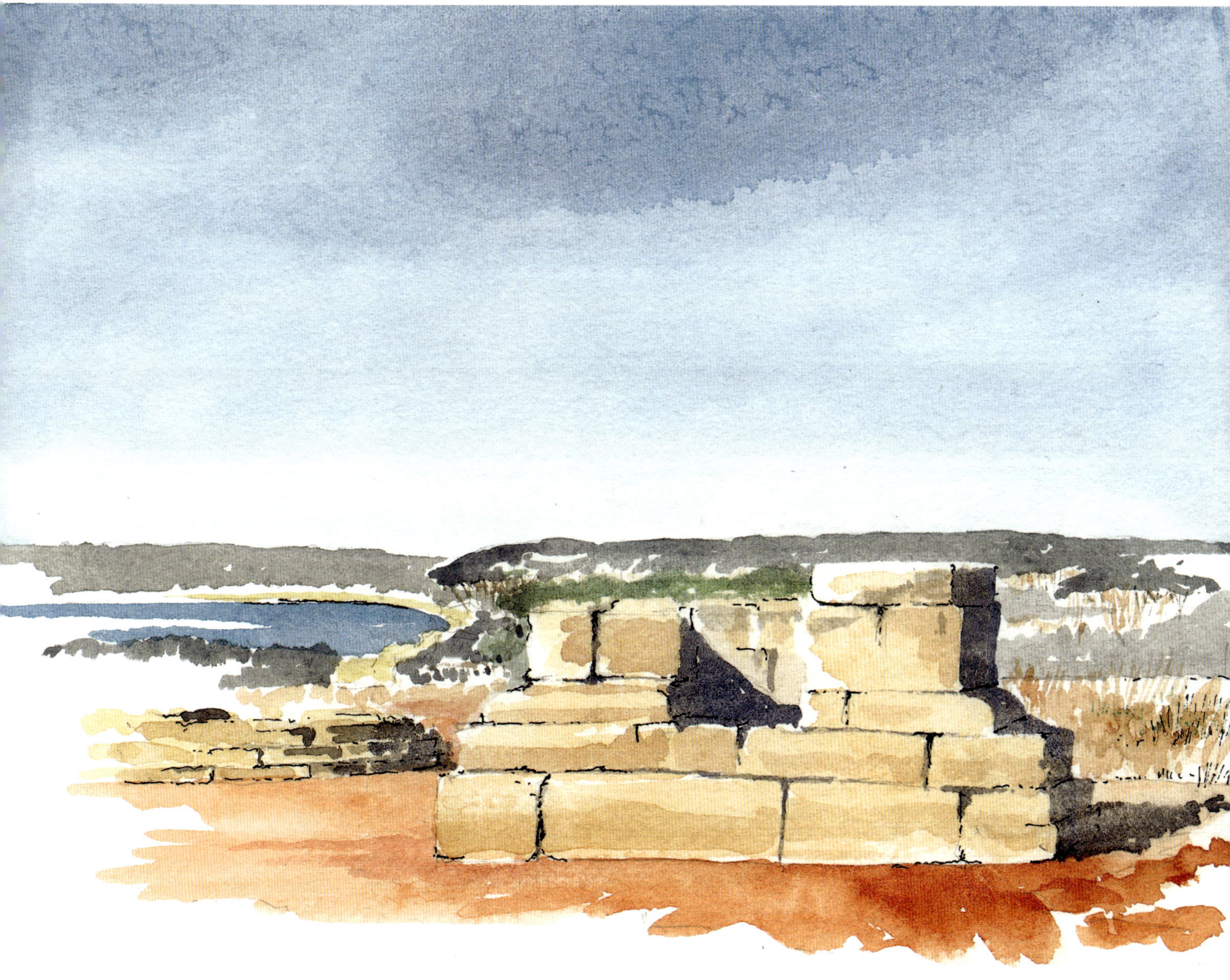

Etruscan Necropolis of San Cerbone, Baratti Bay

 Hilltop farm in the morning mist

Conclusion

The more one explores, the more one discovers the magic and magnetism of this unique area of the world. This is the beginning not the end of a fascinating journey of exploration. There are so many places, buildings, gardens and landscape still to discover.

It is not surprising that Byron, Browning, Shelley and Tennyson and many others found Tuscany to be a very special place. It has been and still is a dynamic area drawing one back to admire the past and explore the present.

The aim of this Book has been to capture a sense of place of a few of the many parts of Tuscany that have left their mark giving me the urge to draw and paint. No other part of the world in my extensive travels has so much to offer concentrated in one area. The Etruscans and Romans left their mark, the medieval period gave us great gothic cathedrals churches and abbeys. The invention of the Renaissance was here coupled with a remarkable collection of art created by some of the greatest artists and sculptors the world has ever seen. It is great to find the Italians still moving forward, treasuring the old but not restricted by it: encouraging the new and never being reluctant to use both side by side.

Most towns have withstood the onslaught of visitors and still have much to offer and their magnetism attracts one back again and again.

To sum up, it is difficult to disagree with D H Lawrence writing of the countryside in his Italian essays, when many years later the tractor has replaced the oxen but the magic of this special area remains:

'Tuscany manages to remain so remote, and secretly smiling to itself in its many sleeves. There are so many hills popping up, and they take no notice of one another. There are so many little deep valleys

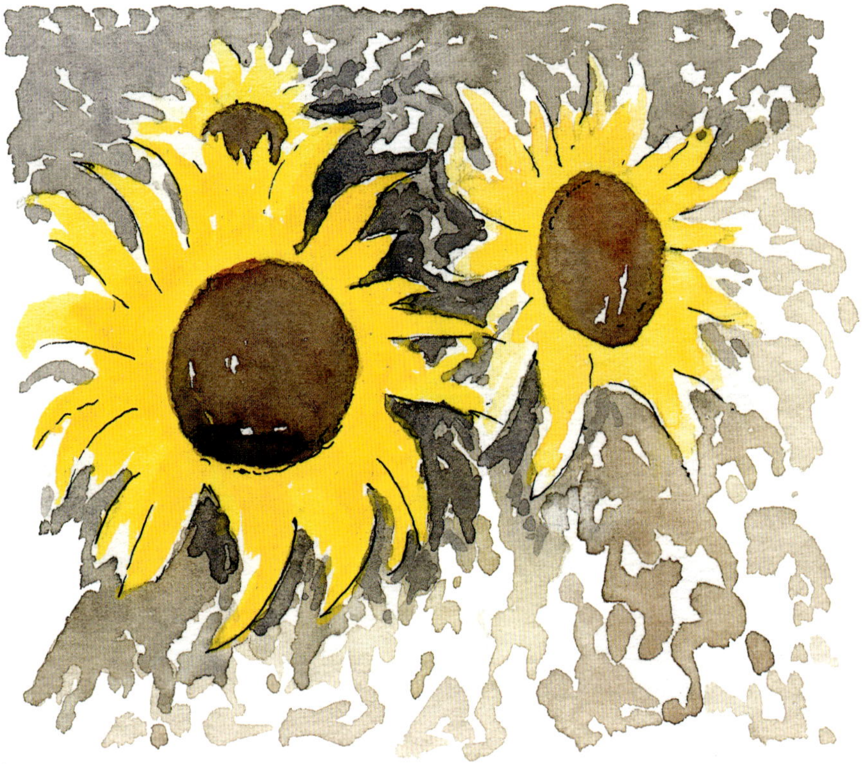

Sunflowers

with streams that seem to go their own little way entirely, regardless of river or sea. There are thousands, millions of utterly secluded little nooks, though the land has been under cultivation these thousands of years. But the intensive culture of vine and olive and wheat, by the ceaseless industry of naked human hands and winter-shod feet, and slow-stepping, soft-eyed oxen does not devastate the country, does not denude it, does not lay it bare, does not uncover its nakedness, does not drive away either Pan or his children. The streams run and rattle over wild rocks of secret places, and murmur through blackthorn thickets where the Nightingales sing all together, unruffled and undaunted.'

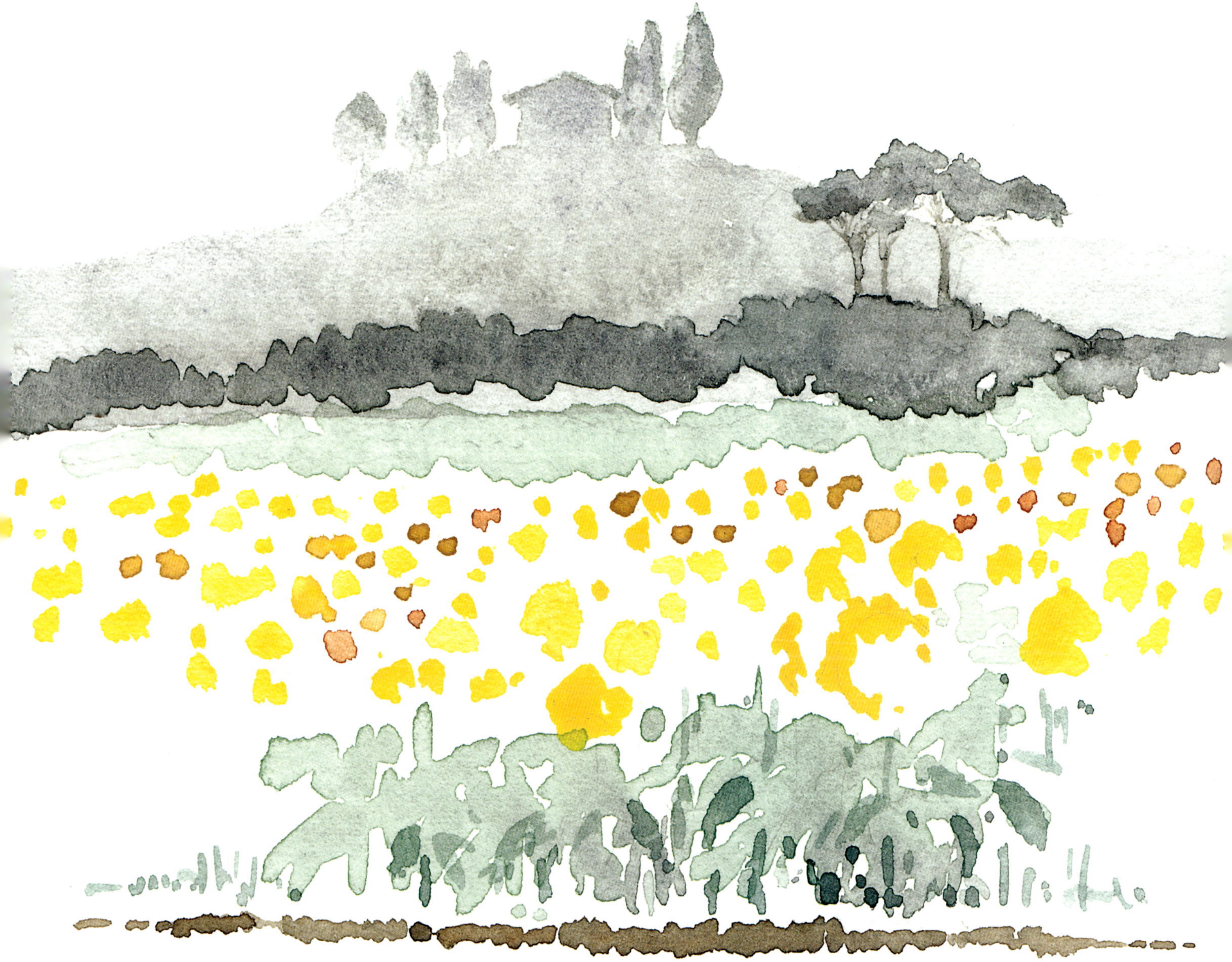

Field of sunflowers

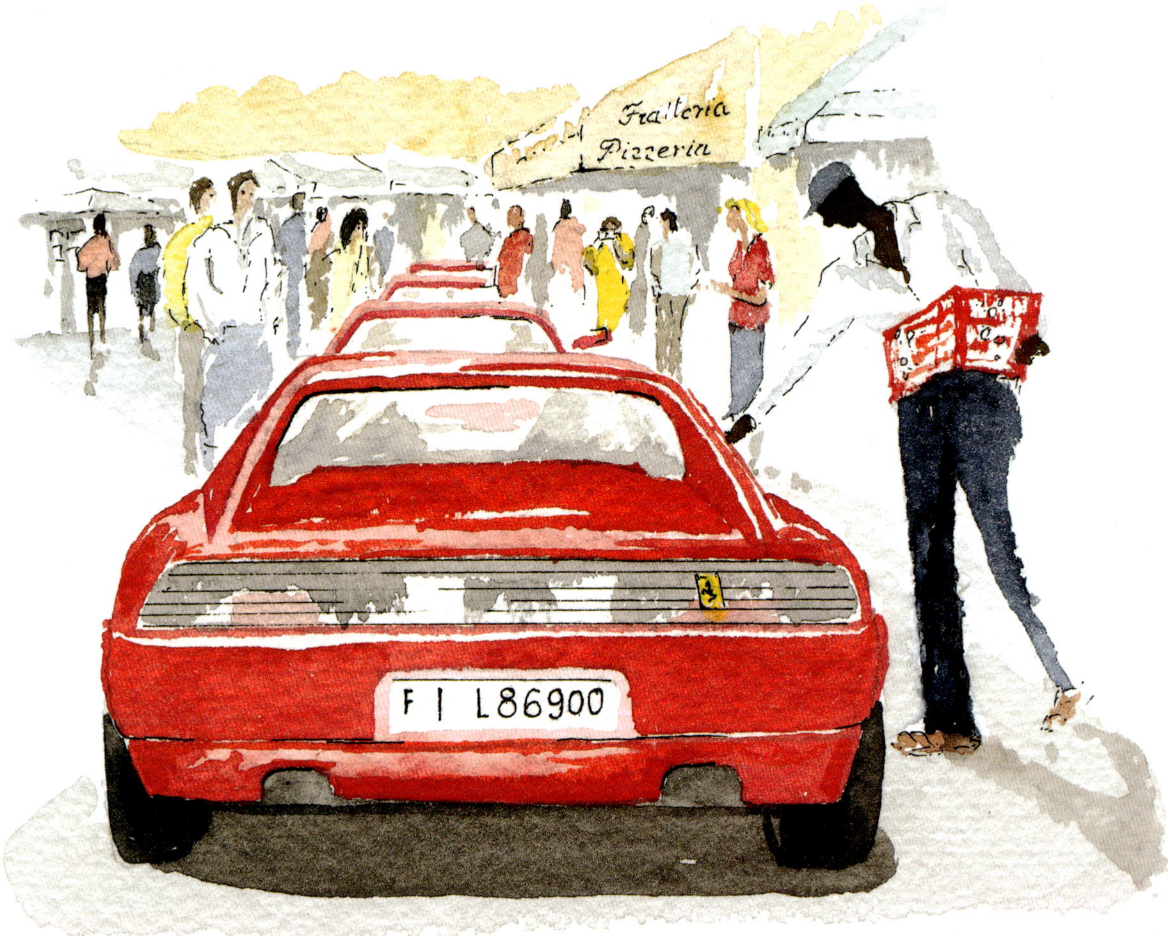

Red Ferraris in Pisa on the weekend of the Italian Grand Prix

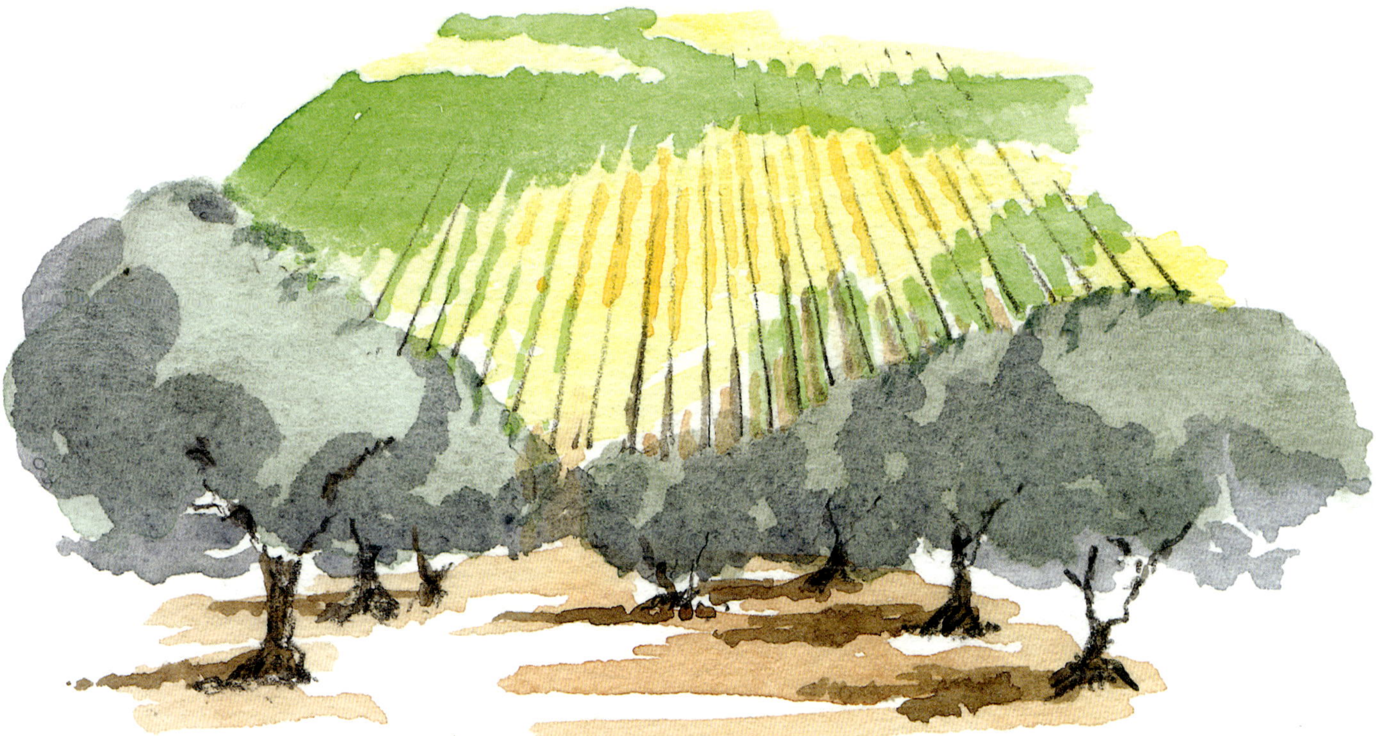

Olive grove and vineyards in the distance

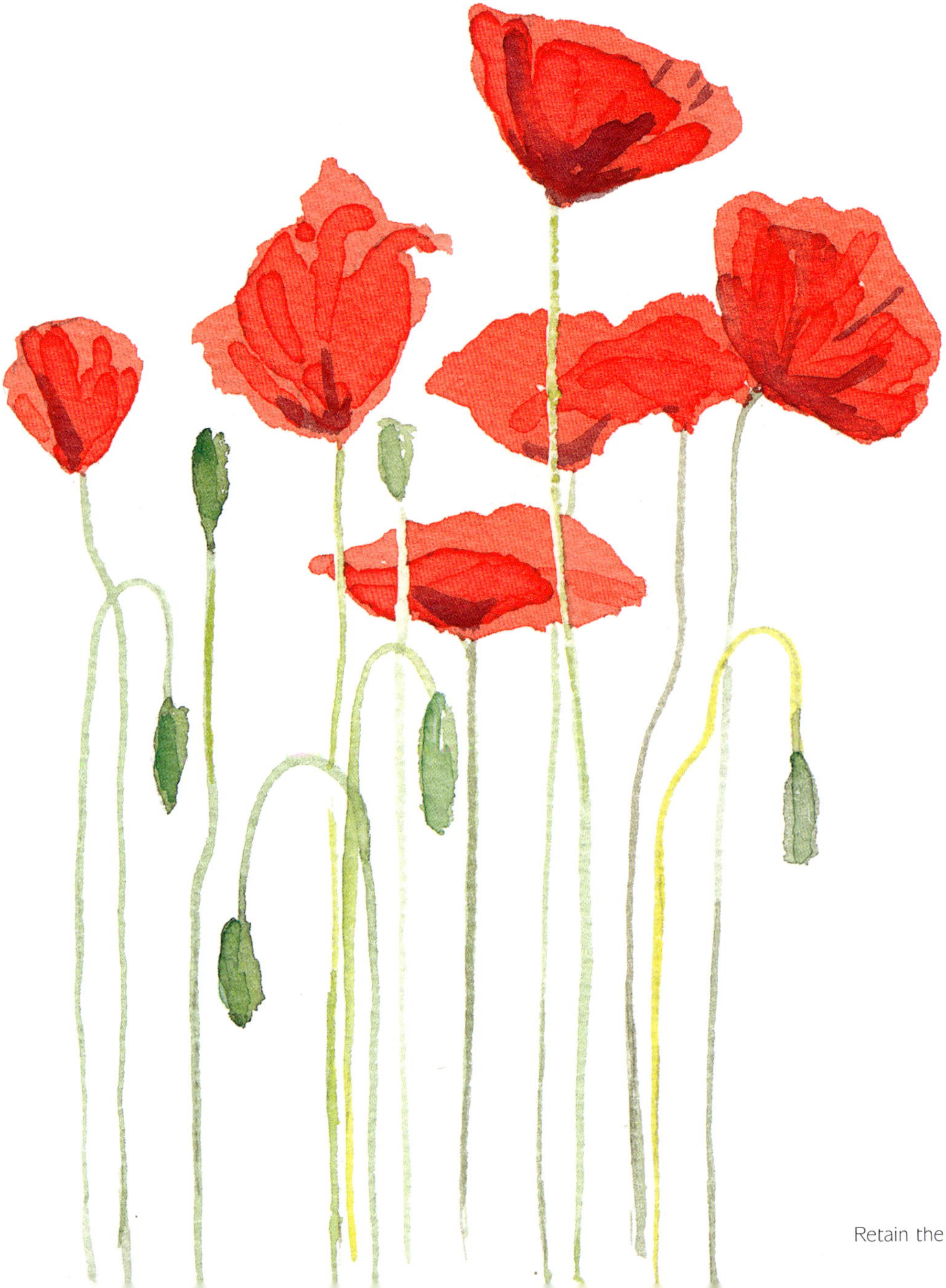

Retain the vision of translucent poppies

Index and Glossary

Buildings, places, architects, artists & designers
Page numbers in Italics indicate illustrations

Brief Glossary

Campanile	bell tower
Campo dei Miracoli	field of miracles
Camposanto	cemetery
Duomo	cathedral
Galleria	gallery
Museo	museum
Palazzo	palace
Palazzo del Comune	Town Hall
Piazza	town square
Ponte	bridge